T0361680

Advance Praise for *Inside the Reagan White House*

"In this gripping story of leadership, Frank Lavin makes clear how Ronald Reagan demonstrated a blend of principles and practicality that made his presidency so successful."

— Ken Khachigian, Reagan's Chief Speechwriter and author of *Behind Closed Doors: In the Room with Reagan and Nixon*

"Frank Lavin was there for much of the Reagan years, seeing the revolution up close and personal. Now, this witness to history has written it down in great detail for the benefit of all."

—Craig Shirley, author of *Reagan's Revolution: The Untold Story of the Campaign That Started It All*

"Frank Lavin's tales from the ramparts of the Reagan Revolution are witty, gripping, and filled with insight into a great president and his times. Prepare to learn what it's like working in the White House and on campaigns from an expert and delightful raconteur."

— Matthew Continetti, author of *The Right: The Hundred Year War for American Conservatism*

"An eyewitness account that's shrewd, attentive to detail, thoroughly engaging, and, here and there, really pretty funny. To anyone interested in the Reagan years—which, of course, ought to be everyone—Frank Lavin's book will come as a gift."

— Peter Robinson, Special Assistant and
Speechwriter to President Reagan

"Reagan's vision, which encompassed his fervent belief in the eventual demise of the Soviet Union's evil empire, shaped his foreign policy thinking. He played a major role in winning the Cold War. Frank Lavin has penned a must-read, can't put down book which provides the inside story and captures both the power of Reagan's strategy and extraordinary oratorical skills."

— Ambassador Paula J. Dobriansky,
former NSC Director of European and
Soviet Affairs, Reagan Administration

INSIDE THE
REAGAN
WHITE HOUSE

A FRONT-ROW SEAT TO
PRESIDENTIAL LEADERSHIP
WITH LESSONS FOR TODAY

FRANK LAVIN

POST HILL
PRESS

A POST HILL PRESS BOOK
ISBN: 979-8-88845-694-1
ISBN (eBook): 979-8-88845-695-8

Inside the Reagan White House:
A Front-Row Seat to Presidential Leadership with Lessons for Today
© 2025 by Frank Lavin
All Rights Reserved

Cover design by Cody Corcoran

Post Hill Press
New York • Nashville
posthillpress.com

Published in the United States of America
1   2   3   4   5   6   7   8   9   10

CONTENTS

Foreword vii

Introduction: January 6, 2021 xi

Chapter 1:   It's Over 1

Chapter 2:   The Background: Explaining Frank Lavin 8

Chapter 3:   The Great Communicator 33

Chapter 4:   1981–82 The Office of Presidential
             Personnel: An Uneven Start 41

Chapter 5:   The Troika: Baker-Meese-Deaver 68

Chapter 6:   1983–84 Office of Public Liaison 79

Chapter 7:   Presidential Events 101

Chapter 8:   1985–86 National Security Council 118

Chapter 9:   Gorbachev and Reykjavik: Things Fall Apart . 165

Chapter 10: The First Lady 207

Chapter 11: 1987–89 Office of Political Affairs 214

Chapter 12: The 1988 Presidential Race 233

Chapter 13: Searching for Jupiter: Explaining
             Ronald Reagan 260

Chapter 14: Afterwords 279

Bibliography 283

Index 287

Acknowledgments 305

FOREWORD

It is commonplace among historians and biographers that we need 30 years at least to come to durable judgments about major historical figures, especially presidents. For one thing, it can take that long—or longer in recent decades—for key confidential documents to be declassified and organized by archivists. The lengthening of time also begins to change our perspectives on both the time and the person. We come to perceive and appreciate certain qualities that were not noticed contemporaneously, or the nature of the challenges of the time appear different as subsequent events play out.

A related challenge to biographers and historians is that senior individuals—cabinet secretaries, senior White House aides, campaign strategists, and so forth—are often unreliable or partial witnesses to events, and can mislead an investigator. In some instances, memories simply fade, but in other instances very senior figures have the mixed motive of having their own reputations and causes to protect. When conducting research for my own two-volume chronicle of Reagan's political story, I began to make a note of when a senior official told me something that was directly contradicted by documentary evidence.

In cases like this you tend to go with the documentary evidence, because documents don't change.

This is not to say that the recollections of senior officials have little value or deserve a deep discount. To the contrary, even partial or reputation-enhancing reminiscences are useful for a historian, for they help put a mosaic together. Just always keep in mind Henry Kissinger's famous axiom that no one ever comes out second best in their recollected conversations. (Kissinger's massive memoirs are literary and historical master-pieces, but no one should ever base a book on his word alone.)

In the course of learning-by-doing, I came to place mem-oirs—along with diaries and letters—as my favorite source for insight into and details of presidents and other eminent his-torical figures. There are two useful rules for approaching such testimonials however.

First, lay aside memoirs written by senior aides while the subject is still in office, because they are often score-settling or reputation-preserving, and written to create a media frenzy. In the Reagan years, think of Don Regan's *For the Record*, with its sensational and overblown claims about Nancy Reagan and astrology, crafted to get on the best-seller list, or David Stock-man's *The Triumph of Politics*, attempting to vindicate Stock-man's disloyalty to President Reagan. Both, it should be added, were produced by ghost writers. Similar memoirs can be found from the Clinton White House, such as Robert Reich's bit-ter *Locked in the Cabinet*, or George Stephanopoulos's *All Too Human: A Political Education*, both written for the purpose of enhancing their post-White House careers.

Some senior figures can be trusted, if they tend to have a high quotient of humility and discretion. But such figures seldom produce memoirs. One very senior and highly loyal appointee once told me that he was reluctant to write a memoir because he was afraid of Nancy Reagan!

Second, therefore, the general rule biographers and historians should follow is that you should seek out memoirs and recollections of people whose names did not appear in the newspapers. They are more likely to tell you things that are true, interesting, original, and insightful. For example, despite the many excellent and probing biographies of Franklin Roosevelt over the decades, the best and most penetrating accounts of his first two terms are still the memoirs of his forgotten aide Raymond Moley, *After Seven Years* and *The First New Deal*.

And this brings me to the memoir you have in your hands. Frank Lavin's account of his time in the Reagan White House tells us what might be the American analogue to British costume dramas, namely what the key people "downstairs" did in the great drama of the Reagan presidency. Here you will hear the names of many unsung heroes of the Reagan presidency. Along the way Lavin relates a number of first-hand encounters with Reagan that I've never heard before, always with a point or lesson that adds to our understanding of "the Gipper". Lavin is candid in relating new details of a number of well-known conflicts inside the White House—the kind of conflicts that are endemic to every administration, but which the hostile media always tried to exploit in Reagan's time.

But it is much more than that: in addition to relating a well-paced, first-hand account of what he saw and did in the wider world of Reagan's presidency, Lavin offers a compelling account of how Reagan profoundly affected his own outlook. This is a rare combination of first-person narrative of people and events, and the deeper meaning of what took place, both for himself and for the world. In this respect it reminds me of one other book, our mutual friend Peter Robinson's *How Ronald Reagan Changed My Life*.

Here and there Lavin pauses to ask enduring questions about the nature of public life that transcend the Reagan years, and thus offers valuable lessons for all times. He offers specific considerations of how certain aspects of presidential administrations work that will be useful to anyone who works in the White House under either party. In other words, this is no ordinary memoir. It is a classic, and worth the wait for Lavin to ponder over and write now that the years have lengthened since Reagan was with us. I am sure you will find it as gripping and memorable as I did.

Steven F. Hayward, author of *The Age of Reagan*

INTRODUCTION

JANUARY 6, 2021

I had been mulling over this book for a number of years, making notes here and there, sketching out chapters, and doing some sporadic research at the Reagan Library. But the assault on the Capitol on January 6, 2021, convinced me that this book must be published. The formal Electoral College tally that day confirming Joe Biden's victory, after a chaotic scene in which rioters mobbed the Capitol and delayed proceedings for hours, should show Americans that a stew of confrontation, disregard for civic norms, and disrespect for the Constitution is poison for Republicans and poison for our Republic.

As Americans survey the 2020 Trump defeat and the chaos in the nation's capital, it should prompt us to reflect on past moments of success and consider how we can recapture the moral high ground, the policy initiative, and the hearts of American voters.

The moment is ripe for us to consider, once more, some of the guiding principles of Ronald Reagan. To be sure, these principles are not exclusive to Reagan, but he seemed to bring the right blend of substance, vision, and communication skills that made these ideas consequential.

America needs a vibrant two-party system, but one based on a competition of ideas and of policies—not a clash of personalities or a clash on the street. We need to reflect on what kind of country we want to see and what kind of political leadership it will take to get us there. Understanding the Reagan presidency is not a bad place to start.

CHAPTER 1

IT'S OVER

It was a sunny June day in 2004. I was at the National Cathedral in Washington, DC, attending the memorial service for Ronald Reagan, one of the four thousand guests paying respects. It was a somber moment, one of memories, prayers, and reflection.

In his eulogy, Reagan's vice president, George H.W. Bush, said of Reagan, "He was beloved, first, because of what he was. Politics can be cruel, uncivil. Our friend was strong and gentle.

"Once he called America 'hopeful, big-hearted, idealistic, daring, decent and fair.' That was America and, yes, our friend.

"And next, Ronald Reagan was beloved because of what he believed. He believed in America, so he made it his shining city on a hill.

"He believed in freedom, so he acted on behalf of its values and ideals.

"He believed in tomorrow, so The Great Communicator became The Great Liberator."

Margaret Thatcher, who served as Britain's prime minister from 1979 to 1990, even longer than the eight years of the

Reagan presidency, spoke next: "In his lifetime, Ronald Reagan was such a cheerful and invigorating presence that it was easy to forget what daunting historic tasks he set himself. He sought to mend America's wounded spirit, to restore the strength of the free world, and to free the slaves of communism. These were causes hard to accomplish and heavy with risk, yet they were pursued with almost a lightness of spirit, for Ronald Reagan also embodied another great cause, what Arnold Bennett once called 'the great cause of cheering us all up.' His policies had a freshness and optimism that won converts from every class and every nation, and ultimately, from the very heart of the 'evil empire.'"

As Brian Mulroney, prime minister of Canada from 1984 to 1993, attested, "Ronald Reagan was a president who inspired his nation—and transformed the world. He possessed a rare and prized gift called leadership, that ineffable and magical quality that sets some men and women apart so that millions will follow them as they conjure up grand visions and invite their countrymen to dream big and exciting dreams. I always thought that President Reagan's understanding of the nobility of the presidency coincided with that American dream."

President George W. Bush summed up, "Ronald Reagan believed in the power of truth in the conduct of world affairs. When he saw evil camped across the horizon, he called that evil by its name. There were no doubters in the prisons and gulags, where dissidents spread the news, tapping to each other in code what the American President had dared to say. There were no doubters in the shipyards and churches and secret labor meetings, where brave men and women began to hear the creaking and rumbling of a collapsing empire. And there were no doubters among those who swung hammers at the hated wall as the first and hardest blow had been struck by President Ronald Reagan.

"The ideology he opposed throughout his political life insisted that history was moved by impersonal ties and unalterable fates. Ronald Reagan believed instead in the courage and triumph of free men. And we believe it, all the more, because we saw that courage in him."

In less than an hour of eulogies, world leaders applauded Ronald Reagan's contributions as president and gave a sense of his human side as well. I was walking out of the National Cathedral after the service and chatting with Peter McPherson, who had served as administrator of the Agency for International Development. The ideas and the values are permanent, noted Peter, but why is there a sense of loss, even beyond the sense of loss for President Reagan?

I agreed with his observation. Yes, the ideas and the values are permanent and live past Ronald Reagan and past any of us. But there was a sense of melancholy—even beyond the fact that this was a memorial service—because as we looked around the cathedral and we saw our colleagues, we realize that what made the Reagan administration special was not just the leadership of Ronald Reagan and the enduring principles, but the particular mixture of individuals. The principles are here forever, but the distinct combination of personalities and how they interacted can never be recreated. We look around the cathedral, and we see shadows of ourselves. Shadows of what we once were.

WHY I AM WRITING THIS

Beyond his policy initiatives, the story of the Reagan presidency is the story of Reagan himself and of the varied cast of characters who worked for him. How does one capture a special moment and a special time? Can we step back from the shadows at the National Cathedral and reconstitute the moment and the personalities of the Reagan era?

Writing this book was like looking at a faded portrait. The Reagan days were ones of wonder, challenge, change, and perhaps some craziness. Today, the portrait has some sparkles left, but much color is gone. This book posed some challenges to me: How could I portray the distinct White House culture, the sense of mission, the camaraderie, and the *feeling* of the White House? Second, how could I assess the purpose, the goals, the wisdom, or the folly of what we attempted?

Jane Austen tells us in *Emma*, "Seldom, very seldom, does complete truth belong to any human disclosure; seldom can it happen that something is not a little disguised or a little mistaken." With that caveat in mind, this book attempts to offer some insight into Ronald Reagan and his presidency from a staffer's perspective. I try to be honest with the facts and honest with myself and others, but this is not an attempt at an academic history. In this book, I alternate between interior chapters that focus on my personal journey and exterior chapters that discuss broader themes that involve the White House or Ronald Reagan.

I write this not to criticize any particular person, so if offbeat notes occasionally surface, it is not for purposes of malice but to illustrate some of the idiosyncratic behavior with which I came into contact. We had a cause that united us, an important cause for our country and, indeed, the world. But we were beset with human flaws, with all of the resulting challenges in judgment and behavior. How to align the noble policy goals of the Reagan administration with the imperfections of the policy process is the story that follows. As for me, there were moments of success and times when I fell short. Against this backdrop of bold policy changes was my opportunity to grow from youth to adulthood, to try to harness my strengths of a high capacity for work and a gift of intelligence and diagnostics, and to control against weaknesses—in my case, a disposition that was, at times, sarcastic, flippant, or impatient; only average social skills and slow-improving communication and management skills. This story will tell how well Reagan did and how well I did.

There are three goals in writing this: to provide some sort of insight on day-to-day life in the Reagan White House; to better understand the Reagan presidency, what it was about and what he hoped to accomplish; and to draw some inferences on the US political system and government as well as how the White House operates.

There are considerable difficulties in evaluating any president because of the subjectivity involved. The first blush of political commentary largely reflects one's personal politics. If the president's views comport with your own, you happen to have a high opinion of him. If the president has a different philosophy than you—well, he could not have done a good job.

The second constraint in political evaluation is that people who cannot evaluate policy will tend to substitute a sort of moralizing. By this logic, there cannot be any reason for a policy different from your preferences, other than that the president is morally deficient. People who advocate less expensive energy do not care about the environment. People who advocate school choice are trying to defund public schools. People who want increased defense spending are militarists or bullies.

So much of the immediate political evaluation of Reagan was along those lines. If you are right of center, Reagan seemed pretty good. But if you are more or less left-of center, Reagan was not so good, perhaps even despised.

As we pass the forty-year mark of Reagan's election, perhaps this first blush of judgment has faded a bit and we can make an effort at being a bit more objective.

Let me suggest a three-fold measurement of a president:

- Did he more or less try to do what he said he was going to do during the campaign? This speaks to his consistency and his intellectual honesty.
- Did he more or less enact his program? This speaks to his competency and his ability to lead a political system.
- Was his program the right program in any event? This can take years to fairly evaluate and even then the analysis can be blurred by multiple causal factors.

I invite the reader to move beyond any personal philosophy and to evaluate Reagan across these three measurements. Perhaps political books need to come with a warning label. *Warning: if you are ideologically rigid and believe it is impossible for someone with different views from yours to be successful in politics except through underhanded tactics, this book is not for you. But if* you are intellectually curious and want to understand how an improbable president could achieve a successful tenure, allow me to share this story.

"There are years that ask questions and years that answer," said the writer Zora Neale Hurston. Journey back with me to the Reagan years as we attempt to make the shadows come to life, attempt to answer some of the questions.

CHAPTER 2

THE BACKGROUND: EXPLAINING FRANK LAVIN

Portrait of myself as a young man, *circa* **1975**

I was riding in a car in Washington, DC. It was 1975, I was a college freshman, and I was with a friend whose name I can no longer remember. The news on the car radio was about the Kama River truck plant in the Soviet Union. The plant was being built with assistance from Ford Motors, and it was to produce heavy trucks that critics said could be used for military purposes, which the Soviets and Ford both denied.

The radio story was that Young Americans for Freedom (YAF)—the conservative student group—was protesting the plan because of the concerns of possible military use of the trucks.

I was intrigued because I was unfamiliar with the issue, and only vaguely aware of YAF. "Who are these guys?" I asked aloud as the newscaster finished his story.

"They're nuts," my friend said dismissively.

"Well, they might be nuts," I reasoned, "but they have a good point on this issue, don't they?"

I joined YAF. Some of their views I might not have been entirely comfortable with, and I was opposed to the confrontational or theatrical politics to which some of its members were drawn. But on the big issues—the Soviet Union was a threat and the government was too big—YAF's positions were spot on. I was thinking like a Reaganite before I was a Reaganite.

The Kama River plant opened in 1976, and in 1979, when the Soviet Union invaded Afghanistan—its biggest military deployment since World War II—it transported soldiers and supplies in trucks built at the Kama River plant.

HOW I GOT HERE

How does one end up in the Reagan White House? An evolving interest in politics, a bit of luck, and perhaps my own personal strengths all played a role. I was fortunate to grow up in a comfortable upper middle-class family in a small city in the Midwest. My father returned from combat in World War II, finished college on the GI Bill, and found his way back home to Canton, Ohio, to join the family meat-packing business, marry, and raise four children. I was child number three, born in 1957.[1] This was lucky because family circumstances meant there was always a roof over our heads and food on the table. Though my father revealed later that in fact we had been subject to the ebb and flow of fortune that might accompany a small business, my parents made sure downturns and economic bad news never had an impact on our lives. Music lessons, summer camp, and family holidays all formed the fabric of a loving and carefree, if unremarkable, existence.

That connects to the other lucky aspect of Canton—the sheer everyday ordinariness of that sort of life helps one grow up with a minimum amount of pretension. My guess is that if you asked my parents what would be the greatest sin a person could commit, they would say rudeness or incivility. They were against any form of prejudice. Mind your manners. Be friendly. Play fair. Do unto others.

Our parents were keen on having us go as far as we could, academically and professionally. My father was the first generation of his family to attend college. My father's father was skeptical of the value of higher education but finally consented to allow my father to go to college on the condition that he attend an Ohio school and study business.

My parents' world was shaped by the Great Depression and the limits it imposed on possibilities, opportunities, and travel. Then the war came, and more limits. That changed in the 1950s with the post-war economic boom and the start of a family. The chief goal they wanted for us was to excel to the best

---

[1] My father's World War II service and family history is relayed in *Home Front to Battlefront.*

of our abilities. Try for the finest education available, including private schools.

I was first sent to parochial school, although we are Jewish, because St. Pete's would take me in first grade even with a birth date later than the public school cut-off. Then, when some people began organizing a local private school, my parents became enthusiastic backers, serving on the board, PTA, and in other leadership roles. It was almost natural that after eighth grade, I followed my two elder siblings to boarding school, Phillips Academy in Andover, Massachusetts. And in the fall of 1975, I found myself entering Georgetown University's School of Foreign Service because, at that time, I was drawn to the exciting lure of a diplomatic career in far-off lands.

As I moved on to boarding school, I began to develop a sense of political awareness. At first it was from a purely historical perspective. I had a small coin collection and became a somewhat serious collector for my age group. (Yes, not necessarily the best way to meet girls.) My dad had collected postage stamps when he was a child and thought it a worthy hobby. We would go to collectors' shows, flea markets, and swap meets as occasional weekend outings. I might every once in a while purchase or swap for an item. I began to notice political memorabilia such as campaign buttons and posters, and I started collecting that material as well. Then I began visiting campaign headquarters to ask for material—even writing candidates and campaigns asking for whatever they could spare. Soon I had an interesting collection as well. Meanwhile, I took to reading more about American political history, focusing on presidential races.

I slowly developed an interest in politics, but it took longer to develop a political philosophy. I remember initially finding the left appealing. I was in fifth grade during the 1968 campaign. Both my parents had disdain for Nixon and were unenthusiastic Humphrey supporters. George Wallace was appalling to them. That approach seemed suitable for me. I couldn't help but notice that at school most classmates took an opposite view. They were unenthusiastic for Nixon and had disdain for Humphrey. Wallace remained appalling. I was skeptical of the right because of the intolerance on its fringes. At school, we studied *The Grapes of Wrath* and several parents protested, keeping their children out of school so they would not see the movie version. To make matters worse, we were assigned to read (in fifth grade) Barry Goldwater's *The Conscience of a Conservative*, which was supposedly a summary of conservative philosophy. It was far too advanced for our small minds and left a bitter sense of conservatives as either narrow-minded and censorious, or overly intellectual and pedantic. The wise course of action in fifth grade was to have nothing to do with them.

By the 1972 election, I was more politically aware and more coherent in my thinking. McGovern seemed the logical choice at first. He was against the war, and the war was wrong, and Nixon (and Kissinger!) were for the war. True, there were a lot of silly things some of the anti-war people were saying and doing, but at base we could all agree that the war was bad and should be stopped.

But beyond any political leanings, I was excited about my growing habit of collecting political paraphernalia. It dawned on me that there would be no better place to collect material than at the Democratic and Republican National Conventions, both to be held that year in Miami, the Republicans approximately six weeks after the Democrats. The Republicans were organizing a charter flight from Cleveland as part of a national youth outreach effort to bring three thousand volunteers to Miami, at discount rates. That clinched it. I would go to the Republican convention as part of this program called "Young Voters for the President." I was neither a voter nor particularly for the President.

We had a lot of policy discussion at the Republican convention, and it somewhat convinced me that Nixon was the right man. Watching the Democratic convention on TV firmly convinced me that McGovern was the wrong man. McGovern personally did not endorse the excesses of his party's convention nor could he be fairly blamed for them. But it was more than coincidence that the radical left embraced him. I was thunderstruck that protestors at a "peace" rally or "peace" march might actually carry North Vietnam flags or pictures of Ho Chi Minh—while we were at war with North Vietnam. It struck me as egregiously bad judgment as well as disloyal. And it was done in a carefree carnival atmosphere that suggested the proponents had not given a lot of thought to North Vietnam or Ho, but that they were simply trying to be as outrageous as possible.

Similarly, I was aghast at the violence that erupted at the Democratic convention. Why were some of the protestors violent? Why did they resort to throwing rocks? Why not just vote for McGovern if that were your preference?

The Vietnam War was a wrenching experience for the United States, and however honest our intentions, it was clear that by 1972 America had little appetite to continue. At the same time, there was genuine anguish over our commitment to South Vietnam, legitimate concerns about human rights in North Vietnam, and questions regarding the political-military implications of the victory of a Soviet ally. It seemed we were keen on counting the costs of continued commitment, but not fully counting the costs of a withdrawal, although by that time a withdrawal was preordained. Yet wherever you stood in this complicated series of trade-offs, it seemed there was no basis for welcoming a North Vietnamese victory. A history teacher at boarding school showed us a "documentary" produced by the American Friends Service Committee dealing with human rights abuses in South Vietnam, including testimony from the "Winter Soldier Investigation," a group of returned Vietnam veterans who testified about human rights violations conducted by GIs in Vietnam. But just as criticisms of *The Grapes of Wrath* turned me away from conservatives four years earlier, blanket criticism of US soldiers and of American society turned me away from the left in 1972.

By the end of the 1972 campaign, I considered myself a Republican, though with my political philosophy still evolving. I was most concerned about foreign policy and in that regard most concerned about the Soviet Union. In 1973, I was a summer intern for the National Republican Congressional Committee. I was a Congressional Page in the summer of 1974. I then interned at the College Republicans office in the Republican National Committee where I worked directly for the national chairman, Karl Rove. With an effervescent personality, a mastery of political trivia, and a dry sense of humor, Karl was an easy person with whom to make friends. What's more, he had assembled in his leadership an eclectic group of high-energy, opinionated, and irreverent people with an impressive array of political knowledge and experience.

I attended various Republican campaign training schools and gatherings. The Young Republican Leadership Conference was one, which featured speakers who told us we were right and others were wrong and the various hospitality suites had open bars at night. The Teenage Republican Leadership Conference was another, whose speakers were even more on the right and told us we were right and others were wrong and there were hospitality suites but no drinking. The College Republican Student Fieldman School was by far my favorite, which featured people talking about how to win elections, making witty asides, occasionally criticizing even other Republicans including jokes about Nixon (growing in disrepute), and at night there were open bars with a chance to meet some intriguing people: some bright, some funny, some ambitious, some chasing girls, and some girls almost seemed to want to be pursued.

Even with the disgrace of Watergate, I relished this environment, becoming increasingly comfortable on the right and increasingly active in the College Republicans. This was a post-disaster moment for the GOP, in which the search for answers was in part an intellectual awakening for conservatives. *The Wall Street Journal* editorial page made a lot of sense. The Heritage Foundation put out timely, punchy papers on policy matters. Norman Podhoretz's *Commentary* magazine had a keen insight on the Soviet threat. It carried Georgetown Professor Jeane Kirkpatrick's "Dictatorships and Double Standards" article that explained the problem in equating an authoritarian with a totalitarian regime. (I was delighted to learn years later that Reagan also enjoyed the article, and it was through that essay he decided to bring Kirkpatrick into his administration.) There were articles in *Commentary* by Edward Luttwak, whose course I took on the Grand Strategy of the Byzantine Empire. For some reason, the lectures on Byzantium seemed to spill into a debate over MX basing systems. There were also articles in *Commentary* by Walter Laqueur, and I would take his graduate seminar as well. Another Georgetown Professor, Jan Karski, who had witnessed the worst of humanity, was a fraternity brother and a friend. *National Review* regularly published superb analysis and editorials, even with more stories than perhaps necessary on the Shroud of Turin. Slowly my political philosophy formed and I evolved into a more-or-less establishment conservative Republican.

My evolution continued. I sent a check into the Committee on the Present Danger because, well, there was a present danger. Whereas only a few years before, *The Conscience of a Conservative* had been a turn-off, Milton Friedman's *Capitalism and Freedom* captured me with its argument that market economics offered not only better economies, but better societies. Whittaker Chambers's *Witness* grabbed me with its combination of high drama, historical relevance, and philosophical discussion on the nature of communism.

At Georgetown, I joined the College Republicans and eventually became president of this four hundred-member club. It was a free-floating polity with a range of opinions, issues, passions, and intelligence. Membership could be grouped into three general categories: establishment, conservative, and libertarian. The establishment types were generally well-to-do and were Republicans because that was appropriate behavior for their socioeconomic class. The conservatives were more ideological and focused on tax cuts, stopping the Soviet Union, and social issues such as abortion. The libertarians were a bit of a mystery and did not always seem to represent a coherent philosophy. You could appeal to the establishment Republicans by quoting Abraham Lincoln. You could appeal to the conservative Republicans by quoting Winston Churchill. And you could appeal to the chemical Republicans by quoting Jerry Garcia.

Popular historians often view the 1970s with disdain, with the seminal political events of that decade being the US withdrawal from Vietnam, the subsequent communist takeover, the Watergate scandal, and Nixon's resignation in disgrace—all of these events running at odds with Americans' self-perception. Weren't the Republicans the party of probity and economic rationalism? When it came to international behavior, wasn't the US always one of the good guys? And didn't we always win? Ho Chi Minh had a different point of view, that communists were always the good guys and they would always—inevitably—win. But when it came to democracy, our system produced people of unusual talent and character, didn't it? Or maybe the open nature of our system also catered to emotion and left plenty of room for hustlers, grifters, and opportunists as well as for noble acts.

But this political turmoil at the national level was in contrast to what was taking place at the personal level. To come of age just after the draft ended meant there was no longer any military conscription. And the national trend to lower the drinking age to eighteen meant that any bar would readily serve a seventeen-year-old. And there was a revolution in sexual mores, even though I never quite seemed to catch that train. Some voices in the women's movement encouraged women to assert themselves through sexual activity just as tobacco companies encouraged women to assert themselves by smoking cigarettes. "You've come a long way, baby," was one brand's slogan. Smoking and sexual activity were each positioned as a natural step in the march of progress, but for me, I never cared for smoking. During the pledging process at my fraternity, I was asked about the number of partners I had, and I reflected that the ideal answer here was "one." Yet my history rounded off to zero.[2] Yes, the decade was cursed with bad music, bad TV shows, and bad hair styles, but no draft and the availability of alcohol meant it was a lot of fun to be staying alive.

And the strangest thing about the 1970s is that, although Watergate damaged Republicans and 1974 was a rout for the Democrats, by the end of the decade there had been a shift to the right. By 1980, core Republican themes of peace through strength, market economics, and traditional values had resonance.

During that period, I became more interested in practical politics. I had read everything Theodore White had written, even his China book. Read Germond and Witcover. Was enthralled with *Fear and Loathing on the Campaign Trail*, *The Boys on the Bus*, and *The Advance Man*. I thought I knew something about

---

[2]   A friend described my approach to dating as akin to the British army in World War I: purposeless, but with great dignity.

campaigns, and I wanted to play a role. I turned eighteen in October 1975 and took a semester off from Georgetown in 1976 to become a fieldman in Senator Robert Taft's reelection campaign back home in Ohio.

1976—ENTER REAGAN

The first vote I ever cast was against Ronald Reagan, when I voted for President Gerald Ford in the 1976 Ohio Republican primary while working for Senator Taft. Yes, what Reagan said made sense. We needed to stand up to Soviet expansion. And the government was too big and too expensive. But there was also a risk with Reagan, wasn't there? And Ford meant no surprises. He wore well, and was an unpretentious, honest Midwesterner. Isn't there something a little off-putting about Hollywood, with its celebrity culture? (There were buttons that said, "Reagan is an Actor.") And in the post-Watergate era, wasn't Ford's predictability welcome? Having just thrown one president overboard, did we really want to throw another?

The Reagan challenge to Ford had its origins before the formal 1975 start of the campaign. In many respects, the split was inevitable; the Republican Party by the mid-1970s encompassed several different philosophical tendencies, as well as different cultural and geographical groupings. And the natural conservative impulse to respect the incumbent hierarchy was shattered by Watergate. Various missteps by Ford (some literal) only sharpened the view that he was not up to the office and further undermined his claim to legitimacy.

No doubt some of these differences were overstated, and Ford and Reagan philosophically had much in common. Other aspects of the differences were accentuated for tactical purposes. But in some vital ways, they represented different outlooks, a different philosophy of government. Reagan was anti-establishment and Ford was establishment. Reagan was a leader and Ford was a manager. Reagan wanted to change the system and Ford wanted to run the system well.

Ford embodied the main street heart of the party, and Reagan represented the Sunbelt future of the party. There were also differences of personality and ideology. Ford had made a career in Washington and brought hope to post-Watergate Republicans who felt we had to get back to basics with a candidate whose integrity was beyond reproach. On the other hand, Reagan captured the imagination of those who felt Washington itself needed to change.

What Reagan was and what he represented demographically is somewhat of an elusive question, though notably he had greater blue-collar appeal than Ford and greater appeal to ethnic voters. Reagan's populist appeal was a neat trick for a movie star. Although Reagan did not have a wealthy lifestyle, it was hard to see that he had much in common with the man on the street due to his Hollywood years. But he did have empathy, coming as he did from a poor background. He did have a lack of arrogance and pretension. And he had a willingness to engage and approach. Nonetheless, his populist appeal must have confounded Gerald Ford, who had also come from a modest background.

In some respects, Reagan's 1976 campaign prefigured both the positive and negative aspects of his presidency. In a positive sense, we see Reagan's leadership gifts: his courage in taking on a sitting incumbent, his vision in seeing the Soviet Union as the key political and moral challenge of his times, his insight in talking about the size of government, his communication skills in television speeches with his powerful appeal to voters, and even his tactical boldness in naming Pennsylvania Senator Richard Schweiker as his running mate.

But we also see some of the less successful aspects of his presidency. During the 1976 campaign, he repeatedly showed a limited interest in management and uneven attention to details. In more than one state, the Reagan campaign failed to file a complete delegate slate. When the campaign was strapped for cash, donations were not processed in a timely fashion, with literally bags of donations left unopened. Similarly, Reagan was generally unwilling to fire people, waiting until internal staff dissensions threatened to sink his entire campaign.

I had—and still have—strong establishment impulses. Not merely to defend the status quo, but I felt one should respect those in positions of leadership. They had paid their dues, they had been proven successful in the polls, and I was loath to join a rebellion. When I was working for Senator Taft in his ill-fated 1976 reelection campaign, I feared that Reagan at the top of the ticket might doom Taft's chances. I might have been right about that, except that Taft lost anyhow that fall, and Jimmy Carter carried Ohio against Gerald Ford. The Taft campaign seemed underpowered, generating limited enthusiasm. Taft himself, though dedicated and bright, had the patrician mannerisms of pre-TV age politicians. He did not warm to crowds, and they did not warm to him. The Democratic nominee, Howard Metzenbaum, seemed to capture the energy of that year. Still,

I had the good fortune to work with Rick Segal, who was my boss in the campaign and a good friend over the years. And the key lesson of 1976 was that nothing was necessarily gained by embracing the establishment. There might be less there than meets the eye.

DESPONDENCY OVER CARTER

The initial promise of the Carter Administration faded quickly. Like Reagan, Carter was also an outsider, and he campaigned, plausibly, as a moderate. Carter joined Reagan in criticizing Ford for not welcoming Solzhenitsyn to the White House. And Carter was a Naval Academy graduate, a nuclear submariner, and a Sunday school teacher, for gosh sake. How left-wing could he be? But we soon discovered that a mainstream lifestyle did not mean mainstream politics.

Despite his native intelligence and his establishment background, it was increasingly clear that Carter was in over his head. America was going the wrong way. The economy suffered perhaps the greatest rise in the misery index in US history—ironic as the term was coined by Carter in 1976 to go after Ford. This misery index was 13.4 percent when Carter was running against Ford and averaged 19.6 percent in 1980, with 12.5 percent inflation and 7.1 percent unemployment. And there was a growing view that the US tilt toward détente had not induced the Soviets to behave better. Indeed, with aggressive military support of communist movements in Africa, Afghanistan, Cambodia, and elsewhere, there was a sense that the Soviets were on the march and that Carter was not up to the challenge. Compared to this picture of a floundering Carter, even

Ted Kennedy looked appealing—he had a vision and a sense of where he wanted to take America.

Carter's "malaise" speech seemed to blame the American public for the problems we faced. His view was one of limits. What a contrast with Reagan's optimism, which saw the American people not as part of the problem, but as part of the solution. One of the irreducible obligations of a leader was to believe in his cause, to believe in his country, to believe in himself. Carter projected ambivalence about the American people and his own mission. He will be remembered by history as bright, honest, and earnest, but simply not up to the job. *TIME* magazine described the Carter presidency as "characterized by small people, small talk, and small matters."[3]

Historian Edmund Morris captured the Carter Administration: "An obsession with allegedly dwindling natural resources; a smallness of outlook, from the cancellation of the supersonic transports to the issuance of bills for White House hospitality; public lights dimmed, cardigans unbuttoned, hemorrhoids proclaimed, human rights called for, the Panama Canal forfeited, fifty-two American hostages in Iran; eight helicopters sent in to rescue them, in a demonstration of dragonfly wrath…the nadir…of American prestige in the post-Eisenhower era."[4]

As for me, I continued with studies at Georgetown, somewhat unenthusiastically. School was but a necessary path to get to the adult world. I remained intrigued by political campaigns

---

[3] Roger Rosenblatt, "Out of the Past, Fresh Choices for The Future," *TIME*, January 5, 1981, https://time.com/archive/6856173/out-of-the-past-fresh-choices-for-the-future/.

[4] Edmund Morris, *Dutch: A Memoir of Ronald Reagan* (United Kingdom: Random House Publishing Group, 2011), 406–407.

and I spent the summer of 1977 working for Walter Craigie, the State Treasurer of Virginia, who was a candidate for the GOP lieutenant governor nomination and lost the nomination in what some saw as a proxy for the Ford-Reagan race of the previous year. Craigie was as bright and dedicated a public servant as you might find, but he was not a natural politician. He suffered from an establishment pedigree and from the desire of some Reaganites for revenge. The party leadership understandably liked him and they were properly concerned about the Democratic nominee, Chuck Robb, a charismatic Marine veteran who had the good fortune of being LBJ's son-in-law. Robb was correctly seen as someone who could appeal to centrist voters and pose a long-term threat to Republicans, and he validated those fears once he became lieutenant governor, by winning the governorship, and then two terms in the Senate.

In 1978, I took another flier on a remote race: the Republican nominee for attorney general of Texas. Frank Donatelli was the campaign manager, and he asked me to help with research. It was my good fortune in future years to serve under Frank in several capacities during the Reagan administration, and I benefited enormously from his wisdom, his even-keeled management style, and his friendship. Yet we faced an uphill task. No Republican had been elected attorney general in Texas in over one hundred years, but the state was increasingly Republican and former Deputy Defense Secretary Bill Clements was the nominee for governor. The other fortuitous meeting I made in that campaign was with the attorney general candidate himself: James A. Baker, III. I saw in Jim Baker in 1978 what Washington, DC, saw in him in 1981—that he was bright and methodical (a bit like his old Princeton roommate, Walter Craigie). But Baker had more of a natural instinct for politics and had superb analytic and presentation capabilities. He had made his mark as chief delegate hunter for Ford during the 1976 primaries, and his 1978 campaign was seen somewhat as a stalking horse for a 1980 run for Bush (41) in Texas.

Baker was not a natural glad-hander—no Bill Clinton, willing to spend twenty minutes chatting with the check-out clerk. But he was a natural when it came to strategy, policy, and prioritization. He showed in the 1978 race a keen attribute of crisis management: deciding what *not* to do. A successful campaign—like a successful administration—can undertake only a finite number of tasks. But ideas, worthy or not—experiments, rumors, demands, and suggestions—vastly outpace a campaign's ability to process, respond, analyze, and verify, so a campaign can be in perpetual crisis. It needs discipline to determine what are the three or four necessary components of the race that could take it to victory and how does it ensure it is allocating resources against those essential tasks? In other words, the ability to say "no" is a key element of management and Baker was a master of this art of discipline.

In many respects, it was a normal campaign with speeches, position papers, and fundraisers. However, at the time, it was the most elaborate and successful Republican campaign for attorney general in history. The number three job in the number three state. I stayed with Jamie Baker, the candidate's eldest son (later a successful attorney in his own right), in a house that had been the family home of Woodrow Wilson's foreign policy advisor, Colonel Edward House. One weekend I was in an Austin barbecue joint with Jamie, when a man next to me grabbed a woman in a highly inappropriate fashion. Ignoring the admonition to mind your own business, I grabbed his wrist and asked him what the heck he was doing. The man properly rewarded me with a rabbit punch and Jamie thankfully hustled me out of there leaving me with a black eye for my troubles. I quickly learned how some people do business.

Bush (43) was running the same year for Congress in West Texas where he had grown up. Clements won, Baker lost—thankfully, I would add, as it allowed him to play a national role—and Bush (43) also lost. I returned to Georgetown. The Baker campaign was a useful proving ground. Several of the staffers went on to the Reagan administration in addition to Frank Donatelli; Jim Cicconi, bright, capable, and not too far out of law school, was the research director and my immediate boss. He went to the West Wing as special assistant to Baker. Pete Roussel, whose easy-going demeanor hid sharp communications skills, became a deputy press secretary. Lisa Stoltenberg was to bring a quick mind and strong diligence to the White House.

LEARNING TO LIKE REAGAN

By 1980, Ronald Reagan stood unrivaled on the American political landscape, though neither his nomination nor his election were foregone. But only Reagan could bring together the three main currents of conservative philosophy—economic, foreign policy, and social—and do so in a fashion that was up-beat and inclusive. Right message; right messenger.

Still, many of his political opponents simply did not take him seriously. Perhaps the single most common fallacy in political analysis is to believe that someone who differs from you on issues is somehow unintelligent, corrupt, or otherwise deficient. Just as the critics of Reagan pushed me away from him in 1976, they pushed me toward him in 1980. He was not unintelligent, though he was plain-spoken. He was interested in ideas and he had a philosophy of government, but he never fancied himself an intellectual. He was not a manager, as he preferred big ideas to government minutia. And he was not narrow-minded. He had a certain traditional view of the world, but his years in Hollywood also demonstrated to him that people come in all shapes and sizes.

Some of the other Republican candidates were also interesting. George H. W. Bush was appealing in some respects, though Reagan's message fit better with my worldview. And I did not care for Bush's depiction of supply side economics as "voodoo economics," a clever phrase, but unhelpful to the ticket and misleading. Bush had a lot of strengths, but Reagan had the vision.

Howard Baker was also running, and he was intelligent, serious about government, and one of the most pleasant people you will ever meet in politics. Bob Dole, Phil Crane, John Connally, and John Anderson also were running, but I did not find any of them particularly appealing. To my mind there was one big question. Who would stand up against the Soviets? There was only one answer: Ronald Reagan.

British political scientist Isaiah Berlin wrote an essay about the fox and the hedgehog, describing different types of leadership models. The fox knows many things. The hedgehog knows one big thing. The fox is the ultimate tactician, who knows the ins and outs of every challenge. Reagan was more of a hedgehog. He knew not one big thing, but a few big things, the most important ones. The Soviet Union was a threat and had to be dealt with. Tax rates were a disincentive. Economic growth is important for reasons far beyond the economy. Rarely did a man fit his times as well as Ronald Reagan fit the 1980s.

Reagan's depiction of the Soviet Union as an "evil empire" is memorable in part for the consternation it caused among certain intellectuals and the disdain that many showed for his remarks. Sometimes when the situation is so bad, it takes a certain amount of guts just to speak the truth. "To see what is in front of one's nose is a constant struggle," stated George Orwell. As a consistently predatory and repressive state, the Soviet Union was evil and it was an empire. That simple assertion seemed a reasonable starting point for any serious discussion of Cold War foreign policy. If we could not get that right, we would not be able to get anything else right. For if we did not consider the Soviets particularly evil, nor particularly an empire, what were they? Why should we care? In this alternative universe, the Soviets were nothing worse than a clumsy version of Canada, having differences with the U.S. perhaps, and capable of boorish behavior, but there would be no particular need to be concerned about them even if they invaded one country, destabilized yet another, spread anti-American propaganda in a third, and arrested dissidents at home.

In 1979, I was in college and my roommate, Gaines Cleveland, and I established a small graphic design firm, creating print ads and letterhead for people on a part-time basis. Karl Rove called us up in the fall and asked if we would design the Bush 1980 logo. This caused great excitement for Gaines and me. It was an honor to be asked. But we weren't certain if we were for Bush. We debated this rather elementary request for several days. We decided we could do this job even with our reservations, as we were providing general assistance not strategic assistance. When we called Karl back to tell him we were ready to help, he told us we were too late, they already had a designer put together the Bush material.

We were annoyed at ourselves for dithering and vowed not to make the same mistake again. An independent conservative group, National Conservative Political Action Committee (NCPAC) called shortly thereafter and asked if we would do some design work for their independent expenditure campaign for Reagan, and we readily agreed. We were working on national presidential ads as college seniors, which we smugly felt was some sort of record until Mike Murphy started producing national ads as a Georgetown college sophomore. One more interesting brush with history occurred when Hugh Hewitt, now a nationally known radio host and columnist, invited me to do research and writing work for Richard Nixon, which was a rewarding activity and gave me the chance to meet Nixon several times.

As I finished at Georgetown, I continued to rise in College Republican leadership, eventually serving as national treasurer, and, in 1979, I was an unsuccessful candidate for national chairman. However, maybe you can learn more from losing than from winning. I developed a lifelong group of friends, many who I worked with in later years, from campaigns to the White House. In 1980, I went to Taiwan to study Chinese, and I returned in the fall, just in time for the elections.

My exposure to China wasn't my main life-changing event while at Georgetown. I started going steady with a girl and it became increasingly serious (Those eyes! That sass!). I had one of the great occasions of good fortune in my life: I fell in love with Ann Wortley, and we were married a few months after graduation. Dickens expresses the feeling better than I could: "I was not merely over head and ears in love with her, but I was saturated through and through. Enough love might have been wrung out of me, metaphorically speaking, to drown anybody in; and yet there would have remained enough within me, and all over me, to pervade my entire existence." Karl Rove was my best man at the wedding.

Dating Ann also brought about inadvertent contact with the 1980 Reagan campaign. I had returned from Taiwan in the fall of 1980 as the presidential campaign was in full swing. Ann's father, George Wortley, was running for the GOP congressional nomination in Syracuse, New York. George was the favorite, but barely; his front-runner status largely stemmed from the fact that he had been the nominee in 1976 and captured a credible 46 percent of the vote as Jimmy Carter carried the state. However, George was being pressed in his attempt for a 1980 rematch by the 1978 nominee, Peter DelGiorno.

Thus the 1980 Republican primary was largely a contest between two former nominees, with two smaller candidates as well. George was the slight favorite in polls and in fundraising, but Peter was energetic and determined to press the campaign.

The weekend before the September 9 Republican Primary, DelGiorno ran a TV ad that had been produced for his 1978 campaign in which he was endorsed by Reagan. The ad ran without any explanation that the endorsement was from 1978 and the viewer was left with the unmistakable, but inaccurate, conclusion that Ronald Reagan had jumped into the Syracuse congressional primary and was now endorsing DelGiorno—a calamity for George Wortley. The ads started on the Saturday before the Tuesday primary, so it looked very unlikely to turn this around in the forty-eight hours before the vote. The Wortley campaign was flooded with unhappy phone calls.

That same day, I called the Reagan campaign to discuss the problem and ended up speaking with the regional political director, Roger Stone. Yes, that Roger Stone. Today known for his connection to Donald Trump and his prison sentence, in 1980, Roger was a well-regarded Reagan operative, responsible for the Northeast states. Roger was justly unhappy at the misuse of an old endorsement and he went on the warpath. And he did a fabulous job. Before the end of the day Saturday, he was able to call *The Post-Standard* in Syracuse and as Roger later related to me: "Governor Reagan is furious. I was able to reach him on the campaign plane and he is quite unhappy that his good faith effort to assist the ticket two years ago is being misused. He insists the ad be taken down immediately."

DelGiorno had to pull the ad and his campaign put out a hapless statement that it had been run "by accident." He looked a bit foolish because, well, he was a bit foolish. George beat Peter 40 percent to 30 percent and went on to win the general election as well.

I returned to DC and started volunteering in Reagan's transition office, "The Office of the President-Elect" after Election Day. I had formally entered the world of Ronald Reagan.

Ann broke her ankle a week before the wedding and went down the aisle in a wheelchair. On the left, my siblings Doug, Maud, and Carl, and on the right are my parents, Carl and Audrey.

CHAPTER 3

THE GREAT COMMUNICATOR

Where did the label "The Great Communicator" come from? Surely other presidents were competent communicators, or had charisma, or a sense of style, even if some were a bit plodding. What made Reagan "great"? Many academics note Reagan's substantive approach to issues and his philosophical consistency.[5] As Reagan stated in his farewell address, "I wasn't a great communicator, but I communicated great things...." No doubt those are foundational elements in communications, but there was more to it. Reagan was a great communicator because he had a great life, meaning there was enough breadth of experience, enough hardship, and enough success that allowed him to flourish, to empathize, and to be creative. Indeed, we can point to three particular life experiences that gave rise to those communication skills.

---

[5] Robert C. Rowland, "Principle, Pragmatism, and Authenticity in Reagan's Rhetoric" (paper presentation, Ronald Reagan Centennial Symposium, University of Southern California, February 2011).

The first was Reagan's experience with radio. Here, Reagan had a great teacher: Franklin Roosevelt. FDR's Fireside Chats were considered revolutionary at the time, but when we listen to them today they might seem a bit ordinary. What was so special about a Presidential radio address? Was it simply the name "Fireside Chat" that was supposed to engender familiarity? Was it that the US was in the Great Depression and needed reassurance?

FDR did two things no one else in the country had ever done (or had ever done methodically). In the short span of radio history, an "address" was typically the radio broadcast of a speech or a rally. The radio network would go to a national party convention, or a university, or the Economic Club of New York, and broadcast the speech that was being given. There was no recording technology in those early days, so speeches were carried live. What FDR understood with his radio address was that the radio audience wasn't an after-thought or a by-product of the actual audience, but the radio audience would be considerably larger than that in-person audience. There was not even a need for a "real" audience. There was no need for the newspapers—frequently unsympathetic—to intermediate and report on what Roosevelt was saying. For the first time, the American public could hear the president directly, without any interpretation from the traditional media. FDR was the first American political leader to systematically craft a message exclusively for radio, exclusively for the radio listener. The man went "virtual" well before our digital times.

That led to the other FDR innovation. Since he was speaking to families at home in the evening, his address was geared toward individual listeners. He used conversational tones, everyday metaphors, references to the household, the fireside. He realized it was more powerful to draw the listener into a conversation that was seemingly one-on-one rather than to have the listener be in an audience listening to the president speak to a large group. Grandiosity and bureaucratese would weaken the effect. Rather than a pretentious, "The President will now address the National Association of Civic Leagues," this radio address was called a "chat," the word that friends use when they talk with each other.

As James Fallows noted: "The most important words in Franklin Roosevelt's initial fireside chat, during the depths of the Depression and banking crisis in 1933, were the two very first words after he was introduced. They were: *My friends*."[6] One was immediately drawn into FDR's inner circle.

It wasn't Roosevelt's majesty that people admired, it was his accessibility. Reagan describes listening to FDR: "His strong, gentle, confident voice resonated across the nation with an eloquence that brought comfort and resilience to a nation caught up in a storm and reassured us that we could lick any problem. I will never forget him for that."[7]

Reagan absorbed this. He voted for FDR all four times, and in the White House when Reagan referred to "the president," he was referring to FDR. Reagan was also a radio man. He frequently framed his remarks in the style of radio broadcasters.

---

[6]   James Fallows, "'My Friends': Communications and a 'National Family,'" *Our Towns*, May 8, 2021, https://www.ourtownsfoundation.org/my-friends-communications-and-a-national-family/.

[7]   Ronald Reagan quoted in H. W. Brands, *Reagan: The Life* (New York: Knopf Doubleday Publishing Group, 2015), 27–28. Kindle.

He introduced a weekly radio address. It was his medium in some respects: cool, controlled, informal, almost intimate. He could have a quick neighborly conversation with you and you welcomed it. Lou Cannon notes that although FDR and Reagan were serious about their policies, "they recognized that the decisive aspect of presidential leadership was inspirational rather than programmatic."[8]

Movies and television were the second life experience that made Reagan the Great Communicator. He came to political maturity not through the age of media, but through the age of *mass* media. You were speaking to the entire nation if you were in a movie, to people from all walks of life and from different political backgrounds. This is in sharp contrast from today's cable TV and social media in which the market is highly segmented and you are only speaking to like-minded people. Reagan's view of communications was that it was the tool to win people over. He wanted his remarks to be as inclusive as possible. He wanted to inject a bit of humor and to avoid friction in his rhetoric. He wanted to make it as easy as possible for people to agree with him or to at least accept as many of his points as possible.

Today, a western movie might be built around a crime story or it might be a romance, but in Reagan's day there was no audience segmentation. Every Roy Rogers movie included both crime and romance. For that matter, it included a song. Every Gene Autry movie was the same. Every movie had a fist-fight, a gun fight, a villain, a hero, a sweetheart, someone strumming a

---

[8]   Lou Cannon, *President Reagan: The Role of a Lifetime* (United States: PublicAffairs, 2008), 85.

guitar, and a lovable animal. There was always a moral lesson as well. The protagonist was always the hero. There was no anti-hero, no counter-culture hero. Virtue prevailed. Happy endings were mandatory, particularly during the Great Depression. Something for everybody. That was how you made a movie. That was how you made a speech.

It was not only the westerns. When the number of babies named "Shirley" tripled from 1933 to 1935 at the height of Shirley Temple's popularity, it showed the hold the movies and popular culture had on our imagination.[9] In the 1934 movie, *Stand up and Cheer!*, the FDR-*doppelgänger* president fights the Great Depression by creating a "Department of Amusement" to lift people's spirits. Shirley Temple's on-screen father announces to the secretary of amusement, "Mr. Secretary, the Depression is over.... People are happy again." Even though FDR's actual campaign song in 1932 was "Happy Days Are Here Again," the movie's over-the-top optimism strikes us today as a bit silly or juvenile. Yet, in 1934, when people around the world had to decide whether to put in their room a photo of Shirley Temple, or Hitler, or Stalin, maybe her idea of how to fight the Great Depression was the least silly of the lot.

There was something else about the film heroes . They were fundamentally establishment figures, but willing, when necessary, to work outside the system. They had a slight contrarian

---

[9] "Shirley" went from fourteen thousand to forty-two thousand in two years. As a reference, "Franklin" went from one thousand to 5,300 from 1931 to 1933 and established itself as a proper name for a child born to parents from the Great Depression, although my parents disclaim this. "Shirley Name Popularity," Our Baby Namer, http://www.ourbabynamer.com/Shirley-name-popularity.html.

bent. Perhaps more of a marching to a different drummer mentality than anti-establishment. But there was a reason why the hero of a new radio show also launched in 1933 was called "The Lone Ranger" and not the "Team Player Ranger" or the "Consensus-Building Ranger." America respected that contrarian, within bounds.

Reagan saw in television what FDR saw in radio. The broadcast was not a by-product of the event. It was the event. Mike Deaver took it a step further. The audience was the by-product. They were in the room only to make the broadcast look authentic. Reagan was really speaking to the man on the street, not to a collective, not to a leadership body. As pollster Dick Wirthlin noted: "People don't like 'speeches,' they like conversations."[10] Everything Reagan said on a broadcast was a statement to an individual person. He placed enormous effort on trying to establish a rapport with the audience.

Reagan related: "Radio was magic. It was theater of the mind. It forced you to use your imagination…. It's sad that we've now had several generations who've never had a chance to use their imagination in the way we did."[11]

And Reagan never lost the cadence of radio. He wouldn't just say: "*Walter Mondale has voted to raise taxes one hundred forty-two times.*" Instead, he would say: "*I want to tell you a story about a man. A friendly man, a man who could be a good neighbor, but a man whose first love was big government. In fact, this*

---

[10] Richard Wirthlin and Wynton C. Hall, *The Greatest Communicator: What Ronald Reagan Taught Me About Politics, Leadership, and Life* (Milwaukee, Wisconsin: Trade Paper Press, 2005), 69.

[11] Ronald Reagan and Robert Lindsey, *An American Life* (United States: Simon & Schuster, 1990), 59.

man was so committed to enlarging the government that he voted to raise your taxes some one hundred forty-two different times. The man's name? Walter Mondale."

Reagan explained it:

> When I was a sports announcer, I learned something about communicating with people I never forgot. I had a group of friends in Des Moines and we all happened to go to the same barber. My friends would sometimes sneak away from their offices or other jobs when I was broadcasting a game and they'd get together at the barbershop to listen to it; after a while, I began to picture these friends down at the shop when I was on the air and, knowing they were there, I'd try to imagine how my words sounded to them and how they were reacting and I'd adjust accordingly and spoke as if I was speaking personally to them.... Over the years I've always remembered that, and when I'm speaking to a crowd—or on television—I try to remember that audiences are made up of individuals and I try to speak as if I am talking to a group of friends...not to millions, but to a handful of people in a living room...or a barbershop.[12]

This takes us to the third element of Reagan's communication success. For Reagan, public speaking was an important

---

[12] Reagan and Lindsey, *An American Life*, 147.

means to an end, but it was also an end in itself. It was part of his identity, not only a professional tool. His skill at using that tool masked the deeper value.

That deeper value was this: growing up in limited circumstances, with parents of modest means and no particular social stature, and with his father Jack Reagan having his share of unemployment and drinking problems, perhaps the only time Jack and Nelle Reagan received any public accolades throughout their adult lives was when they performed in community theater. They could smile and take a bow, and the audience—the town—smiled back and applauded.

I think young Dutch Reagan absorbed a key lesson from that experience: public speaking is magic. It moves people. It teaches people. You can make people laugh. You can build a movement. And you can rise above your circumstances in life, regardless of how lowly you might have started. Take it seriously, and it is your key to a better life. When you lift others up, you are also lifting yourself.

Reagan took pride in personally writing and honing his remarks. Staff Secretary Richard Darman once noted he was as much of the Great Editor as the Great Communicator. Reagan was a craftsman and he respected the craft. He respected the technology and the medium. He respected Franklin Roosevelt. He respected the movies and television. He respected his mom and his loving, alcoholic dad and their life lessons. That's what made him the Great Communicator.

CHAPTER 4

1981–82 THE OFFICE OF PRESIDENTIAL PERSONNEL: AN UNEVEN START

One of my chores in the Office of Presidential Personnel (OPP) was to conduct the courtesy interviews. This was the term used for a chat with people whom the higher-ups had already determined were not a good fit, but who deserved the courtesy of a meeting. Yet if the

purpose of the meeting was to be polite, would it not be impolite to signal a false message?

This was a lead-the-horse-to-water exercise. I would start out subtly, "You know, this is an extremely competitive position." That was too subtle for many. "Extremely competitive," I repeated, attempting to dampen expectations. But Americans in general are not always easy to convince of their own limitations, and there is something about politics that can attract delusional personalities.

I met with a high school French teacher who wanted to be ambassador to France. "If that isn't open, I'd take Belgium," he added helpfully.

And a Kentucky highway patrolman who wanted to be a CIA officer, and showed up in full dress uniform. "But the president doesn't personally select CIA officers. You have to take a test and go through the interview process."

"C'mon. If the president wants to do it, he can do it."

The key to success in this job was to keep an absolutely straight face and deal with everyone in a sober, polite, and professional fashion.

Not surprisingly, whatever segment of the population that was most unrealistic in its expectations was also most likely to not take the news well. The first rule of the Dunning-Kruger club is that you do not know you are a member of the Dunning-Kruger club.

***

My duties did not change significantly with the inauguration. I continued doing roughly the same tasks, but I was working for the president rather than for the president-elect. I was a volunteer in the Office of Presidential Personnel, essentially a clerk.

I had no salary, no title, no assigned desk, no phone, nor did I have any sort of plan. But I knew a lot of people from the campaign, and it was a busy time. As the saying goes, nothing *propinks* like propinquity. If you want to be in on the action you had better find a way to get close to the action. The Transition Office shut down and I moved to the Old Executive Office Building (OEOB).

There was action. In 1980, the country wanted a change and Ronald Reagan provided it, bringing into his administration a range of enthusiasts who projected their hopes and their ideas into the new government. Now that Reagan had been elected (or more commonly, now that "we're in"), we were finally going to see some change in foreign policy. Some action at defense. Some pro-life movement. The tax cuts we need. An economic policy that moves America ahead.

The institution that would make sure the right people got into the right positions was the Office of Presidential Personnel, responsible for screening candidates and making recommendations to the president, cabinet secretaries, and independent agency heads. The civilian federal workforce in 1981 was about two million people, of which some three thousand were political appointees. Presidential Personnel was responsible for filling those positions.

The "eighteen acres" of the White House complex is comprised of the White House and the Old Executive Office Building (OEOB). The White House in turn is comprised of the West Wing, the mansion, and the East Wing. Perhaps close to two thousand people work in the White House complex, but that includes the grounds crew, the tour guides, the telephone operators, the Secret Service, the White House pastry chef, and hundreds of others who are part of the permanent edifice that helps the White House run. The substantive work of government is undertaken by a smaller group of three to five hundred specialists, divided among about a dozen White House offices. Each office is run by a member of the senior staff stationed in the West Wing. The West Wing also hosts the Press Briefing Room, the White House mess, and the NSC Situation Room. Most famously the West Wing hosts the Oval Office, the Cabinet Room, and the Roosevelt Room, named after both presidents Roosevelt, where senior staff meetings take place. The East Wing is primarily the Office of the First Lady and the Visitor's Office.

Moving into the White House complex were Reaganites—excited, motivated, burning with hopes, some burning with personal ambition, and representing all walks of life. California preppies. Texas ranchers. Ohio small-town merchants. Middle America children of firefighters and mailmen. Aristocrats, plutocrats, true believers, and Democrats. Some were longtime Reagan supporters ("Long Marchers"), some were very talented people, and some happened to be in the right place at the right time. Probably more of an amalgam of Americans than existed in any previous White House staff. They were an eclectic mix with not always a lot in common except a deep abiding belief that America needed help and that the Reagan administration would be the vehicle to make it happen.

The challenge for any new administration is how can all of this energy be harnessed productively and channeled into a government system? Campaigns are full of forward-leaning types who can be strong in initiative and creativity, but not always strong in thoughtful analysis. There is a "move fast and break things" attitude that might make sense in certain circumstances but might lead to problems in a government setting. "Better to ask forgiveness than to ask permission," one senior White House staffer told me. Yes, but...

That journey from campaign mode to governing mode was not always a smooth one, but there were any number of capable participants who made it work.

Down the hall there was Jim Warner in the Domestic Policy Office. An unassuming guy in an unassuming position. In fact, he was so low-key that you would have to really get to know him to know that he had served as a US Marine in Vietnam and had been a prisoner of war in North Vietnam for several years, held captive at the Hanoi Hilton. The American woman he married was a "red diaper baby" who grew up in a household where both parents were members of the Communist Party USA. She had seen the light and broken with her parents' faith. So both Jim and his wife knew communist party songs: those he learned while held captive and those she learned on her parents' knee.

Down the hall the other way was Morgan Mason, son of movie star James Mason (*Rommel!*), and future husband of rock *diva* Belinda Carlisle. Morgan was serving as Associate Director of the Office of Political Affairs. My wife, Ann, was working in Presidential Correspondence, the office that responds to people who write to the president, where one of her colleagues was Shirley Temple's son, Charles. Fess Parker's daughter, Ashley, worked in advance. These offspring of stars were unaffected, though the word might have a different meaning for someone from a Hollywood background than it did for other people. They were hard workers who were there to serve the president.

In the counsel's office was Wendell Willkie III, a top-notch attorney with a lofty pedigree, and throughout the building were friends, offspring, and relatives connected to past administrations and near-greats of history.

A stone's throw away was Dean Godson, a fast-talking Cambridge graduate with a clipped British accent, who ended up working as assistant to Navy Secretary John Lehman. Dean was then an American citizen who had grown up in Britain and continued to mystify his American colleagues with his British habits. He gained notoriety on his first day at work when he climbed into the back of a taxi and asked the driver to take him to the Pentagon. A quarrel quickly ensued, and Dean was somewhat rudely kicked out. Only later did Dean realize he had mistakenly climbed into the back of a DC police car. There is more to the story, but Dean went on to reclaim his British citizenship, run one of the leading London think-tanks, and become ennobled: he is now Baron Godson and sits in the House of Lords.

Joining the NSC was a Georgetown professor, Jose Sorzano. Fleeing Cuba as a kid, he worked his way through a PhD and earned a tenured professorship at Georgetown, giving it up to serve as Jeane Kirkpatrick's deputy at the UN. When I worked with him at the NSC, he told me of his arrival at the refugee camp in the US through Operation Pedro Pan, helping families get their kids out of communist Cuba. They arrived famished after the multiple legs of the evacuation and each kid was given an unfamiliar fruit—an apple—to tide them over until mealtime. "You don't eat the core," explained the camp staff. "What's a core?" asked Jose, as he had already eaten the apple whole, a combination of hunger and of never having seen such a fruit.

Most of the campaign leadership joined the administration. Campaign spokesman Lyn Nofziger grappled with the FBI clearance forms that asked him to list the residences he had held over the past fifteen years. True to his style, Lyn wrote on the form: "If you're so smart, you tell me." The FBI failed to see the humor in that comment, and even a year later Lyn was still wearing a temporary pass.

In the Office of Public Liaison, there was a Washington operator *par excellence*, Wolf, we'll call him. Wolf calls me over one day and in a hushed conspiratorial tone pulls out a folded gas station map of the greater DC area. On the map, Wolf has hand-marked Xs with various notations. "Oh are these bookstores?" I ask in one of my more naive moments and his head swivels toward me so quickly you almost hear the neck bones snap. I correct myself, "I mean restaurants?" Wolf is dismissive. "These are the *bimbos*. you need to know where the bimbos are. Can't be too far away from a bimbo." Wolf had the geospatial equivalent of a little black book.

And in a building in which people carried, sometimes ostentatiously, policy journals, CBO papers, CEA forecasts, and BLS data, campaign veteran Lee Atwater would carry the tabloids—*News of the World*, of the "Elvis found on Mars" headline variety. Lee had served as regional political director in the 1980 campaign and was now in the Office of Political Affairs. Lee was one of the more capable political operatives in the country, and he went on to serve as campaign chairman for George H. W. Bush's presidential race in 1988. Lee's point in reading the tabloids: *You are trying to understand where the world is going with data, but I am better able to understand where the world is going through the tabloids.* If you want to study animal behavior, you better understand what the animal eats. There is desk truth and there is street truth.

In addition to courtesy interviews, my initial job was moving paper, literally. Incoming resumes had to be processed. By today's standards, this was all pretty low-tech. No imaging, no scanning, no emailing, no tagging, no electronic storage and retrieval. Files were stored in, well, filing cabinets. Copies were made using a photocopier. Material was placed in an interoffice envelope and other clerks took it around to other offices. A pneumatic tube carried material from the OEOB to the West Wing. It was a reasonably efficient nineteenth century set-up. A resume came in from a scientist who might be a good candidate for Assistant Secretary of the Air Force for Science and Technology. One copy of the resume would go into an alphabetical system, one would go into a file created for that AF/AS/S&T spot and then we would also retain his resume in both the Army and Navy S&T positions because you never know and then we would make another copy to place with the Defense Department undersecretary's file, because that erstwhile Air Force assistant secretary could alternatively be an interesting chief of staff or science advisor to the undersecretary.

And there were the ghosts of the previous administration. You could see on the interoffice mailers the scratched-out names of officials of the Carter administration. You could find form letters from them on your Memory Selectric, the highest tech item available in the White House. The standard equipment was the IBM Selectric II. It had "auto-correct," a special key that would erase a letter without having to stop typing, paint over the error with correction fluid, wait for it to dry, and continue on your way. The Selectric II was a marvel, and the Memory Selectric better still. It was essentially a Selectric with a dial on the front panel. The dial had twenty settings and at each setting you could actually store a one-page letter or document. These were not widely in service and were generally reserved for executive secretaries.

I first worked for Rick N, an Associate Director of Presidential Personnel, though still unpaid. My job was to review incoming resumes and try to determine where they should be considered. Then make appropriate files and copies and route them. The Office of Presidential Personnel was divided into clusters or directorates, each representing a group of departments and agencies. There were over a hundred staffers in Presidential Personnel, many absorbed in the labor-intensive work of processing incoming resumes, phone calls, and interviews. Other staffers were working on identifying key vacancies that had to be filled, still another group interfaced with the political shop to make sure the campaign types got placed. The Office of the Vice President had a liaison to make sure the Bush people were taken care of.

I was working pretty full days; the fourteen-hour days weren't so bad, but the seven-day weeks got to be fatiguing— simply moving paper. I was doing all of this standing up in a room that was filled entirely with banks of file cabinets. I mentioned to Rick after about a week that if I had some sort of bureau or desk on which to sort I could do a better job. He agreed and a desk appeared. I mentioned to Chris H the secretary, that if I had a telephone, I could answer the phone when she was already on a call. She agreed and a phone was installed. I found a swivel chair in a hallway. Within a week I had seemingly progressed from low-level clerk to upper-level clerk.

Fortune intervened again, this time in the form of Lee Atwater, who strolled down from Political Affairs. I had known Lee since we both worked for Karl Rove in the early 70s in the College Republicans. "How ya doing?" he asked. I was doing fine. "You on staff here?" "No, I'm a volunteer." "We'll take care of that." Lee had some extra "120-day" appointment slots and he kindly threw one my way. Desk, phone, chair, paycheck. Bingo. I went to the White House administrative office and ordered business cards. I had moved from White House volunteer to White House staff, but seven years later Lee would present a bill (see Chapter 11) when he was put in charge of Vice President Bush's 1988 presidential campaign.

DR. YES

I later worked for "Wildman," another of the associate directors. He was a dramatic person, and religiously wedded to false positives. He was given to telling people on the phone, "I'm pulling for you. I'm doing everything I can. It's difficult but I'm going to the mat." Besides being overly theatrical, he typically ended up giving false hope to candidates. The easy thing to do was to be positive to candidates, but it could also be misleading. I felt this was bad management and ultimately unhelpful, playing on hopes in an attempt to be polite and I decided to search for a way of giving an honest response should it ever fall to me.

It did fall to me. My work for Rick and Wildman was deemed to be of strong enough quality that I was promoted to working for Willa Johnson, one of the associate directors of the entire Presidential Personnel shop, responsible for the defense and foreign policy cluster. Promotion is a bit of an elastic term here because I was still a file clerk. The files were in her office, there were rows of them, and it meant I was frequently running in and out. Sorting, filing, pulling. I was asked by Willa to do the courtesy interviews.

A typical candidate for a position would be a county Republican chairman or a Reagan delegate who was, surprise, of Irish ancestry and wanted to be ambassador to Ireland. In fact, ambassador to Ireland was the top spot sought in the foreign policy/defense cluster where I worked. My job was to try to let people down easily. Some were indignant. Some were angry. I finally hit on an approach that would let them down, and not cause ill-will.

I went to the resume bank and selected the four resumes that threw off the most sparks. One such person had multiple PhDs, spoke several languages, had written a number of books, done great volunteer work for Reagan, and so forth.

I would take the courtesy interview for a candidate who wanted to be ambassador to France and whisper to him, "Well, I'm really not supposed to do this, but let me show you the other candidates for the position." Then I would hand him these three or four of these high-energy resumes and let him flip through them.

Usually there would be a low whistle or a groan. "Gosh this guy looks pretty good."

"That's what I'm telling you."

"I don't have a PhD in French history and another one in French literature," they would continue.

"I see what you're saying."

"Well, what about the Belgian position?"

"These resumes are for the Belgian position."

One advantage of working for Willa is that she saw I was always there. And it turned out to be essentially seven-days-a-week work, from dawn to dusk. The work itself was not intellectually demanding, but it was draining in terms of the time. It was one of these routine bureaucratic positions in which no one would notice if you did a good job, but would if you did a poor one. At least given my proximity to Willa, she would be aware of the hours I was putting in. With heavy doses of coffee and no free time to socialize, I ended up losing about twenty pounds over three months.

A second advantage of this proximity was a habit Willa had of thinking out loud. She was regularly referring to a matter on her desk and would wonder aloud, "Who is so and so?" She was dealing with tens of thousands of job seekers, among which there might be several thousand serious candidates, each of whom had political supporters, and the supporters themselves would contact Willa, as would political leadership, campaign leadership, members of Congress, and policy types.

She had to keep straight in her mind that there were thirty candidates who might be interested in being deputy director of the United States Information Agency, of which there were actually eight who were plausible, and three who were quite strong, but there were also about sixty people who were trying to contact her on behalf of one of the eight, or one of the broader group of thirty, and there were also journalists trying to cover this and just as you were winnowing down the list someone would walk down the hall and say you need to put this person on your short-list. He was supposed to be deputy secretary of agriculture but got knocked off the list because he wouldn't sell his family farm, and you'd say, "C'mon you gotta be kidding, what connection does agriculture have with USIA?" And he'd say, "If you wanna argue with Deaver, go right ahead. This guy is Deaver's pal and was deputy ag sec for California. Just give him some thought for USIA." And if you are thinking quickly, you could say, "Look, isn't it a better fit to plug him into AID, where there is the Food for Peace program, and at least we can draw on his ag background?" If you were not thinking quickly, you'd have to see Mike on Friday afternoon at the weekly management meeting, and maybe you could pull him aside and plead with him to take this dep sec of ag for California (excuse me, the *former* dep sec) off your hands and find another job. Of course, there might be a cost to this as well, if you pursued it clumsily.

So-and-so wanted to serve on the President's Council on Physical Fitness? Hmmm, who is she? I see, an aerobics instructor from California. But wait a second; she is the instructor of Ursula Meese, Ed's wife. Is she any good? Does she have a policy background? Does Ursula Meese support her efforts? Does Ursula even know the instructor is making a play? And what about Ed Meese, who always struck me as a genial and professional, but maybe he's not particularly genial when it comes to how his wife's aerobics instructor is handled. Better tread carefully. (From everything I saw, Meese was indeed professional and ethical in his conduct, but you don't always know this in real time.)

But the real value in working for Willa was that I had a strong memory and a gift for names so I could frequently answer her out-loud questions. Who is so-and-so? *He headed the Missouri Reagan campaign in '76, but was only honorary chairman in '80.* Why? *Because the governor wanted to head the campaign, and the national people deferred to the governor, wisely in my view.*

Who just called? *He's in the DC bureau of the* Dallas Morning News. *Not sure how friendly he is, but he's not hostile.*

Who is this guy who wants to be an ambassador? *He served as lieutenant governor of Ohio in the 1970s.*

Once she was talking out loud and said, "Now what's the number for so and so?" and I rattled it off the top of my head. She was a bit startled. "Where did you get that?"

"Well, you called the fellow yesterday."

"But I must have made thirty other calls since then—did you remember all of them?"

Not all of them, just those you were stating aloud. She quizzed me on several phone numbers, and I got them. I don't think I have a photographic memory, but odd things will stick in my mind. I will chalk it up to the endless caffeine.

***

As central as the Personnel Office was to the success of the Reagan administration, the most critical developments of 1981 were in other offices. James Baker itemized the top three priorities of the new administration: the economy, the economy, the economy.[13] The president had put forward a rather ambitious economic plan to get the US economy out of the doldrums. Reagan's plan involved spending cuts to shrink the size of government (more accurately, to slow its rate of growth); deregulation to spur growth; sound monetary policy to kill inflation; and most controversially, tax cuts both in rates and absolute amounts to spur growth. The tax cut proposals were the most contentious politically because they were rather ambitious—the final version was a tax cut spread over three years—and because they were based on a reduction in tax rates, those paying taxes would benefit proportionately. Reagan needed Democratic votes to get his bill through. In negotiations with Congress, the tax cut was reduced from an annual 10–10–10 percent reduction over three years to 5–10–10 percent, and the framework for economic growth was put into place.

***

It began with an unusual scurrying of feet. Nothing to panic about, but it was noticeable. The sort of soft noise that might accompany some sort of surprise birthday cake for a senior staffer. Then more feet, louder. People were running. Then voices. *The president's been shot.* It was first more of a murmur. Then it was a question. Then an affirmation. Such an odd statement, raising more questions than it answered. No clarity; just a chant. *The president's been shot. The president's been shot.* I was in my office in the OEOB. TV sets went on in every office. Junior

---

[13] Steven F. Hayward, *The Age of Reagan: The Conservative Counterrevolution* (United Kingdom: Random House Publishing Group, 2009), 95.

staffers crowded into the offices of the senior staffers to watch the news. The communications office had a bank of three television sets, each one tuned to one of the three major networks.

The news gripped us, though early reports were positive. *He was nicked. He's at George Washington Hospital. People say he's okay. He was cracking jokes as they wheeled him in.*

Secretary of State Al Haig bounded into the White House briefing room and gave the most un-reassuring speech possible. The least calming words in the English language might be: "Stay calm." But second place to that phrase was Haig's statement of that moment: "I am in control here." He looked red in the face. He also misinterpreted the constitutional order of succession. Not huge mistakes, but ones that contributed to an image of a man in over his head, or not quite a team player.

The vice president turned Air Force Two around from a Texas event to make an emergency return to Andrews AFB. He wisely decided not to return to the White House grounds by helicopter, a privilege normally reserved for the president. In contrast to Haig, Bush knew that a crisis was a time for a subdued presence and a reaffirmation that the system was working. Chaos did not benefit anyone.

More bad news. Press Secretary Jim Brady had been shot, and it turned out that he was permanently disabled. Advance Man Rick Ahearn was tackled in the scuffle but OK. But Secret Service Agent Tim McCarthy and DC police officer Tom Delahanty had both been shot.

It was shattering for the White House staff as well, and some of the life went out of the building until Reagan was released from the hospital twelve days later and returned to a rousing welcome home reception on the front stairs of the OEOB.

Ronald Reagan had an almost magical resonance with the public, or parts of it. After he was shot, a Special Forces veteran Master Sergeant Roy Benavidez mailed Reagan the Purple Heart medal that he had received after being wounded in Vietnam. "You have earned this more than me," he wrote with magnanimity. When that gesture was publicized by the media, hundreds of vets from across America mailed their purple heart medals, echoing MSG Benavidez's statement. Reagan had a hold on our imagination, and his connection with the average American evoked a powerful desire among people to share in his story.

We saw that spirit a few months later when a member of the press shouted a question to Reagan as he was boarding his helicopter on the south lawn. It was in December, so the logical question was, "Mr. President, what do you want for Christmas?" Reagan answered, "A train set." Was this political positioning in that it was a quintessential holiday gift? Was it sentiment, in that one could imagine a kid in a small town in Illinois in the 1920s wanting this ultimate expression of power, of freedom, of adventure, of technology? It might have been any of those reasons, or it just might have been an innocent answer. In any event, several dozen Americans sent train sets to the White House. The White House set them up on the ground floor of the Old Executive Office Building and had them all running simultaneously during the holiday season.

Despite the intense schedule and the responsibilities of helping shape the new administration, much of my work in

Presidential Personnel could be called normal office work. But there were also occasional incidents, some minor, that helped shape my view of government service. This began with my exposure to Wildman and his habit of white lies. But there were other events that drilled home the importance of integrity. Common sense tells you that you only add value to the system if you bring principles. Former Chief of Congressional Affairs Bryce Harlow put it simply: "Integrity is power—I'd put integrity first."[14] (Harlow served in the Eisenhower administration, having earlier been congressional liaison for General George Marshall during World War II.) But there were occasional glaring examples to the contrary.

For example, we had a system of sending three recommendations to the president for openings on Boards and Commissions. It was only a matter of time before someone would try to outsmart the system by sending forward two weaker candidates and one stronger, violating guidelines to send forward the three best candidates. But be careful about playing games. I was talking with someone who did this with a nominee for the Corporation for Public Broadcasting, who related after the fact that Reagan picked the wrong one. "We sent him two turkeys and a good guy, and he picked a turkey."[15]

Sometimes these misplaced efforts took on a sense of the absurd, as was the case with "Hardy." As part of my in-processing

---

[14] Bryce Harlow quoted in Hedrick Smith, *The Power Game: How Washington Works* (New York: Random House, 1988), 65. Kindle.

[15] Fully aware of this gamesmanship, Kissinger would joke that a bad National Security Council would send three foreign policy recommendations to the president, the first of which might lead to nuclear war and the second might lead to surrender to the Soviets, leaving only the third option for the president to consider.

work, I manned the front lines of incoming resumes, handling the initial letters and resumes and routing them to the appropriate directorate for processing. I also had the authority to simply reject an application out of hand. One day I received a letter from Hardy of Mississippi. It had been hand-typed and consisted of essentially one sentence, with no punctuation. "I would like to help President Reagan by serving on the United States Parole Commission I work on an oil rig seven days on and seven days off so I have time to help out."

This was not exactly a fact-filled letter, and no additional information, such as a resume, was enclosed. Nonetheless, I was familiar with other recent incidents in which highly qualified or well-connected individuals would approach the administration quite informally, as had Hardy, so I did not automatically dismiss his letter. He is either very well-connected or just not very bright I thought. And not everyone has good grammar. I called him up.

He was genial enough, though he did not come across as highly qualified. He repeated the basics of his letter that he liked Ronald Reagan, and that he worked on an oil rig, and he wanted to serve on the US Parole Commission. He mentioned that Lanny Griffith could attest to his credentials.

This was encouraging because Lanny was an old friend from College Republican days who was then the executive director of the Mississippi Republican Party. I called Lanny and he told me that Hardy was just about stone cold nuts, though he meant well. Lanny told me his last extensive discussion with Hardy was the summer of 1980 when Hardy had approached him in hushed tones. Hardy told Lanny conspiratorially that he had "infiltrated" the John Anderson for President campaign as a volunteer. Anderson was an independent candidate for president who finished with about 8 percent of the national vote, and about 4 percent of the vote in Mississippi, which happened to be one of Ronald Reagan's best states. Reagan needed no help at all in Mississippi, and he certainly would not have viewed Anderson as a factor to worry about, in addition to the legal and moral issues involved with "infiltrating" someone else's campaign.

Luckily, Lanny kept a cool head. "Hardy," he said, "this is such a vital role you are playing that it is important that we protect it at all costs. From now on, you and I cannot meet. We cannot even talk. Not even on the phone. And don't write me a letter. We can't have anyone know the deep cover role you have taken on. At the proper time, in the proper way, we will contact you. For now, carry on your mission. Stand by for follow-on instructions. And remember: do not contact me."

This was brilliant. There never were any follow-on instructions. Hardy faithfully kept far away from the Reagan operation. John Anderson got free help from a hard-working, if slightly demented, volunteer. It was win-win.

But now it was post-election. Lanny related that Hardy had no particular background in criminal justice matters. Was not a lawyer. Was not from law enforcement. Was not a college graduate. Was perhaps not a high school graduate. Did not do anything to help Reagan. But everybody sort of liked him as that part of southern culture in which a colorful personality could be viewed as a plausible alternative to competency.

I related to Hardy that it did not look likely there would be a fit on the Parole Commission. His heart was broken. Then he started his spring offensive. Letters and phone calls to me, daily, asking if there had been any change. This assault went on for weeks, then months. I finally got it. Lanny fended him off with the indirect defense and I would have to do the same.

A few days later, he called the office and asked for me by name. I answered that "Frank Lavin" had been fired for stealing typewriters. Hardy was surprised with the news, but it did allow me to say that the White House was shutting down the entire Parole Commission process until the FBI finished its investigation.

It did the trick in getting rid of Hardy, but it was a bit of foolishness, wasn't it? Of course, you have to differentiate between foolish behavior that was simply a waste of time and foolish behavior that crossed a legal or ethical line. I was up on the fourth floor of the OEOB filing, copying, moving paper, and responding to requests, and there was a person about my age across the hall, also working for Presidential Personnel, but I wasn't quite clear what his responsibilities were. One day he waved me over. "*Psst*, look what I've got here." It was a large crate, almost a footlocker, of bags of jelly beans.

"That's terrific," I said. "Where did those come from?"

"The company sent them to me."

"Uh-huh. Well, why did they send them to you?"

"Just because I asked."

"Just because you asked?"

"Yep."

"C'mon. A company isn't going to send you jelly beans, at least this many, simply because you requested."

"They will if you do so on White House stationery," he said.

"You are kidding me."

"No. I just wrote them a letter telling them I was at the White House and asking them for sample bags."

"You can't do that."

"I already did."

"This can't possibly be right," I insisted.

"It's not a problem. You just write to people asking them for help, and you get it."

"That can't be right."

He was quite proud of his trick. I was appalled. Though I was not sure what rule had been violated, I was pretty sure that you should not be using White House letterhead to get "gifts" from people. Apparently this fellow did it more than once. A few weeks after our jelly bean conversation, I saw George Saunders, a retired FBI agent who was the longtime White House security consultant come by to visit this person. Unlike the typewriter thief who was fiction, the jelly bean thief was for real. He was unceremoniously fired and escorted immediately from the building.

LETTER TO THE EDITOR

Here is an additional mistake, driven by naivete more than anything else. There was a nominee for an assistant secretary position at Health and Human Services. The newspapers discovered that he had previously served as the general counsel for Liberty Lobby, a now-defunct rightest group that dabbled in anti-Semitism. Let's just say it had an inordinate fascination with public officials who happened to be Jewish. It was a fringe group, but it would not redound to anyone's credit that he had worked there. Immediately the candidate was under fire.

Of course, this was debated in the corridors. Nobody defended Liberty Lobby, given the odious nature of the group. But how long had the individual worked there? Had he known what the group did? What were his personal responsibilities? All were plausible questions. But to my mind, this fellow was in pretty deep because he had served for several years as general counsel of the organization. He was not simply the piano player in the bordello, but he had to accept responsibility for the actions of the institution.

Some of the press criticism was pretty harsh, impugning the Reagan administration for nominating this person, making broader allegations about Reagan's ethics or policies. This struck me as unwarranted. A turkey had been nominated, and the nomination would have to be withdrawn.

My boss in Presidential Personnel was very unhappy. This whole thing was terrible. We were getting killed. I agreed. In fact, I wrote a letter to the editor of the *Washington Post*, essentially criticizing the nominee and defending the administration. The next day my boss continued the discussion. What was unfair to her mind was not the degree of the criticism, but the fact that he was getting criticized at all. She thought the nominee was a good guy and was being unfairly tarnished because he spent a few years working for Liberty Lobby.

I was appalled at her judgment, but what frightened me was the realization that I had the day before sent a note to the *Post* essentially contradicting her view though defending the administration. It was amateurish on my part, not fully appreciating that once in government you were no longer a free agent.

Still, since I was defending the administration, I would not be getting into trouble, would I? Well yes, I probably would, because I was going against my boss in a public fashion. Because I was injecting myself in an area where my opinion had not been sought. And because I went to the media without any sort of approval or clearance.

But my letter was sent in a private capacity, on personal letterhead, and without my being identified as a member of the administration. That was OK, wasn't it? No, fool. If you are a member of the administration, you give up your independent status, at least in public. It is just inappropriate for a White House employee to be offering public comments on White House business in such a fashion.

I remember rushing to the letters page of the *Post* for several days thereafter searching for the letter and running through my head what I would tell my boss and others when confronted. (Must be a different Frank Lavin?). Fortunately after several nervous days it became clear that the letter would not run. I had dodged the bullet.

WHAT DID IT ALL MEAN?

Personnel is policy, the saying goes. Hire good people and you will get good decisions. We could see this in the Reagan administration where we had some terrific advocates of policy in George Shultz, Colin Powell, and Caspar Weinberger. There were also weaker and even forgettable characters. Some had good management skills; others had a good sense of policy. To be effective you needed capabilities in both realms. Know where to go and know how to get there.

The Presidential Personnel position initially required the white lie, minor but distasteful. But as I grew in experience and self-confidence, I moved toward more helpful responses and undertook never to be put in a position where dissembling might be required. Did I learn anything from my experiences with Wolf, Wildman, Hardy, jelly beans, letters to the editor, and others?

- Always tell the truth because your reputation is your most important asset.
- Let people know when you cannot deliver.
- Think through commitments carefully, but if you make a commitment, you must honor it.
- How people are treated matters. If the matter is important to the other party, it should be important to you. (If a senator calls you up regarding "a small matter," it is not a small matter.)
- Victory or defeat is rarely absolute. Coalitions are rarely permanent. Even a loss on an important piece of legislation can be overturned or mitigated. You have to be able to work with everyone. People will be with you on one vote and against you on another.
- Look for a way to say "yes."
- Responsiveness matters. Return every phone call.

- Trying to be too clever can be self-defeating. Prevailing for a moment is frequently less important than establishing a long-term relationship.

Many of the rules seem common sense, but as I moved on through other positions it was striking to me that their purest expression was in my White House assignments.

Ann, working in the Office of Presidential Correspondence, related that the president was receiving ten thousand letters a day. After the assassination attempt, it climbed to twenty thousand a day. Several thousand of these were resumes, and they each had to be handled professionally and promptly. American business culture can be very informal, so we were well aware we might have prominent Americans, or even personal friends of the president, writing to him directly in unadorned language and on plain white paper. Sifting through these letters, getting a courtesy response back—"The President asked me to let you know that we have received your letter and it might be a while before we are able to get into the points you raise given the hectic pace of events…"—and making sure the letter got routed to the right directorate were all vital parts of the job.

Presidential Personnel had an enormous sense of mission combined with grueling hours. The sense of mission was driven by those early days of the Reagan administration, in which the president set an ambitious tone from the start: renew America's self-confidence, get the economy going again, and stand up to the Soviets. "Make no little plans," advised Daniel Burnham, "they have no magic to stir men's blood." Reagan understood this adage. His vision and the drama of the assassination attempt combined to give a compelling sense of purpose to the presidency during those early days.

At base, there are two kinds of people in politics: those who make something happen and those who do not. Reagan was in that first group.

Presidential Personnel's mission was to find the best people from that first group but it was. Reagan who personally selected the three most important people in that group.

CHAPTER 5

THE TROIKA:
BAKER-MEESE-DEAVER

*There are two competing theories of political popularity: Is popu-
larity toothpaste or is it capital? The toothpaste theory holds that
popularity is an expendable asset. After you deplete it, it is gone.
You have squeezed the tube and now it is empty. If that is the case,*

you better hoard it. Don't ever expend your popularity on something that might be unpopular. Pragmatism should govern behavior.

The capital theory holds that popularity is an investment to be deployed. You use your popularity to advance your agenda. You are not intrinsically opposed to risking some popularity as long as it is purposeful. As your agenda works, you build the popularity back again. Aspirations should govern behavior.

Let's leave the personal narrative for a moment and discuss how the Reagan White House operated. Every president needs a White House team that shares a convergence of interests and tactics to be effective, but the team also needs to have enough divergence in its approach that the president hears a range of views and there is some capacity for experimentation. Ronald Reagan brought that together by embracing both true believers and pragmatists.

Ed Meese summarized the two groups: "It was essential that the President have stalwart backers who understood him and his program and were willing to stay the course no matter what. It was also essential that he have people on his team who understood the ways of Washington..."[16]

One of the smarter guys in the White House, speechwriter Peter Robinson, builds on Meese's taxonomy: "Broadly speaking, the White House staff divided into two camps, the pragmatists and the true believers. The goal of the pragmatists was simple. They wanted to persuade Ronald Reagan to stop acting like a conservative, becoming a moderate instead.... The goal

---

16 Edwin Meese, III, *With Reagan: The Inside Story* (Washington, DC: Regnery Publishing, 2015), 103.

of the true believers was just as simple…[t]hey wanted the President to pursue every aspect of his conservative agenda."[17]

Counselor to the President Ed Meese was a true believer and helped make sure Reagan stayed on course with a conservative agenda—high impact, ambitious, but achievable—and even if it were not entirely achievable, it started a dialogue and opened minds and hearts for possible long-term victories.

Chief of Staff Jim Baker was a pragmatist, and highly effective to boot. It is not just that he was intelligent, because there were plenty of bright people in the West Wing. His singular contribution was that he was disciplined and methodical. Baker was not there to be a cheerleader; there were plenty of those around as well. As a good lawyer, it was his responsibility to caution his client or point out where the client might not be likely to prevail. This discipline allowed him to winnow out less important initiatives, in effect setting the priorities for the administration. There were plenty of good ideas out there, but only a handful might make a lasting difference.

Deputy Chief of Staff Mike Deaver was responsible for the schedule, for events, and other personal elements of Ronald and Nancy Reagan's activities. As a longtime confidante of both, he could serve as a reality check for various ideas and initiatives.

The result: Meese's perspective was that there was value in overshooting a bit because you never know what might be achievable until you start the process and because you can use the issue to communicate. Baker's perspective was that at some point you take what you can get and move on to the next issue.

[17] Peter Robinson, *How Ronald Reagan Changed My Life* (New York: Harper Perennial, 2004), 207.

And Deaver's perspective was what would, or would not, fly with the president and first lady (both of whom needed to be on board). That is why this troika of power worked. They each brought a distinct point-of-view to the decision-making process.

None of the three had rough edges. Baker, Meese, and Deaver were typically pleasant and businesslike. Baker is the one I knew the best. I was not a close confidant, but I worked with him during his Texas attorney general race in 1978 and had regular opportunities to work with him in the White House as well. I knew him to be a strong performer.

Others had different views. Some Reaganites were suspicious of Baker's Ford-Bush pedigree. Others saw his business-like tone and corporate lawyer background as camouflage for cutting deals and lowering expectations. Would Baker "Let Reagan be Reagan"? Simplistically, some more ideological supporters evaluated the seriousness of an effort by the amount of friction it created, whereas Baker by training and nature tried to avoid friction.

Beyond the ideological questions, there were territorial questions. Where did one person's authority end and another's begin? This speculation about relative power is not irrelevant, but it can be overstated. Was Meese being squeezed out? Nofziger? Bill Clark? Who was making the calls? Was Reagan being manipulated? These questions rose and fell on the barometer from week to week. Deaver, through his public relations lens, tended to side with Baker but was less active in this jostling, focusing his efforts on messaging, advance work, and the president's schedule. Deaver had always been less ideological. Ten years before I voted against Reagan for Ford, Deaver voted against Reagan in his very first race, opting instead for George Christopher in the 1966 Republican gubernatorial primary.

Meese and Baker did have differences, naturally enough, but any successful White House should welcome different points of views. I never saw anything but professionalism in their relationship, though more mid-level and junior staffers could have sharper elbows. That is how it goes. The people who have the power know how to handle it smoothly. Those who don't might try to elevate their status by pretending they have it.

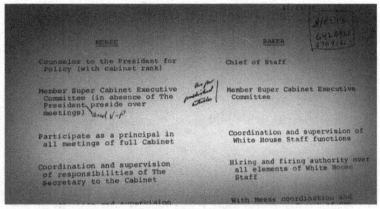

Helping delineate responsibilities, Meese and Baker created a memo specifying their roles.

Were the staff splits simply a tug-of-war between the true believers and the pragmatists? Did the TBs know Reagan's soul and the pragmatists want to cut a deal?

The reality was more complicated. Reagan wanted—needed—both the true believers and the pragmatists. The value of the pragmatists was to manage the system, to attain the best outcome possible in a given situation. The value of the true believers was to improve that given situation and not settle without a fight. One group managed a system and the other group changed the system. Reagan without pragmatists was rhetoric, like the Goldwater campaign. Reagan without true believers was operational effectiveness with no anchor, like the Nixon presidency. Reagan saw each as falling short.

The true believers focused on the upside. What could the Reagan administration be? What America could it be? This spoke to Reagan's heart. His presidential ethos and personal outlook on life was one of optimism. He was idealistic by nature and his presidency was designed to be aspirational. You don't always want to aim for the middle of the bell curve, even if that is where you might end up. Sometimes you can shift the curve.

Reagan was also smart enough to know he needed someone who focused on the downside. What might go wrong? What can we salvage? This is where the pragmatists brought value. We actually need to pass a budget, to deregulate, and to confirm nominees. We have to bank our wins, minimize our losses, and move on to the next issue. In that vein, Nancy Reagan offered support for Baker's approach: "Some people are so rigid in their beliefs that they'd rather lose than win a partial victory, and I always felt that Meese was one of them."[18]

Early in 1981, Office of Management and Budget Director David Stockman pushed a Social Security reform proposal. It was dead on arrival on the Hill, with both Democrats and Republicans

---

[18] Nancy Reagan and William Novak, *My Turn: The Memoirs of Nancy Reagan* (New York: Random House, 2011), location 4090. Kindle.

rising against a threat to Social Security payments. Reagan was able to quickly sideline this proposal and regain momentum on his signature issue: tax cuts. If Baker had not sensed a looming calamity in Stockman's initiative, the administration could have wasted precious political capital on this issue and undermined its broader agenda. Score one for the pragmatists.

On the other hand, in 1987, Reagan upended US foreign policy when he visited Berlin and challenged Gorbachev to "tear down this wall," over the objections of Chief of Staff Howard Baker and Secretary of State George Shultz. The thrust of the speech was how do we aspire to a better world, one that values human freedom, rather than how do we manage the world we have. The speech was written by the talented White House speechwriter Peter Robinson. Score one for the true believers.

The true believers and the pragmatists might have had more in common with each other than one might suppose. The Baker-Meese-Deaver troika was characterized more by cooperation than by friction. Every workday, the troika met at 7:30 a.m. in Baker's office. At 8 a.m., the meeting was expanded to include the rest of the senior staff in the Roosevelt Room. At 8:30 a.m., each member of the troika met with their immediate subordinates (their "direct reports" in White House speak) in their offices, and at 9 a.m., the troika reconvened to meet with the president in the Oval Office. This West Wing mitosis and meiosis could only work in a system that reflected discipline and hierarchical management. Management required segmentation and coordination required integration.[19]

Some elections are *status quo* elections and some are change elections. In a *status quo* election, the middle of the bell curve probably does tend to win. The voters like the direction of the country and want to keep a good thing going. But in a change election, voters are open to alternatives. They might want a clean sweep. In 1980, the voters wanted change. Carter was widely viewed as having fallen short, and voters had an appetite to try something new. Reagan had to show that he had a vision of where America needed to go and that his approach to change was in response to that public hunger.

By the same token, Reagan had to convince the voters that he was the acceptable face of change, that his presidency did not represent risk, or amateurishness, or extremism. He knew what he was doing; he was going to lead America to better outcomes, and his presidency would take people along.

Did Reagan delegate too much to the troika? To say that Reagan was not a manager misses something important. He had a secret weapon: he had a compass. He knew where he wanted to go. Reagan managed by leadership, using his unparalleled communication skills. He could articulate a vision (for the true

---

[19]   Did Reagan's strategy of balancing different approaches play out in other areas? In foreign policy, Shultz led the soft-liners; Weinberger, the hard-liners. Reagan embraced the two and negotiated successfully after he had the defense program, INF deployment, and SDI in place. In economic policy, Paul Volcker led the monetarists; Paul Craig Roberts, Larry Kudlow, and Arthur Laffer, the supply-side school; and Martin Feldstein and David Stockman, the budget-balancers. Reagan tied them together and brought down inflation (monetarists), and sparked robust growth (supply-siders). After he won the Cold War, budgets came into balance with the dramatic drop in defense spending.

believers) and a framework (for the pragmatists). This allowed him to build a team of sympathizers, supporters, technocrats, and, yes, true believers. Articulating that set of beliefs over twenty-plus years and field testing it in a series of political contests allowed him to refine his beliefs, his team, and you could say, his management. He knew where he wanted to go and he knew how to get there.

Add to this a set of cultural codes in the White House. We had a sense of mission. We had professional pride in our work. We knew we had four years, maybe eight, to make a difference. This allowed for high-energy, high-cohesion, high-performance outcomes. There were mistakes and bad calls along the way, perhaps inevitable with the pace of the White House. But the Reagan administration also developed a sense of excellence in its White House operations, with a seasoned and highly capable senior staff that allowed President Reagan to pursue his agenda as effectively as possible.

Since Baker was responsible for White House staff, he could build out his management purview with a team of strong lieutenants: David Gergen handling communications, John Rogers running administration, Margaret Tutwiler running the political affairs during the re-election. Jim Cicconi was Baker's executive assistant, having worked for him in the 1978 Texas attorney general's race, and the man who frequently ran interference for Baker on day-to-day White House matters. All were highly capable, sure-footed, and loyal, but perhaps none more important as a force multiplier than Staff Secretary Dick Darman.

The Staff Secretary Office is a strange beast, with little direct power, but with a great deal of indirect power. It ran no programs, was responsible for no budget, and only had five or six total staff. The indirect power was considerable because the secretariat was essentially the president's inbox and outbox. Darman was not just bright, but more important to his role, he was an integrator. He saw how the pieces fit and he saw second-order effects, two elements frequently lost to those more silo-oriented.

Sherlock Holmes describes his brother, Mycroft:

> Well, his position is unique.... The conclusions of every department are passed to him, and he is the central exchange, the clearinghouse, which makes out the balance. All other men are specialists, but his specialism is omniscience. We will suppose that a minister needs information as to a point which involves the Navy, India, Canada and the bimetallic question; he could get his separate advices from various departments upon each, but only Mycroft can focus them all, and say offhand how each factor would affect the other.[20]

Overstated, but you get the point.[21]

The staff secretary was responsible for the interoffice review and approval of all documents going to the president—tasking, tracking, integrating. Darman controlled what the president

---

[20] Sir Arthur Conan Doyle, "The Adventure of the Bruce-Partington Plans" (December 1908) 1–2. https://sherlock-holm.es/stories/pdf/a4/1-sided/bruc.pdf.

[21] Darman's reputation went on to suffer during the Bush 43 administration, where he is viewed as one of the proponents of President Bush's abandonment of his "no new taxes" pledge, arguably setting the stage for Bush's 1992 defeat.

saw and who had input into the decision. Al Haig noted in his memoirs, perhaps with exasperation: "There are three main levers of power in the White House, the flow of paper, the President's schedule, and the press."[22] We are told that Walter Mondale consented to be Jimmy Carter's running mate in 1976 only after a commitment from Carter that the vice president would see all papers that went to the president, a privilege we have difficulty seeing Nixon offering Agnew. The staff secretary is supposed to function as an unbiased umpire, mediating among different White House offices. This became a powerful position under Darman, who had a natural sense of how best to use this seemingly staid process to shape outcomes. Running the process might be a bit like being an umpire. But what if the umpire was adept enough that he could occasionally shape the game? Or at least offer a little coaching for a key player? The game runs a little smoother, doesn't it?

Baker, Meese, and Deaver all moved on from the White House for the second term, but this troika provided Reagan with the leadership he needed for a successful first term, with a mixture of collegiality and competition that largely, but not always, stayed in balance—a point brought home to me as I moved to my next assignment in the Office of Public Liaison.

---

[22] Alexander M. Haig, Jr., *Caveat: Realism, Reagan and Foreign Policy* (New York: MacMillan, 1984), 83.

CHAPTER 6

1983–84 OFFICE OF PUBLIC LIAISON

I met Reagan for the first time early in my Office of Public Liaison tenure. I do not remember all of the details, but I recall it was a good meeting, except for when I overshot.

I knew that Robert Service was his favorite poet. (Somewhat predictable, as Service's poetry combined a strong narrative with western themes.) So, I thought of memorizing a few verses of "The Cremation of Sam McGee." I have a generally reliable memory and before too long I had the first few verses down pat. I figured I would find an opportunity in the course of the event to rattle them off.

At the presidential meeting, I became aware quickly of two developments: that my reasonably good memory failed me almost completely. I could only recall the opening line of the poem. Second, it is more difficult than one might suppose to subtly weave poetry into a casual conversation.

It is easy enough to say, "Nice unemployment numbers, Mr. President," or "Great rally in Pennsylvania, Mr. President." There was no easy way to observe that "The Northern lights have seen queer sights, Mr. President." There simply appeared to be no opportunity to invoke the poem without it appearing completely contrived, which of course it was. Reagan was as always polite, tolerant, beaming, and he leaned toward me, recognizing I had something to say. Of course, I had something, but at the same time I had nothing. The words wouldn't come, and the words didn't fit anyhow. An awkward pause and the moment passed. A friend observed, perhaps unkindly, that it was sort of a perfect Frank Lavin vignette: solid factual premise, over-engineered response, no regard for context, low emotional intelligence, and failed execution. A bit harsh, perhaps, but I could not dispute the analysis. The only saving grace was that the meeting was successful in getting the right people into a productive discussion with the president. Only my private efforts were unsuccessful.

***

It is an ongoing question in politics: should you work primarily with your core political support and largely ignore other points of view? Working with your base seems to be the default approach to political communications today, but in the 1980s we viewed outreach and communication to the general public and especially to swing constituencies to be important. The theory was to work with whatever coalition you could on whatever issue was in front of you. The business community might be supportive of President Reagan's economic policy and efforts to rein in regulations, but only mildly supportive of foreign policy, and generally not interested in the social issues. There was a significant element of the Hispanic community that cared about social mobility and prosperity, and also sought the dignity and respect to be expected from a group composed of minority members and immigrants. Many were sensitive to foreign policy issues as well. Veterans' organizations were concerned about defense policy in addition to the core veterans' issues. It was worth engaging with most groups as we believed we could earn some respect and gain ground politically by regular interaction, cultivation, and communication.

The most striking difference between outreach strategy in the 1980s and today is that in the 1980s, we viewed politics as building coalitions which included explaining positions to undecided groups, neutral, and even unsympathetic groups. If we could take Reagan's share of the Hispanic vote from 30 percent to 35 percent, that would be a worthy endeavor. Besides the practical gains, isn't it a healthy civic exercise to reach out to all groups? By the same logic, shouldn't the White House be open to opinions and requests from all segments of society?

The thought was that every constituency was worth some sort of appeal. Even constituencies which might in general tend to support Democrats, such as the African-American or the Jewish community, could be cultivated through meetings and communication, and this could result in at least relative progress.

In 1983, I joined the Office of Public Liaison (OPL) as an associate director. Formally, OPL was the White House office responsible for constituency outreach. In addition to the groups mentioned above, we had other occupational groups such as farmers, as well as demographic groups like women, ethnic, and religious groups. There were other leadership groups, such as conservative organizations. Under the Carter administration, there had been outreach to the gay community, but in the

Reagan administration this was conducted informally, without a designated contact in OPL.

In the era before the internet, organized outreach was perhaps the most important alternative communication channel available to the president. The traditional media outlets were the primary source of news for voters, but organized groups also had newsletters and events, providing an alternative channel for the president to get his message out.

Outreach and constituency messaging was our main task, and there were three overriding management points that defined my term at OPL. First, the White House Chief of Staff Jim Baker and the Director of the Office of Public Liaison Faith Whittlesey did not care for each other. Whittlesey was a true believer but lacked the geniality of Ed Meese. Second, the critical mission of our office at that moment was building support for administration policy in Central America (aiding the Contras in Nicaragua and bolstering the democratic government in El Salvador). Third, we were going into an election year.

The first point, the Jim Baker-Faith Whittlesey split, is largely why I ended up in OPL. Jim Baker brought in Frank Donatelli to be deputy director of the office, and Frank brought me in, the three of us having met during Baker's unsuccessful campaign for attorney general of Texas in 1978. Frank was the right person for this job, not just because of his high intelligence and capacity for hard work, but also because of his unimpeachable Reagan credentials. His even-keeled temperament recalled the comment that, if a person were any more low-key, he would be capable of photosynthesis. So, amidst various slights, conspiracies, and efforts to marginalize, he held his own with quiet competence. Always practical, always a rationalist, Frank was the glue that made OPL effective. Despite the fissures and drop in trust, the office managed to function reasonably well through the election although there was a clear cleavage between the Faith loyalists and the rest of the OPL staff.

This unhappy marriage could spill over into general office effectiveness. With the exception of the statutory bodies such as the National Security Council and the Office of Management and Budget, no White House office has demarcated responsibilities. For most White House offices, governance is by stated responsibilities. Office power stems from reputation, effectiveness, and collegiality. Your ability to get something done depends a lot less on the title on your door and a lot more on what others think of you and their willingness to work with you. In a sense, you only do what the chief of staff wants you to do. Some people are more effective and more collegial, and they grow in responsibilities. Others shrink.

As OPL engaged with various organizations and constituencies and communicated the administration's views back to them, we would host national leadership groups. We would send speakers to events. We would have roundtables, panels, and discussions to keep the gears of government moving smoothly with appropriate input, as we tried to mobilize friendly groups and explain ourselves to those we thought we could win over.

The National Restaurant Association needed a speaker for their board meeting. Not surprisingly, they were opposed to efforts to raise the minimum wage, the same view as the administration. They also were opposed to efforts to make tips income taxable, a difference with the administration. Who from the administration would attend the National Italian American Foundation annual dinner? We want more than one; Democratic nominee Walter Mondale's running mate is Geraldine Ferraro, remember? A chronic disease charitable organization wanted its leadership to meet with the president. A veterans' organization needed an overview of military issues. A winning sports team gets a photo with the president because, why not? Americans like winners, and Reagan likes to smile, and it is right in the Rose Garden, and the TV networks love this. Will the winning team present Reagan with their team's jersey? Maybe the jersey will have "Reagan" or "Gipper" emblazoned on it, and perhaps the number on the jersey will be "1." Sometimes we might be pretending to be generating something newsworthy just as the media might be pretending to be covering something newsworthy.[23]

The point was to help people talk to the White House and help the White House talk to people, usually through some sort of structure that would maximize the impact. People want to connect with you if you are in the White House. They want to meet with you, to see you. They had a problem, an issue, a relative, a favor, or an opinion. They had to report to their company, their team, their firm, their faction. "I'm talking this over with the White House." "I have a meeting on this very topic tomorrow at the White House." "The White House has asked

---

[23] In 1962, historian Daniel Boorstin published *The Image: A Guide to Pseudo-Events in America* in which he coined the term "pseudo-event," which he also called a "media event," referring to an event which might be devoid of news, but has been orchestrated simply for the media story. The president welcoming a sports team or pardoning the Thanksgiving turkey are two common such events.

me to come over and work with them on this issue." And all these people are friends, allies, friends-of-friends, or potential friends. Nobody is unimportant. The demand for individual meetings easily out-stripped time available, so by necessity people had to be brought in as part of a group.

As a White House staffer, if you were a bit clever and a bit forward-leaning, you could serve as ombudsman and help with problems, with people, with other meetings. If a state party chairman needed to see someone at a cabinet department, you could arrange that. You could certainly help with internships. Can you actually stop or start legislation? Not a chance, but you could host lunch with someone from Legislative Affairs at which the matter could be discussed and the pros and cons could be evaluated in a friendly setting. At least your party could get a hearing and a reasonable explanation. If you were nimble, you could be a minister without portfolio.

For me, it meant a lot of events and a lot of direct involvement with the president—from introducing him, to escorting VIPs, to general assistance at meetings. Although my first meeting with the president had been modestly awkward, the second meeting, soon thereafter, was more successful. I was still learning, and Reagan, ever-friendly, was glad to be the teacher. I got to introduce President Reagan to a now-forgotten leadership group. We were hosting a meeting in Room 450 OEOB, the theater-style room that can hold perhaps 150 people. Reagan came on stage, all smiles, to a nice applause. We shook hands and the applause built. The handshake went on as long as needed, and I relaxed my hand to let go. He looked at me with a nod and a smile: *Don't you get it? Keep the handshake. Ride the applause*. I chuckled because I got it, and I reestablished my clasp and kept the shake going. He chuckled because he saw that I got it (finally!). The applause built when they saw both of us having a small laugh and a few in the audience joined in the laugh as well. We were on a Möbius strip of handshakes, smiles, applause, and soft laughter. It was over in ten or fifteen seconds, even though it felt more like ten or fifteen minutes. At this point, the handshake wasn't a formality or a greeting. It was a sign of belonging, the president, the audience, and me—we were all supposed to be here. And the laughter? We were all in on the joke. We were all friends.

Reagan gave some remarks. A nice balance of a few hard facts and an anecdote or an emotional appeal. The point of the speech was to move people his way, to make it as easy as possible for people to agree with him. He did it with some solid evidence, then added a joke, or a quote, or a historical example. He kept the smile going. The cock of the head that carried two or three messages. It was a wink to the audience. Now you were in on it as well. And he paused at the right time and smiled again as if he had just thought of that punch line. And those in the audience felt like they were the first to hear it. A secret joke between them and the president.

Up close it was a delight to work with Reagan. He understood the room; he could read the audience. They say that bad teachers teach a course; good teachers teach the students. Reagan always taught the students. The first thing you had to do was to win the room. Easy, usually, but still a necessity. When he received visitors in the Oval Office, he radiated *bonhomie*. His deportment before and after the visitors was striking. I would typically slip into the Oval Office before a formal meeting, run through a few points with the president and his personal aide, Jim Kuhn. I'd say something like, "We'll do a handshake and a photo as they enter. Then you offer a few remarks to welcome. Then they have a brief presentation. And that is it." The president was all business. He would ask a question or two of clarification if necessary. I'd duck back out to get the visitors from the holding room. When the meeting started, it was almost as if there was a different Reagan. The lights were on, so to speak, and the cameras were rolling. President Reagan was on top of his game. His face would light up as if he had been waiting all day for this particular meeting.

In fact, the chief risk in a presidential meeting was not the president, it was the visitor. One of the challenges for a president in connecting with people is that a president, any president, is so intimidating that he can freeze the room. People freeze. Conversation freezes. Time and space seem to freeze. It was all a bit ironic given Reagan's natural warmth, but people literally did not know what to say or do. Was it polite to ask a question? Was it consistent with protocol to make a point? What was the best way of raising a subject? It became extremely difficult to get practical value from some meetings because it could take a while for the normal rhythm of discussion to resume. Reagan was there to talk through an issue, to hear someone's point of view, but his personal presence in itself could disrupt the meeting. He was the human Heisenberg principle, unwittingly limiting the assessment he was trying to reach.

People still had a television image of the president, and it could be several minutes before they realized, *Heck, I am not watching him on TV. I am actually talking with him.* People forgot their message. Or they agreed when they meant to disagree. As a result of all this, meetings with the president could be very uneven.

We had to develop mechanisms that would allow the meeting and event to take place as planned. The most important element of this would be to spend a few minutes in planning with the visitor in order to avoid repetitive or inessential behavior during a visit.

A national trade association would spend months trying to get on the president's calendar. The president would ask them what was on their mind, and the remarks could be off-message or trivial. It was worth everyone's time to have a pre-meeting to ensure the meeting itself would result in the right information being conveyed.

Reagan was quick to recognize this problem himself and if the conversation was frozen, he would use his secret weapon—jelly beans—to unfreeze the discussion. Just when the pause went on long enough that it risked becoming awkward, the Gipper would jump in. "I just realized I've been a bit impolite. Let me offer you some jelly beans," he would say, moving the bowl to the guest. If that did not do the trick, he would continue to riff. "Do you prefer the red ones or the white ones? Here, try some of each." At this point even the most frozen guest could mumble something to the effect that the white ones were fine, and the conversation was jump-started.

If this secret weapon did not work, he would help move the event along typically by telling a self-deprecating joke or making an amusing comment. There were a few stories or observations that he would tell repeatedly.

There is the story of the two brothers; one is an incurable pessimist, the other an incurable optimist. The parents are so concerned they take the boys to the doctor who arranges a special treatment. For the pessimist, they arrange to present him with a room of the best toys. They show him the room and immediately he starts crying, "I'm afraid if I play with any of these toys, I'll only break them."

Then they try the optimist, and to cure him of that problem, they take him to a room filled entirely with horse manure. The boy runs joyfully to the pile and starts flinging it around. The boy states with a smile, "With all this manure, there's got to be a pony in there somewhere."

Or Reagan would make a point about American inclusiveness and distinction: "America represents something universal in the human spirit. I received a letter not long ago from a man who said, 'You can go to Japan to live, but you cannot become Japanese. You can go to France, and you'd live and not become a Frenchman. You can go to live in Germany or Turkey, and you won't become a German or a Turk.' But then he added: 'Anybody from any corner of the world can come to America to live and become an American.'"[24]

---

[24] Ronald Reagan, "Remarks at a Republican Campaign Rally in San Diego, California," transcript of speech delivered at San Diego Convention and Performing Arts Center, California, November 7, 1988, https://www. reaganlibrary.gov/archives/speech/remarks-republican-campaign-rally-san-diego-california#:~:text=America%20represents%20something%20universal%20in,and%20not%20become%20a%20Frenchman.

Or he would talk about the differences between the US constitution and other constitutions: "Because their constitutions are documents by the Governments telling the people what they can do. And in our country, our Constitution is by the people, and it tells the Government what it can do. And only those things listed in the Constitution, and nothing else, can Government do.[25]"

These simple homilies were authentic. They were Reaganisms, capturing his own incurable optimism and his belief in America.

Frequently, there was a movie connection in a presidential meeting. Remember, while he was awaiting surgery after being shot, he let loose with saying, "Can we rewrite this scene beginning at the time I left the hotel?"[26]

Stand and Deliver was a movie made about Jaime Escalante, a math teacher on the south side of Los Angeles who took his disadvantaged students to top ranks in AP calculus. It was a story as true as it was endearing, and no surprise that President Reagan had Escalante in for an Oval Office visit. The movie's message of optimism and social mobility clearly fit with the president's. As a farewell gift, Escalante left a college calculus textbook on Reagan's Oval Office Desk. I eyed it when I was in the office a few minutes later and I could not resist, "Catching

---

[25] Ronald Reagan, "Remarks and a Question-and-Answer Session With Area Junior High School Students," transcript of speech delivered at the State Dining Room at the White House, Washington, DC, November 14, 1988, https://www.reaganlibrary.gov/archives/speech/remarks-and-question-and-answer-session-area-junior-high-school-students.

[26] Reagan and Novak, *My Turn*, location 231, Kindle.

up on some reading, Mr. President?" He didn't miss a beat. "Yes, I like to leaf through math textbooks in my spare time."

Another episode had its start in 1952. By that time, Reagan's movie career was past its peak and he starred in a sports biopic, *The Winning Team*, about the life of baseball great Grover Cleveland Alexander. Doris Day played the loyal wife. This was not edgy new-age cinema, but beneath the corn there was an important message. Alexander suffered from epilepsy, at the time not a well-known disorder, and his epileptic attacks were thought to be bouts of drunkenness. When Reagan made the picture, it resulted in a broader public discussion of epilepsy, and, as a result, Reagan became affiliated with the Epilepsy Foundation. Over the years, he regularly headlined their events and fundraisers.

I brought in the leadership from the charity to meet with the president, along with the poster child of the Epilepsy Foundation. As was always the case, Reagan was warm and sunny. "Y'know, I feel a personal connection with this problem," he said, "because one of my earlier films was about Grover Cleveland Alexander, the biography of the famous baseball player who had this condition. He was first thought to be an alcoholic, but eventually it was diagnosed as a disease. At that time not much was known about the disease and the movie did a lot to raise consciousness. Stop me if I have told this story before."

This final comment was clearly a rhetorical aside, but, ineptly, the man from the charity decided to take it literally and stopped him. "You told us about that last time we met," said the man, cutting the president off. Reagan was about as genial a personality you could find, but the one unforgivable sin in his world was to step on his line. The president had lobbed a softball to his guest, and his guest muffed it. Clearly, if there was one thing this charity did not want to hear, it was annual praise from the president. The president retained his smile, but gave me a sideways glance that could freeze water. As the show must go on, the president turned his remarks to some words of support for the child. Reagan would always bend down and greet children at their level. And he had the gift of making the conversation one-on-one, having a pleasant back and forth with the child. This simple gesture saved the day for this event.

Indeed, Reagan was so dedicated to working with these charitable groups that every Thursday afternoon we would bring in a chronic disease or afflicted constituency, usually headlined by a movie star who was connected with the issue, typically as a survivor or through a family member who was a survivor. There was frequently a child along, also a survivor and frequently the "poster child." The reception developed a pattern. Reagan first instructed the White House photographer to put down the camera. He would get on his knees and embrace the kid with a hug. After a chat and a smile, then he would say hello to the movie star. Finally, he would tell the photographer to pick up his camera again and get some photographs. *The great cause of cheering us all up.*

And meetings did not have to involve the president. We could organize a White House briefing or discussions at different levels of the government. Even office calls could be helpful in communicating. Given the nature of government and American society, there is a considerable range of opinions, interest groups, requests, and advice. People would not hesitate as individuals to visit to make their case. One day, the RNC called to ask if Frank Donatelli could meet with someone they felt was important, suggesting he was a donor or a potential donor. Frank asked me to sit in, fortunately, as it turned out. After courtesy openings the gentleman gave us a pitch as to why the president should pardon Reverend Sun Myung Moon, the erstwhile leader of the Unification Church, then in prison for tax fraud. There was no particular reason to pardon Moon, and there was even less of a reason why the Public Liaison Office would be involved in the matter, but the man was free to make his case. We had a polite brief meeting, and, as he left, he presented Frank with a small box. Opening the box after the man had left, we saw it was a diamond. Frank and I went swiftly to the Counsel's Office to report the gift and turn it over.

***

In a fundamental sense, Reagan was a wholesale politician. He gave a great speech. He connected with the audience. He understood delivery, staging, and sequencing. And he was nimble enough to deal with Q & A.

By the same token, he was less comfortable as a retail politician in one-on-one conversations. Surprisingly, he was not a natural extrovert in small group settings. Events that were unstructured were harder for him to deal with and could make poor use of his time. As we see today, the least effective way to get people to network is to label a reception a "networking event." It was harder for him to deal with individual personalities in an open setting. Sure, he maintained his pleasant disposition, but it can be a challenge to try to establish a rapport at the individual level, and it was easier for Reagan to do so at a group level. Age might be a factor here, and decades of television-movie-radio work meant there was always a wall with the audience. Friendly with everyone; friends with no one. Reagan's genius was his complete lack of pretension, his self-deprecating humor, and his geniality.

Indeed, the two nicest people in the West Wing were Ronald Reagan and George Bush. If you were in a hurry and bumped into one of them rounding a corner, despite your horror, it would be Reagan or Bush who would apologize to *you*. The White House had a lot of important people in it, and a lot of people who thought they were important. But the two most important of all were also the most rigorously polite—a reminder that manners do not hinder, but enhance, the exercise of power. Secure people are polite. Insecure people use their power in a petty fashion. Both men were so naturally friendly and conversational that even courtesy chats with staff could make them late for appointments. The White House Office of Administration had to send a memo to staff asking staff not to stop either the president or VP in the corridor for a conversation to keep them on time.

Other people had less warmth. I was always surprised how enormously accomplished men like George Shultz could be so indifferent to his nominal colleagues. I remember once running up to the Chief of Staff's Office to leave something for Don Regan, responding to an inquiry. Shultz was in the outer office, waiting to see Regan, as I arrived. I said, "Good morning, Mr. Secretary," as I entered that outer office, and Shultz turned his head to look at me and said...nothing. It was a bit awkward as now we were each looking at each other, him waiting for his meeting and me waiting for some sort of response to an inquiry. Time passed slowly, but after thirty seconds or so someone came back with the response to my question. I thanked the chief of staff's person, and then I said, "Goodbye, Mr. Secretary," which again brought no response. His taciturn nature earned him the nickname "Buddha" from his staff. As one State Department aide stated, "If you want to know the true meaning of silence... you should be alone in the elevator with George when he's on a bummer."[27]

RE-ELECTION

The unstated goal of OPL was to bolster the president's re-election campaign by working with key constituencies. We had a good message of economic growth for the middle-class, but in 1982, the recovery had not yet started. Republicans got bested in the midterms, with Democrats picking up one Senate and twenty-seven House seats. By 1983, the recovery was moving along but slowly. And some public opinion polls showed Reagan losing to former astronaut Senator John Glenn and even being pressed hard by former Vice President Walter Mondale.

As 1983 turned into 1984, the recovery strengthened as did Reagan's poll numbers. As the approval of the economy grew in the polls, so did positive views of Reagan in general and the view that America was on the right track. More surprisingly, even support of foreign policy became more positive as the view of the economy brightened. As unemployment declined, support

---

[27]   Morris, *Dutch*, 475.

for the administration's Central American policy grew. Pollsters may poll on many issues, but there was one dominant issue. Or to put it another way, voters will give a president broad leeway on policy as long as the economy is performing well.

In terms of electoral politics, the office was restricted. We could not advocate for anyone's election, nor ask people to vote for Reagan. All we could do was to explain administration positions. Nonetheless, we wanted to make a special effort to explain it to swing constituencies in swing states, mainly southern traditional Democrats and northern ethnic Catholics.

In terms of Central America, it meant our message was *all Sandinistas all the time.* Almost every event we held had a speaker on the program with this topic, regardless of the stated purpose of the visit. It is difficult from the vantage point some forty years later to convey the importance of this issue, but it might be a bit like the 2022 Ukraine conflict, with a predatory power attempting to dominate a smaller nation.

In one sense Central America was the center of the whirlwind for the entire Reagan Doctrine. Reagan had sought an approach to the Soviets different from that of most of his predecessors. The Cold War had been defined by a demarcation of the developed world, with an Iron Curtain separating the west from the Soviet sphere. A nuclear standoff guaranteed the peace between the superpowers, unsatisfactory and strained though it was. It was an ugly stalemate, one that consigned much of the world to communism, and put the entire world at permanent risk of a nuclear war, be it by miscalculation or mechanical failure. Yet the Cold War dynamic was reasonably well-established across the foreign policy spectrum. We would hold the line against the Soviets in Europe, where the countries were prosperous and the political systems were mature and resilient.

This meant, however, that the East-West contest merely shifted to the third world, and particularly in the 1970s we saw Soviet advances in Angola, Afghanistan, Central America, and elsewhere. It became apparent that a "standoff" with the Soviets wasn't a standoff, and protecting the *status quo* with the Soviets wouldn't protect the *status quo*. Indeed, one of the key problems of the Western strategy was that it conferred to the Soviets the ability to choose the time and place of where it would try to gain ground.

Reagan knew this. The United States, the West, the Free World, could not afford to organize its foreign policy only on defensive grounds. We had to go on the offensive. The Reagan doctrine, at its simplest, was this: "If you will shoot at the communists, we'll buy you the gun." Reagan was committed to raising the costs to the Soviets of their expansionism by arming anti-Soviet groups around the world.

Needless to say, this was a controversial shift. Governments don't like change, and Reagan heralded change. The leadership class was vested in deterrence, the catchphrase of which was "mutual assured destruction," so this was somewhat a repudiation of the foreign policy establishment. The Soviets were quick to point out that Reagan's aggressiveness was bound to raise tensions. If the US was going to add friction to foreign policy, it would likely bear some of the costs of that friction. It was also clear that not all anti-communist fighters had a sterling record on human rights.

These issues became heated in public discussions as well, perhaps prefiguring some of the polarization we see in America today. One morning, I was driving in through the White House South Gate, and there were protesters there with signs, "US out of Central America." One approached my car as I waited for the gate to swing open. "You're a war criminal," he yelled. I rolled down my window—something I would recommend against today—and asked him why. "Because you support the illegal war in Central America." Once a difference in political views is described as "criminal," one more element of civility is removed.

I never had any problem with Faith Whittlesey personally, nor did I see that she had any with me, but she knew I was there as Frank Donatelli's assistant, and there did not seem to be a great deal of trust. Nonetheless, I did the best job I could and stayed out of her way. The only specific difficulty I can recall was one day when her staff circulated a memo stating that we were all going to chip in to purchase a birthday gift for Faith. I did not feel particularly inclined to do so, and I felt it had to violate the conflict-of-interest rules for someone in her immediate office to solicit a gift from subordinates. I went down the hall to the White House Counsel's Office and talked with Sherrie Cooksey, Associate Counsel. She agreed. And shortly a memo went out from the same person retracting the original memo.

The lack of a good working relationship in the West Wing between James Baker and Faith Whittlesey resulted in a drop in communication and morale. The effectiveness of the office held up despite this less-than-ideal environment. Many of the people in it were highly motivated and talented and did a good job despite the weak management.[28]

There was a plague of ethical issues that materialized later. Cathi was in charge of the Hispanic outreach. She went on to serve in a high government capacity and then to serve a jail term for fraud. Doug was in charge of outreach to the Christian community, and after he left government, he was also convicted of fraud. Zev was a junior staffer who was frequently called upon to give VIP tours of the White House to visiting dignitaries. Occasionally, recipients of tours would give him a token gift in appreciation (the White House has strict rules governing the acceptance of gifts). Zev took this far over the line when he registered at a gift shop, as one would register for wedding gifts, and referred people to the shop if they cared to select a gift for him. He was fired.[29]

But there were happier stories as well, with OPL staffer Mary Jo Jacobi moving on to serve as assistant secretary of commerce in the Bush administration and then directing global

---

[28] A favorable assessment of Whittlesey came from White House Personnel Director Helene von Damm: "She was a warrior for Reagan's policies across the board.... In the process, she alienated all of the pragmatics in the White House, who were less than enthusiastic about the President's steadfast insistence on supporting the Contras." Helene von Damm, *At Reagan's Side: Twenty Years in the Political Mainstream* (New York: Knopf Doubleday Publishing Group, 1988), 248.

[29] A version of this was attempted by Hillary Clinton at the end of the Clinton presidency when she had just been elected to the Senate. She wanted to furnish her new home and registered with a company to allow friends and others to purchase items for her. She could not accept gifts of this sort once she took office as a Senator or if she served as a White House staffer, but there were no rules governing gifts that a first lady could receive. George Lardner, Jr., "Clintons Say They'll Return Disputed Gifts," *Washington Post*, February 5, 2001, https://www.washingtonpost.com/archive/politics/2001/02/06/clintons-say-theyll-return-disputed-gifts/accd07f5-3cd2-4ebf-ba49-b3ac30a35a7d/.

government affairs for Shell and BP. Mona Charen became a nationally syndicated columnist. Judi Buckalew had a successful career in health policy. Frank Donatelli directed a major practice for a national law firm. Marshall Breger went back to academia. Linas Kojelis, Todd Foley, and Mel Bradley had successful careers in business and government affairs.

And most importantly for us in OPL (and for America), Reagan won re-election handsomely, carrying forty-nine states. It is difficult to evaluate the extent to which our work contributed to this outcome, but we saw repeatedly that the more familiar people were with Reagan, the more they understood his program, the more comfortable they were in supporting him. This familiarity countered the image painted of him by his opponents, echoed by some in the media, that he was some sort of ideologue with no sympathy for the less fortunate—and doddering as well.

And on the Central America issues, we made headway as well. "In April 1985, Congress reaffirmed the complete ban on *contra* aid that it had instituted the previous fall; in June, it made exceptions; in the summer of 1986, it authorized new funds."[30]

But the happiest moment was outside the White House. Ann and I were blessed with the birth of our first child, Abby, in 1984, which brought no end of joy and made the repose of the home even more important as an oasis from the growing demands of work. As I turn to next, not all consequential events involve the president, but all presidential events could be consequential.

---

[30] Stephen Sestanovich, *Maximalist: America in the World from Truman to Obama* (New York: Knopf Doubleday Publishing Group, 2014), 232.

CHAPTER 7

PRESIDENTIAL EVENTS

Air Force One landed in Cleveland, and because of positioning requirements for the motorcade, we had to park away from the terminal, so we needed a ramp truck to disembark. The driver of the ramp truck pulled up to the plane, but at a slight angle away from the perpendicular that was required. After realizing he undershot, he quickly backed up to try again. All of this was watched by the president and team waiting in the aisle to exit. On the second attempt, the unfortunate man over-corrected and had a slight angle the other way. He would have to try a third time. The tension was building a bit on the plane, and there seemed to be a steam of impatience rising from some of the senior staff, though the president was not bothered. He offered an offhand comment: "I don't know who that man is…but I bet he had trouble getting his wife pregnant."

And the plane dissolved into hoots of laughter. The man got it on the third try.

***

There are two great truths in the White House, desk truth and street truth. Most of the White House deals with desk truth. What does the Council of Economic Advisers have to say about inflation? What is OSHA doing about regulating smoke alarms? How do we deal with the issues that the Cattlemen's Association raised at their White House meeting? That is all desk truth. Let's get some bright people together and figure it out.

But where should the president travel, and why? That's street truth. Presidential travel requires the right strategy, the right message, and the right event. When all three elements come together, the effect is magic. Indeed, a presidential visit can be dubbed the magic wand of American politics.

Regarding strategy, Mike Deaver pioneered many elements that are now so widely accepted that it is easy to believe they had always guided advance work and scheduling. But Deaver began the process of organizing a schedule so that it fit with policy goals, differing from the long-established view that the purpose of travel was solely to reach an audience, the more people you talk to, the better. Deaver knew that every event had a message, a theme, and a purpose—in addition to an audience. Make sure the event fits with the president's agenda. The audience for an event is not local but national. Stay on message. Avoid non-strategic rationales, such as, "Let's go to Cincinnati because we have not been there in a while." Or, "Let's go to Denver because the mayor is a friend." Or, "We always get a big crowd in Baltimore." You go places where it helps the agenda and everything else is a wasted moment.

Pushing the farm bill? Better have a farm event. Helping a candidate with middle-class voters? What about a suburban high school basketball game? Are ethnic voters key? There are plenty of special holidays and food events that convey the message. And to top it off, make sure the visual reinforces the message. Where is the "money shot"? Use a banner: "Iowa Farmers Welcome Ronald Reagan." Or "Jones Junior High Welcomes President Reagan." Deaver would note that the press could go off-message and write whatever they wanted, but the photo would capture what we wanted.[31]

Except in the middle of a political campaign, you were typically not visiting a locale to win support in that locale. You were visiting a locale to form part of a national news story. The audience was the backdrop. This is an overstatement because Reagan liked chatting with people, but he also understood the power of the message and the photo. Say it this way—you were going to Wichita to speak to the people of Wichita and *also* because Wichita would provide a good stage for a national press event.

Only occasionally, the national audience didn't matter. Reagan took time off from a swing in Alabama to visit a school for

---

[31] As Mike Deaver recalled: "[I]n '76 I was convinced we lost the nomination because Jerry Ford could own the evening news. He could get on television. He was the President of the United States. So I spent a lot of time between '76 and '80 talking to producers of the evening news. I just understood that if I could produce a picture that was so good that the producer in New York couldn't refuse it, I could get on the evening news every night." Michael Deaver, "Michael Deaver Oral History," interviewed by James S. Young, Steven Knott, Russell L. Riley, Charles O. Jones, and Edwin Hargrove, UVA Miller Center, September 12, 2002, https://millercenter.org/the-presidency/presidential-oral-histories/michael-deaver-oral-history-deputy-chief-staff.

kids with special needs. No media was invited along, given the nature of the event. He offered a few minutes of remarks and took questions from the kids. It was a terrific—dare I say, *Reagan-esque*—moment because simply by spending time with these kids, he was endowing their experience with a bit more worth. These kids did not get a lot of joy in their lives, and they might have spent their brief childhood without many people listening to what they had to say or trying to make them feel important. Here was President Reagan taking questions, nodding along, answering the points, telling jokes, and conveying to the world that there was no place he would rather be that moment than right there with them.

Then came a moment of terror. The last kid to ask the president a question had a severe speech impediment. He asked his question, and no one in the room could understand it. The president asked him if he could repeat it and again no one could understand what was said. The staff froze. The teachers froze. What was to have been an upbeat day was potentially a disaster. Instead of allowing these wonderful kids to forget about their disabilities, this kid was going to be reminded of it.

Reagan was quick to come to the rescue: "I'm sorry," he said with a smile, "but you know I've got this hearing aid in my ear. Every once in a while the darn thing just conks out on me. And it's just gone dead. Sorry to put you through this again, but I'm going to ask one of my staff people to go over to you so you can tell him directly what your question is. Then he can pass the question back to me." Rather than make the kid feel small, Reagan brought his own handicap to the forefront.[32]

---

[32] Frank Lavin, "More Than a 'Great Communicator,'" *The Wall Street Journal*, June 8, 2004.

In general, we had to respect the news cycle, meaning one television event a day. It did not do you any good to have two or more events in a single twenty-four-hour cycle. Regardless of how many events you had, you were only going to get one story a day. The flip side of this rule was the zero-defect advance system, originated by Bob Haldeman in the 1968 Nixon campaign: The press would focus on the biggest error of the day, so there could be no errors.

Was this all started by Deaver? After a talk I gave at the Nixon Library, we discussed Deaver's view that the purpose of political events in the age of television is essentially for TV reach. The Nixon Library director explained that H. R. Haldeman gave similar advice to Nixon in 1967. He disappeared for a minute and returned with a memo:

> *A candidate for any…national office can't afford the old 'tried and true' methods of campaigning: six speeches a day, plus several handshaking receptions, a few hours at factory gates and a soul-crushing travel schedule. Just because it has always been this way doesn't mean it always has to be this way…*
>
> *But what do you do—quit campaign travels and sit on the front porch? Not at all. You plan a campaign that is designed to cover the important localities, provide excitement and stimulation for your supporters, generate major news every day…*[33]

---

[33] H. R. Haldeman to Richard Nixon, June 20, 1967.

David Gergen provided details on the Nixon approach: "We had a rule in the Nixon operation that before any public event was put on his schedule, you had to know what the headline out of that event was going to be, what the picture was going to be, and what the lead paragraph would be."[34]

[34] Smith, *The Power Game: How Washington Works*, 501. Kindle.

Haldeman saw that the main transformation between Nixon's 1960 and 1968 campaigns was the emergence of a national media market. Deaver refined that idea to reach specific constituencies and messages. And every president since then has followed the model. There must be a strategy behind the event.

The second component of street truth was the White House speechwriters. They were the most well-read, the most intellectual, and the most agenda-oriented members of the White House. They understood the magic. Reagan managed by message. He sounded the trumpet. As Peggy Noonan noted, "Speechwriting was where the administration got invented every day."[35]

Here's how speechwriting works for people outside the speechwriting office. When I wanted to make sure a speech captured a particular point, I had to engage with that speechwriter informally as that first draft was being prepared. We could always grab coffee or explore ideas in the office and try to build a general consensus about the themes that would be central to the speech. Whether you plugged in with the speechwriter or not, he or she crafted the text and the staff secretary sent it around the building for clearance.

If you were less nimble, you would only see the speech after the staff secretary had circulated it, already late in the process. The rest of the White House might see the speech as a big empty box. The whistle is blown and everybody starts putting things into the box, the State Department, the NSC, and other outside groups. At the same time, everyone starts to notice things in the box they don't like or that don't fit with the speech as they

---

[35] Peggy Noonan, *What I Saw at the Revolution: A Political Life in the Reagan Era* (New York: Random House, 2003), 67. Reprint.

perceive it, so they furiously start taking things out of the box just as they also work to furiously put other things into the box. The pace and emotions pick up so the process evolves into a shapeless, formless mass of energy, with ideas being simultaneously inserted and removed from the box of a speech. The pace increases until it is white hot, and people start making phone calls and engaging in corridor chats to work out the last bit. Over time, people have their needs met, accepted, or rebuffed; or they give up and stop calling; or there is a compromise on a word, a clause, or a theme. Then the whistle blows again, and the speech is done. But it all sort of works because enough people were in enough agreement on the speech throughout the process that the box process is more of a refinement exercise, a rock tumbler through which the speech is polished.

And Reagan had a top-notch speechwriting crew: Tony Dolan, Clark Judge, Josh Gilder, Peter Robinson, Mari Maseng, Peggy Noonan, and John Podhoretz—many of whom went on to produce prizewinning writing and bestselling books. Dolan received the Pulitzer as a reporter before he joined the White House; Noonan received it after she left. Clark Judge established a leading communications firm. Josh Gilder did much the same, independently. Peter Robinson wrote a number of well-received books and helped run communications for the Hoover Institution. Maseng went on to run the Public Liaison Office and then to be Assistant to the President for Communications. John Podhoretz continues much the same cause as editor of "Commentary." These are just the ones I had the pleasure of working with. There were giants like Ken Khachigian and Ben Elliott with whom I did not directly collaborate, but, collectively, this was the 1927 New York Yankees. There's never been another team like them.

The third great element of events was the advance team. They were the most fun to work with and, after the Secret Service, the most operational office in the White House. They understood Reagan. Or was it that they understood how Deaver understood Reagan? They took the theme and made it real. Let's find a physical event to reflect a particular point, be it a legislative initiative or a demographic reach. We spent a lot of time concentrating on jobs and working with the Reagan Democrats. Deaver's genius was to realize that he had to put together events that would transcend the media's predisposition to interpret.

If the speechwriters were who I wanted to have lunch with, the advance people were who I wanted to have a beer with. You will not find more capable organizers than Rick Ahearn, Jim Hooley, Shelby Scarbrough, or Joanne Hildebrand. Grey Terry, Gary Foster, and Andrew Littlefair brought their strengths to this all-star cast.

Jim Hooley worked to fill VFW halls for the underfunded Reagan 1976 effort. Rick Ahearn started on the Hubert Humphrey campaign plane in 1968 and gained fame for having to retrieve his clothes and personal effects from a sealed hotel room that the 1974 Ralph Perk Senate campaign had not paid for. He did so by climbing outside the ledge of the Cleveland hotel, just like in the movies, to steal back that which had been stolen from him. Rick was the lead advance man when Reagan was shot, so viewers of news footage would typically see Rick in the middle of the presidential party as Reagan walked to his car. In a flash, the shots rang out and Rick was in the middle of a scrum as simultaneously Reagan was pushed into his limo and John Hinckley was tackled.

With that background, I listened closely when Jim gave me a great piece of advice as I became part of the traveling party. Always talk with the Secret Service detail. One rule of thumb when you are working with people who carry guns: make sure you know their names, and they know your name.

We need to tell the small-town mayor that he will not introduce the president, but the president will mention him in his remarks and he will get a photo and a handshake with the president. We have to make sure the chief of police is working the right way with the Secret Service. We have to plug in with the political office because the state Republican Party chairman and the governor of the state do not like each other, and they each want to be in the welcome party when Air Force One lands. The chief fundraiser needs to realize that this is not his event just because he raised the money, it is the White House's. This is all street truth.

More street truth: Frequently on the road, a host city mayor would want to offer a toast, a plaque, or read a famous quotation or a bit of history. The best way to handle this would be for the president to incorporate those thoughts into his remarks. The president would show respect for the city (and the mayor) by referencing them. This would be an efficient use of everyone's time on an extremely tight minute-by-minute schedule. There is no more effective way for a mayor to waste a president's time than to take a few minutes to explain how honored he is to greet the president. We can see why every White House moved to off-stage "Voice of God" announcements with "Hail to the Chief" to save a few minutes of platitudes and stage movements.

And on top of the local diplomacy, the fixing, and the finesse, there is the real job—the event itself. Does it flow right? Do we have enough time for the motorcade dismount? Is there a green room for the president when he's not on stage? Does the Secret Service have "overwatch"? Who has done due diligence on the hosts, the sponsors, the dais? The lighting, the TV angle, the run-of-show for proper sequencing? Is the photo line organized and ready to roll, and are handbags gathered and nametags off? The program is always too crowded. Everybody wants to say something. Everybody wants to get in the photo. Discipline is critical to keep on schedule.

Housing starts were up—the first economic indicator that the recovery was underway—and they were up the sharpest in Fort Worth. It was to Fort Worth we went, and the president was walking though some framed-out housing starts. The president was in the middle of the visual and it was dead center on-message. Advance put it all together—from who was greeting Reagan as he stepped off the plane, to who was on the dais, to the warm up music, the balloon drop, the local sports figures and political leaders, the press perspective, the photo angle, the crowd, the donors, the entrance and exit, the security, the entire package. And if they did it right, no one even would notice they did it. Some of their work bordered on genius. And if you could do all that, why not have a beer when it was all over? And, for the single staffers, if you met someone attractive, and he or she was somewhat dazzled by all of this—the White House, the motorcade, and Air Force One—well who could blame? It *was* dazzling.

Some of this event management ended with John Hinckley. After Reagan was shot, there were no more grand entrances through the front of hotels. Too open, too vulnerable. In fact, these hotel main entrances were designed with a grand perspective in mind. Anyone could see the arrival which also meant anyone could, literally, take a shot. From then on, for every president, the motorcade went into the hotel garage and the president walked through the kitchen to the event. This provided an additional opportunity for photographic visuals of Reagan greeting service workers as he sailed through their kitchens and hallways, and gave people who might never have the chance to be near a president the opportunity to meet him.

The president got this right away, but some visitors had trouble with this notion. The Chinese, in particular, were baffled that their president should have to enter through a hotel kitchen rather than be greeted in the lobby with full honors. Yes, international diplomacy was even a factor in entering and exiting hotels.

CAMPAIGNING WITH THE PRESIDENT

Nothing else had the drawing power of a presidential visit, be it for publicity or fundraising. Nothing else could match the enormous stature of a sitting president, the support (at least among Republicans and swing voters) that the president enjoyed, and his ability to command media attention. Having said that, there were times and circumstances at which a presidential visit would be more helpful and situations in which it would be less so. Ignominiously, there might be times where it might not be helpful at all. A visit could be a magic wand, but not in every situation.

For candidates, the publicity of a presidential visit meant that it would be more helpful for those without much stature—a challenger going against a well-known incumbent, for example. The strength the president had with the Republican base meant that the visit would be helpful on the heels of a divided primary, where the president could bring Republicans together. And the publicity of a visit meant it gave a candidate with fundraising ability the chance to bring the most important fundraiser in the land to his state.

There is something seductive about a presidential visit—Air Force One, a twenty-car motorcade, and national television covering the arrival. Reagan stepped off the plane and at the top of the stairs greeted everyone with his broad slow wave and the friendly slow smile. He'd done it countless times before, but it looked as if that was the first time he'd ever done it in his life. Indeed, his joy at arrival allowed you to believe he was waiting all day just to step off the plane. Sure, there were a few thousand people in the crowd at the airport, but you were pretty sure he was looking right at you just then, and his head tilted a little. The lighting was good. The crowd was electric, with signs and balloons setting the scene.

And on a personal level, what a splendid opportunity. I remember my first time in a presidential motorcade and it *was* damn exciting. I was with the Secret Service in one of their chase cars, always a Crown Victoria, maybe the best production line car made in America for this sort of work. The Secret Service had an upgraded pursuit-interceptor model and their own training program with a track in West Virginia. The agent knew what he was doing.

I asked, "Where do we go if there is an incident?"

"*We* don't go anywhere."

"But we are with the president."

"No. You are with the motorcade but you are not in the *bubble*. The bubble gets taken care of, but you do not." It may have been a momentary jolt into reality as I reassured myself that I was unlikely to be the target in any event.

***

Air Force One was the old 707 that first went into service in the Johnson administration, not the new 747 used today. It was a bit cozier, with fewer compartments, and easier for the president to circulate. And indeed, Reagan being Reagan, he came back to the staff lounge as he normally did to say hello.

We were chatting in general, just passing the time, and I ventured, "Mr. President, would you mind if I tell you an off-color joke?"

The president demurred...*well*...with that same slow smile.

I realized even as I spoke the words that I have asked a fundamentally stupid question, or rather, asking the question is fundamentally stupid. Because it is impossible for a sitting president explicitly to request someone tell a blue joke. Beneath the dignity of the office. However, if such a joke happened to slip out in casual conversation, and if it were all in private, and if we were all friends, or at least compatriots, and if parts of it perhaps could not be repeated in church, well what would be the harm?

The point is, don't formally ask permission because the answer can only be no. Just go ahead.

Fortunately, presidential speechwriter John Podhoretz (now editor of *Commentary*) was there. Whether he had simultaneously also figured out this *uber*-logic of my presidential dirty joke permission granting theory, or whether he just wanted to hear the joke, I cannot say, but he had the presence of mind to nudge me and say, "Go ahead."

"What's twelve inches long and hangs down between Michael Dukakis's legs?"

"What?" asked the leader of the Free World.

"His necktie."

Every visit offered somewhat the same architecture: The local candidate was at the bottom of the airplane stairs to greet the president. It was a warm embrace, a two-handed handshake. It went on for a while, in case someone didn't get the idea (reminiscent of my meetings with the president in Room 450 of the OEOB). It came with a nod of the head, a well-timed shrug, and the grin broadened to a smile with a well-timed joke. The crowd saw the chemistry, and the TV cameras were rolling. A few pleasantries, then it was into his limo (brought in on a separate car plane) for a quick dash downtown.

Was it Cleveland, St. Louis, San Diego, or Atlanta? It didn't matter, the motorcade barreled down the freeway to the downtown hotel or convention center, then through the kitchen, of course, and inside there were ten thousand, sometimes twenty thousand, applauding, standing, hooting, and hollering supporters. Frequently we were able to do photo ops beforehand, maybe a special hello for people who donated $5,000 or $10,000 to a soft dollar organization. Then it was into the ballroom for the large event. These events were timed literally minute-by-minute on the schedule.

Reagan knocked them dead. He was at a point of public stature at which he just had to be himself and he carried the moment. A courtesy opening, followed by praise for the local dignitaries and elected officials. Thanked the audience for their support. Some self-deprecating humor, usually about how old he was. The crowd loved him. Then it was back to the Reagan themes. *Government is too big and expensive.* Lots of applause. *The Soviet Union remains a menace.* More applause. *Traditional values are the backbone of the country.* The applause continues. *And that is why we need the candidate to join me in Washington. Someone has to keep Ted Kennedy in line.* Laughter. Applause.

Then, it was back to the airport. The event just raised $800,000. Or a million. Or maybe two million plus. It blanketed the state in positive news, likely for an entire twenty-four-hour news cycle, and it galvanized the base with a direct-from-the-horse's-mouth message: *if you like Reagan, you need to support this candidate.* It also left the White House staff feeling good, if not elated. We had done some more good for the cause, one more step ahead. Cumulatively, however, I knew that it was time to move on. With the re-elect over, I needed to move to a position with more of a policy component.

CHAPTER 8

1985–86 NATIONAL SECURITY COUNCIL

I was taking a polygraph and I was not good at this sort of thing. I have a natural anxiety level that almost ordained me to fail.

"We just need to calibrate the machine," the technician explained in a reasonably friendly, reasonably professional, third-person-plural bureaucratic voice.

The technician hooked me up and said, "We are just going to ask some baseline questions to see how the machine works."

"Fine."

"Is your name Frank Lavin?"

"Yes."

"Do you live in Washington, DC?"

"Yes."

"Did you kill Abraham Lincoln?"

Pause—I was frozen.

"We are just calibrating the machine so you need to answer the question."

He repeated the question. "Did you kill Abraham Lincoln?"

Oh my God. Oh my God. Was I saying this out loud or just to myself?

"*This is an easy one, just answer in a normal tone.*"

Oh God oh God oh God.

"*Please answer the question. Did you kill Abraham Lincoln?*"

"*No!*" *I exclaimed, but a bit too rapidly and a bit too loudly.*

BUZZ. The machine registered my statement as a lie.

I changed tack.

"*I didn't mean to do it,*" *I blurted out.*

BUZZ. The machine again registered a lie.

"*I just meant to scare him.*"

BUZZ. Another lie.

Oh God oh God oh God.

I was desperate now. Perspiring a bit. Drawing sharp, short breaths.

"*I was just showing him the gun and it went off.*"

BUZZ.

I was in a hole I could not possibly get out of. In a panic, I changed tack again.

"*I don't know what happened. I don't really remember.*"

The polygraph man looked at me with a tired expression.

"*Well, which one was it? Was it an accident, or don't you remember?*"

Oh my God, oh my God, oh my God. "I did it. I shot him."

No buzz.

I was on a roll now, and confession was good for the soul: "I feel terrible. I shot Garfield and McKinley as well. I killed them all."

The polygraph man did not break his role. "Well, what about Kennedy? Didn't you kill JFK as well?"

"No," I said quite straightforwardly. "That was Lee Harvey Oswald."

"Right," he said.

I didn't think I would ever be good at the intelligence game. Yet somehow the officer decided I probably was not some sort of reincarnated John Wilkes Booth-Leon Czolgosz-Charles Guiteau Frankenstein's monster, and I was given a top secret codeword clearance and joined the National Security Council (NSC) as deputy executive secretary.

***

What is the purpose of foreign policy anyway? Across the political spectrum, the answer would be "peace and prosperity." But that inarguable response raises more questions than it answers. US foreign policy typically flows between realism and idealism. Realism means respecting core national interests and maintaining peace through a balance of power. Idealism reflects a belief in human rights and democracy, and maintaining peace through a political system that is transparent and inclusive. Realism is based on interests, and idealism is based on values. Most US presidents adopt elements of both in their policies. Reagan's contribution was that he could fuse these two ideas, thanks largely to the Soviet Union. For the USSR represented not only a politico-military threat to the US and its allies, but also a threat to American—and universal—values, with a totalitarian government repressing political freedoms, freedom of speech, and freedom of religion. This allowed Reagan to talk in idealistic terms, to label the Soviet Union an "evil empire," and still stay true to geopolitical goals. Indeed, Reagan could move away from idealism, notably in his cultivation of China and his willingness to work with Latin American governments that had weaker records on human rights. True to UN Ambassador Jeane Kirkpatrick's "Dictators and Double Standards" essay (See Chapter 2), Reagan saw communist governments as totalitarian and not capable of reform, whereas he believed the authoritarian governments could become democratic—as had happened in Taiwan, South Korea, and Chile. Idealism for Reagan was both a means and an end, but the idealistic impulse at times competed with the balance-of-power reality.

In one way, working for Reagan on foreign policy was simple: the direction was clear. In an equally significant way, working for Reagan on foreign policy was complicated: you were trying to change the world. Reagan had a core set of beliefs around which his foreign policy was built. First and foremost was an attitude toward foreign policy. He was not serving as president to preside over a system or to perpetuate a set of arrangements. He was in office to change the system, to alter arrangements, and to take us to a better place. He did not like the stalemate of the Cold War. He knew that conflicts in the developing world could be debilitating. He was keenly aware of the budgetary drain of defense spending. He also knew that with the right approach, the right tools, and the right initiatives, the Soviet Union would be the one worried about a stalemate, or developing world conflicts, or economic pressures. Their system could not survive an all-out competition. When asked his view of the Cold War, he replied: "We win; they lose."[36]

---

[36] Hayward, *The Age of Reagan: The Conservative Counterrevolution*, 102.

Reagan adopted six tactics to push back against the Soviets:

- Get the economy moving again: to reassure the general public, bolster political support, and pay for the budget increases.
- Articulate an affirmation of liberty and Western values: to remind the world that this was not merely a geopolitical rivalry, but that there was a profound moral dimension as well.
- Rebuild America's defenses: to meet or best the Soviets in every sphere of military competition.
- Focus on technology: so that the US could out-compete the Soviets.
- Raise the cost of Soviet adventurism in Central America and elsewhere: the Reagan Doctrine.
- Do all this in an alliance structure that would earn the support of the Free World.

Through my good fortune, I was to be a part of it.

I got to the NSC through an elaborate game of musical chairs. David Stockman was the *wunderkind* Office of Management and Budget director whose fall stemmed from an interview with William Greider in *The Atlantic*, in which Stockman said, "None of us really understands what's going on with all these numbers," among other indiscreet remarks—eventually leading to his resignation. Stockman was replaced by Jim Miller, who had been chairman of the Federal Trade Commission. Jim Miller was replaced at the Federal Trade Commission by Dan Oliver, who had been general counsel of the Department of Agriculture. Dan Oliver was replaced by Chris Hicks, who had been serving as director of the White House Office of Administration. Chris Hicks was replaced by Johnathan Miller, who had been at the National Security Council. I replaced Johnathan Miller. *The Atlantic* interview was bad news for Stockman, but it turned out to be good news for me.

In every administration, the NSC has three jobs. First, it must present foreign policies for presidential consideration. Such proposed policies can arrive from many sources, with the NSC staff presenting the choices in a fair and balanced way. Second, after the policy has been decided, the NSC staff has a role in making sure that the executive departments or the military services are complying with the president's instructions. Third, the NSC staff acts as the personal foreign policy staff for the president by preparing talking points for meetings and trips and handling many routine matters involving other countries. It was in this third area that I worked.

The executive secretary of the NSC, like the staff secretary of the White House, was in charge of process, meaning that the papers for the president were in order and had been properly staffed out and approved, that interagency views had been harmonized, and that the president was getting an honest paper that fairly presented the issue. It also meant that the president's meetings and international visitors were managed properly. What did the president need to see from the foreign policy community? Had all the departments and agencies approved or "cleared" the document? How did meetings of the NSC translate into action and how was that action monitored and managed? It fell to the executive secretary to stay on top of it all.

As deputy executive secretary, my job was not primarily to work on paper flow but on external meetings and events, specifically inbound and outbound presidential events, such as state visits and overseas trips. The main responsibility was to work with the US policy community to set the goals and agenda, and negotiate that with the other governments. We had to make sure both sides agreed on the issues to be discussed; the number and size of meetings; the nature of any ceremonial events, meals, and so forth. The point is that a presidential event is the peak of foreign policy execution, making "summit" an apt term. It is arguably the most important diplomatic tool the United States has. The most precious resource in the White House is the president's time, and we needed to ensure that its use was effective.

There was also the drafting of remarks and talking points to buttress the events, to articulate the policies or decisions. If the president meets with the prime minister of Italy, there is a separate set of documents for each session of meetings, a dinner toast, a statement for a joint press conference, and the sometimes-sensitive formulation of the guest list. Corridor chatter still carried the story of when Rep. Norman Mineta, a Japanese-American, was not invited to the state dinner for the Japanese prime minister because the Carter White House thought he was Italian.

I quickly learned that there is a special kind of NSC-speak—a dry, detached writing style that avoids subjects and adjectives and sometimes avoids objects and verbs. Instead of writing "The president should not make these remarks until after he meets with the French president." You write, "The president's speech would have a greater impact if it were delivered after the meeting with the French president." Instead of saying "no" to a request from the Japanese Foreign Ministry for a joint press conference, the NSC writes, "A joint press conference is not normally held in conjunction with a lunch." A bit of "Voice of God," a little passive voice, with a dash of weird bureaucratese. Memos are sent; but no one sends them. Decisions are made; but no one makes them. Everything just sort of flows anonymously along, evoking the old State Department aphorism: never sign anything you write, and never write anything you sign.[37]

The NSC might have hosted the strongest policy expertise in the White House, composed of scholars, authors, diplomats, military personnel, the world of intelligence, and other accomplished specialists. Unlike the rest of the White House staff, the NSC staffers were not there exclusively because of political pedigree or a longtime affiliation with the president, but some were there largely on the basis of their policy depth.

This internal planning and coordination with foreign counterparties made all the difference in presidential meetings. It did the United States little good for the president to travel to Tokyo, only to ask the Japanese prime minister, "What's on your mind?" All of the issues had to be floated beforehand, and this would ensure that the president would be properly briefed

---

[37] The requirements of feeding the system the paper it required perhaps reached its apotheosis when I was tasked by the national security advisor to develop his talking points for his POTUS meeting and shortly thereafter tasked by the staff secretary to develop POTUS talking points for his meeting with the national security advisor. I might be at my best when I can script both sides of the conversation.

and the respective departments would churn out the papers. The point of visiting Tokyo would be to finalize an agreement, not to begin the discussion.

Indeed, by determining that the president would be meeting next month with the prime minister of Canada and fishing rights would be one of the items discussed, it gave both governments an enormous incentive to work out the issue. From the staff point of view: you are the president's assistant. He is not your assistant. Don't push your work up to him; he has already pushed it down to you.

My job encompassed initiatives such as overseas travel and negotiations as well as more mundane matters, such as presentation of diplomatic credentials. I worked across the NSC, and with the State Department Protocol Office, the Advance Office, and various other groups in the system. The first lady's staff was particularly useful in talking through issues because Nancy Reagan did not like surprises.

My immediate boss, the executive secretary of the NSC, was a retired Navy captain, who was a confidant of Admiral Poindexter and had served at the CIA under Admiral Stansfield Turner in the 1970s. This gave him broad government experience. The erstwhile Carter administration link made him suspect in some quarters, but I only saw professional conduct from him.

However, the captain did have a nervous tic in one eye, which caused spontaneous winking. This could result in unsettling situations for people who were unaware this was merely a physical condition and not a sly political statement. I participated in at least one meeting in which the tic played an unfortunate role. The captain would make an innocuous state-ment to visitors: "A nuclear war can never be won and must never be fought." So far so good, a statement in perfect accord with common sense and administration policy. Then…wink.

The visitors would be a bit perplexed and seek clarification. "The Reagan administration is committed to doing everything it can to avoid nuclear confrontation?"

"Absolutely," asserted the captain, to the momentary relief of the guests. Then another wink and all reassurance evaporated.

The guests tried again. "Nuclear war is not an option?"

The captain would respond, "Not an option." Wink.

The captain cautioned me on protocol as I came on board. Referring to a recently departed NSC staffer, he said, "All that fellow wanted to do was to eat in fancy restaurants and fly around the world with the president." I had not envisioned my job as having either of those privileges, but now that he men-tioned it, both seemed like worthwhile goals. Still, I could tell from his tone that he disapproved of this type of activity. And he didn't wink when he said it. "I see," I said, which was the best I could muster without veering into hypocrisy. It was evocative of H. L. Mencken's description of Puritanism: "The haunting fear that someone, somewhere, may be happy."

THE RON-YASU RELATIONSHIP

The Japanese and the Israelis were the most demanding coun-tries we worked with. They were meticulous in reviewing the details of events and challenging at every point; they needed to debate the rationale for every activity and treated the entire discussion with suspicion, as if we might be inviting their prime minister here to humiliate him. We would rehash the same points at repeated meetings. The Israelis had the charming idiosyncrasy of using a White House meeting to complain they did not have enough White House meetings. Yet somehow it all worked out and more than one Israeli minister stated that Reagan was the most effective president Israel had seen on Middle East issues.

The Japanese, on top of their normal anxiety, insisted that every meeting with the president and the prime minister must somehow represent an "improvement" over the previous meeting. A bit like how Soviet agricultural results always had to result in an "improvement" over the previous year. Since the Japanese went through prime ministers relatively quickly and since relations with the US—though strong—had not markedly improved, this would be a difficult goal to reach. The Japanese Foreign Ministry was in a sort of arms race with itself. On top of this, the gaps of language and culture mitigated against genuine personal friendship, though Reagan knew the Japanese were good allies and he had a high opinion of the relationship.

Particularly wounding was a recent event in which King Hussein of Jordan had gone horseback riding with Reagan. Reagan was an expert horseman, as was the king. The photos were well published, and anyone could see that the two leaders had a bond. This struck a note of anxiety in the Japanese.

What can we do? Our prime minister does not ride horses.[38]

What about something involving baseball, which might be about the only cultural element the prime minister may have in common with the president?

But we have done it before.

We might have to do it again, fellows. We don't have a lot to work with here.

Japan had revolving door prime ministers at times, but for most of the Reagan administration (1982–87), the prime minister was Yasuhiro Nakasone, whose five-year tenure as prime minister was considered a very long time.[39] The relationship was a key one in many senses. As with the Israelis, this focus on minutiae with Japan paid off for the United States.

Although there was not an easy mechanism to reflect personal chemistry between Reagan and the Japanese Prime Minister, the NSC team devised a solution: President Reagan would host Prime Minister Nakasone at Camp David and in addition would ask the PM to call him "Ron," which thus launched the "Ron-Yasu" relationship. They had many direct meetings over those five years, and Reagan respected Nakasone very much

---

[38] Horse diplomacy might have reached its zenith in 1982 when Reagan had a state visit to the UK. As both President Reagan and Queen Elizabeth were "horsey people," they went for a pleasant ride. Notably, the Queen's horse passed gas, a bit loudly. The Queen was a bit startled and said, "Pardon me." Reagan said, "That's OK, ma'am. If you hadn't said anything, I would have thought it was the horse."

[39] At that time, Nakasone's five years was second only to Satō's seven-year tenure in the modern era. Subsequently, Koizumi and Abe have both broken this record.

as a seasoned, experienced, and popular national leader who was taking Japan in a significantly improved direction as far as American policies were concerned. For example, Nakasone would note that Japan and the US were *allies*. Indeed, we were from at least 1960 onward, but prior PMs would not say so.

While Ron and Yasu were having lunch, the remainder of the team ate in the staff mess at Camp David. The US side from left: John Poindexter, George Shultz, George Bush, Don Regan, Mike Mansfield, Jim Kelly. The Japanese foreign minister is Shintaro Abe, father of the murdered former prime minister.

If Israel and Japan were more demanding, at the other end of the spectrum was Uruguay, whose president, Julio Sanguinetti, we had the pleasure of hosting. Indeed, the only issue that arose was that Uruguay has what is believed to be the longest national anthem in the world, clocking in at a solid thirty minutes, as it provides an epic recapitulation of the history of Uruguay. Needless to say, thirty minutes is a bit long to stand during a welcome ceremony and perhaps more of a history of Uruguay than necessary to make one's life complete. Fortunately, the good people of the Uruguay Foreign Ministry understood this point immediately. It seems there is an abbreviated version available for ceremonial purposes.

CAMP DAVID WITH PRIME MINISTER THATCHER

I had only been at the NSC a few weeks when there was a note in my inbox. It was unsigned, though the note said it had been prompted by a phone call from US Ambassador Charles Price, and it noted that Margaret Thatcher wanted a meeting with the president to review East-West relations, proposing the president host her at Camp David. This handwritten note ended in part: "I'd like this if it could be done."[40]

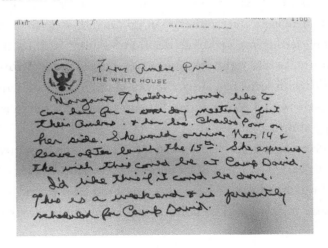

---

[40] Note Regarding Prime Minister Thatcher Visit in Coordination Office, NSC Records, RAC Box 13.

Not only was the note unsigned, there was no salutation. Yet I had to believe it was from a senior staffer if they would have the boldness to propose a Reagan-Thatcher Camp David meeting. I assumed the note was from National Security Advisor John Poindexter or perhaps from Chief of Staff Donald Regan.[41]

There was an easy way to find out. I dashed out of the Situation Room to the White House staff secretary, now David Chew who had replaced Dick Darman. I reminded him that I was relatively new and asked him if he could recognize the handwriting. "It's the president's," he said.

The president was sending the most innocuous note possible to his own staff. Rather than directing us to prepare for a Camp David meeting, he simply stated a preference, adding a gracious "if possible." Talk about a light touch. A reminder that authority is more impressive if whispered rather than shouted and the use of rank to get one's way can generate problems. Good managers steer rather than command. Reagan was, in a sense, letting me make the decision for him, trusting that I would make the right decision. Over time, I learned Reagan did this with some regularity. He would often preface a written comment with a gentle nudge, "If you will permit me to make a suggestion…"

Planning for the visit proceeded. The president wanted to present Mrs. Thatcher with a personalized Camp David jacket, and I was asked to find her jacket size, a request I passed to our embassy in London. The political officer asked plaintively how

---

[41] Owing perhaps to the handwriting, the more fastidious reader will note this note refers to "Charles Pow" in place of "Charles Powell," the prime minister's foreign policy advisor.

he was supposed to know her size. I wished him good luck. Whether by spy satellite, telephone taps, or simply asking her personal assistant, the embassy got the specifics. Indeed, I was awakened at home at around 2 a.m. with a call from London reporting the details.

Camp David is not ornate or even plush. In fact, many holiday resorts in the US might have more nicely appointed facilities, but the setting is spectacular. It is isolated, there is a sense of serenity, and the scenery of Maryland's Catoctin Mountains is breathtaking. Remember, in Washington, the president cannot normally take a walk outside. He cannot engage in any outdoor activities short of a major Secret Service mobilization. He cannot reflect amidst nature. At Camp David, he can undertake all these joys, so the true luxury of the facility is that it allows the president to escape the golden cage of the White House and act like a normal human being. It certainly illustrated why the president enjoyed returning as frequently as possible to his California ranch.

Reagan liked Thatcher. He respected her, and he enjoyed her company. As for "Maggie," I was at first shocked to see the familiarity with which she treated him. "Now, Ronnie, here's what you need to do..." she said at one point. I wheeled to look at him, expecting a glower, but he was taking it all in. If you are the president of the United States, there are basically no peer relationships. Thatcher was perhaps the only leader in the world who shared the president's philosophy, spoke native English, and had the self-confidence to assert herself. Reagan would have successful meetings with government leaders from around the world, but these were diplomatic exchanges and negotiations.

With Thatcher, he was with someone who had also climbed up from a modest background, thrown out the establishment leadership of the party, and, once getting into office, had tackled economic reform and dealing with the Soviets. Reagan had a soulmate. Howard Baker put it: "I believe Maggie Thatcher was the only person who could intimidate Ronald Reagan."[42]

We worked out that the two leaders would have a "four-eyes"—just the two of them (as with Ron and Yasu). Then, the larger party—to include our secretary of state and their foreign minister and policy aides—would join the two leaders for lunch. I would be at a staff lunch table.

Given that the relations between Reagan and Thatcher were so warm, it was odd that the Camp David meeting was difficult to arrange with the British embassy—their actions very much in contrast with the graciousness and professionalism of Antony Acland, the British ambassador. Their "head of chancery" (in effect their number two) was designated to work with me and kept suggesting he also participate in the Reagan-Thatcher meeting. It was blindingly clear that Reagan did not want anyone else in the room while he chatted with Thatcher, and my impression from Thatcher was that she had no particular use for the British diplomat. Still, he insisted, he needed to be in the room. I checked again, in case my instincts were wrong. Reagan's personal aide Jim Kuhn reminded me the two leaders had had a number of similar one-on-one meetings, and that the president valued the occasions. Admiral Poindexter observed that the larger policy group would be meeting at lunch immediately thereafter, so there was no need for note-takers in the

---

[42] Brands, *Reagan: The Life,* 401. Kindle.

small meeting. We all agreed it was appropriate to let them have their privacy, though the head of chancery would not accept my decision. What to do?

The plan was that Thatcher would arrive in a Marine helicopter, part of the Nighthawk Squadron that includes Marine One. The president would greet her as she disembarked, and then drive her to their meeting in his modified golf cart. The head of chancery stated he would follow in the motorcade. I directed him to get into the second sedan, a car with no other passengers. Thatcher arrived, right on time. The president greeted her, looking a bit jaunty, and off they went. The appropriate motorcade went right along, with the exception of the second car. I had arranged for the Secret Service driver to take the head of chancery directly to the staff lodge. As soon as he got there, he exited the car, got his bearings, ran over to the meeting room, and—too late, the meeting had already started. Sometimes a few words and a stroke of timing are all it takes to explain things, albeit a few words repeated: "No, I am sorry, sir. We cannot permit the meeting to be interrupted. I am sure you understand. No, sir. No, I am sorry. I am sorry. I am sorry." He seemed incandescent.

We moved together back to the staff room in the main building, waiting for the staff luncheon, the sidelined chancery official in high dudgeon. I was feeling a bit clever but hoping it was not showing. It was a bit petty on my part, but his adamant refusal to go along with the president's (and, we assume, Thatcher's) wishes left me few options. To my surprise, he made another stab during lunch. We were just sitting down to eat at the staff table while the VIPs were in the next room having cocktails before lunch. "I need to take a message to my minister," he exclaimed, as he sprung from his seat. I sprung up as well. His statement had more than a ring of falsehood to it, since I had been with him since he had arrived and no one had passed him a message. He jumped to the Reception Room, and I was right behind him.

He approached Foreign Minister Douglas Hurd, a pleasant, seasoned professional, and they exchanged a few words. I had no idea what he said, but I suspected it was closer to "I was able to find a jar of the blueberry jam your wife likes," rather than, "Please remind the prime minister that the number of warheads matter more than aggregate throw-weight when calculating the destructive capabilities of Soviet ICBMs." The conversation broke off, and the head of chancery took a drink from a waiter. As he was momentarily without the shield of his minister, I pounced. "It's time for us to go back to lunch." I smiled and gestured toward the ignominy of the staff table.

He was not to go down without a fight. "I cannot leave this room without the approval of my minister," he said with a note of finality that almost made you want to believe him. It was as if Hurd were reflecting this very minute on whether to send the Royal Navy to the Falklands, and this vital message could only be communicated through the head of chancery.

Of course. "Let's go talk to the minister," I said, and started walking toward Hurd. The head of chancery was a bit alarmed, realizing that he was on someone else's turf and not entirely sure of what I might say to the minister. He wisely sprang in front of me and wheeled the minister away from me in a huddle. Again, it was unclear what he was saying, but after a few seconds, he turned back to me and announced, with a bit of pride, "My minister has given me permission to join you at the staff table."

VICE PRESIDENT'S TRIP TO GERMANY

US relations with Germany loomed large in the Reagan administration. It was the height of the Cold War, making security issues and NATO solidarity paramount. The central strategic issue in that relationship was the pending deployment of short-range nuclear missiles, "theater nukes," by the Soviets. If the Soviets were to do so, NATO needed to do the same and deploy its Pershing II medium-range ballistic missiles. The concern was that, if the Soviets had theater nuclear weapons and NATO did not, NATO deterrence would be less credible.

To base the US missiles in Europe would require firm political support from each of the host governments. This was a challenge because no nation wants nuclear weapons on its soil, even as they needed the security guarantees the weapons provided. Germany was lucky to have Helmut Schmidt and Helmut Kohl as back-to-back chancellors who understood this obligation and helped lead their country to deploy these weapons. Indeed, when this issue first emerged in the late 1970s, Schmidt was more committed to Pershing II deployment than Jimmy Carter, realizing German security was at risk if NATO did not go toe-to-toe with the Warsaw Pact. Reagan and Kohl got along well, though there was not a great deal of personal chemistry. Both took the Soviet threat seriously, and both were prepared to stake their political careers on the importance of security. Buttressing the Reagan-Kohl relationship was the national security advisor relationship. Poindexter and his German counterpart Horst Teltschik did have chemistry, and sometimes spoke several times a day. Interoperability was so strong that we at the NSC could regularly receive taskings, questions, and directives directly from Teltschik through Poindexter, in as distilled an example of friendship and alliance coordination as one could hope.

Of course, the Soviets knew all this, and they were doing their best to undermine the Pershing deployment. There were legitimate pacifist and anti-nuclear groups that organized against deployment, there was a range of leftist and anti-American groups, and there were even pro-Soviet and violent organizations. These groups led massive rallies, street demonstrations, protests, civil disobedience, and political movements as the deployment drew near. Still, Kohl and Reagan held firm.

As part of the outreach activity for the Pershing deployment, Vice President Bush was tasked with a German trip. He would speak to the Bundestag and also do some community outreach activity. This mixture of high politics and street politics was a common formula, allowing Bush to connect with senior decision-makers and to bring a message of goodwill and common cause with the man on the street. It is almost impossible for a president or vice president to visit a city, be it domestic or international, and not give some sort of public speech, visit a school, or meet with a public group. Polling data showed us that, despite the protests, most Germans agreed with the US on deployment, seeing the folly of allowing the Soviets to have a monopoly of theater nuclear weapons. We wanted to reinforce the point that the US enjoyed goodwill in Germany despite the occasional anti-Americanism. A public event would send the right message, but with this particular trip we had a problem.

Anti-American fever was running high, and German security officials were concerned about public events. They might just turn into a protest. They might even turn violent. In any event, it was too risky to bring the vice president in front of students, for example, for questions and answers.

This did not sit well with us and we thought it would not play well, either in Germany or the US. Capitulation on this point would make it look as if the anti-American forces had won. Either a majority of Germans were against the deployment, or the Americans were too afraid or too arrogant to connect with the public. The vice president should have some sort of interaction with the German public, but how?

The vice president's advance people had an idea. As the vice president's motorcade was to depart Bonn to return home, there was a farmer's market on the way to the airport. What if he hopped out of the motorcade for a few minutes and chatted with farmers at the market—perhaps even bought something at one of the stands?

We ran that idea past the Germans. "Sorry, it won't work," was their response. Too many security concerns. It is an open event, and there is no way to screen the attendees.

Receiving a German veto, the Americans made a counter-proposal: What if Vice President Bush stopped at the farmer's market but without any public notice, what we in the US call a *drop-by*? This significantly improves security because with no prior notification there is no way for violent protesters to prepare. With this modification, the Germans relented. We keep the side trip as a *close hold* event. It won't appear on the schedule. It will just happen.

The proposed event was about as spontaneous as you can find in this business. The motorcade would pull off on the way to the airport, and the vice president would spend a few minutes chatting with farmers. They'd love it. And the TV camera would love it. The vice president would be in and out before anyone knew.

The day came, the schedule change had not been publicized, and the motorcade pulled into the farmer's market. As planned, the vice president got out to roam the grounds and started talking with one of the farmers, a young man with short hair and a genial disposition. After a few sentences of friendly chat, Bush went to the next booth to repeat the exercise, and the farmer there was also a young man with a short haircut and a friendly disposition. In fact, looking around the farmer's market, you would note that every single farmer was a young male with a short haircut and a genial disposition. They all seemed to have earpieces as well. In fact, every shopper and visitor at the market seemed to have these same attributes. When the German liaison officer was given a quizzical look from the US advance people, he confessed with a small note of pride, "Yes, they are all ours—German security officers. Once you told us that your vice president was going to make this stop, we felt that we had to replace every farmer with one of ours. And we had to replace all of the regular people with our people as well. We just put them on a bus to remove them for the duration of the vice president's visit. They will be allowed back as soon as he is gone."

We were dumbfounded. Were the Germans able to rear-range an entire market with a few days' notice? Were we fooling the Germans, or were they fooling us? Sort of defeated the purpose of a visit to the farmer's market, didn't it? German logic prevailed: *Well, it is what you wanted. It is still a farmers' market, just without any farmers.*

FIRST FAMILY

One ancillary duty at the NSC was to coordinate first family international activity. The Reagan children might occasionally travel overseas or be invited to an international gathering, and we wanted to make sure that their travel and their messages were consistent with administration policy. To the credit of Maureen and Ron Jr., they were dutiful in coordinating their activities through the NSC. Patti Davis was estranged from the family at this point and did not communicate.[43] The children had a reputation for being high maintenance. Ed Rollins opined that he had had Maureen Reagan as a friend and he had had her as an enemy, and it was just easier to have her as an enemy. I never found her difficult, although she made it a practice to have her way, and she never gave the impression of being overly solici-tous of other points of view.

The first lady made no solo trips overseas during my tenure. However, given her stature, various foreign dignitaries would

---

[43] One of the more poignant sentences in President Reagan's memoirs: "I still dream and hope for a day when Patti and I will develop a close relationship again.... [B]ut so far she's made it plain to me that she thinks I am wrong and that she is against everything I stand for." Reagan and Lindsey, *An American Life*, 566.

seek her out for a meeting as they visited the United States, and it fell to the NSC to make a recommendation to the First Lady's Office as to the desirability of such encounters. Demand vastly outpaced supply as many first ladies and former first ladies and other spouses of senior people from around the world found themselves in the US regularly, perhaps to visit a relative, perhaps to see a child at college, or perhaps for medical treatment or a holiday. Rarely did a week go by without an embassy notifying the NSC that their first lady would be visiting NY and would be available to visit DC if there were an invitation from the White House.

Many of these were easy to dismiss but some required a bit of detective work and *clientitis* reared its head. The least objective person one could ask for a recommendation as to whether the first lady should meet her counterpart from Argentina would be the Argentina desk officer at the State Department or the US Embassy in Buenos Aires. But we had to make an independent call as to whether such a meeting was really in the national interest. Indeed, the volume of requests was such that the suspicion grew that certain first ladies around the world were fishing for a White House invitation that would make their US trip a necessity.

Routine notification to the First Lady's Office

One day, I received a referral from the First Lady's Office. There was an inquiry from a DC lawyer who stated he was transmitting a note from Princess Jeanne of Romania, and the note requested a meeting with the first lady to discuss a matter of "utmost importance."

Dennis Ross was the NSC director for Near Eastern and South Asian affairs, and he and I sat down with the lawyer in the White House.

Meanwhile, we asked State for background on Princess Jeanne. Nothing. We asked the CIA. Nothing. State asked the Library of Congress. Nothing. The Library of Congress was asking various academics, and nobody had any insight. The entire matter began to smell.

The meeting with the attorney did not clear the air. His story was that Princess Jeanne wanted the first lady to know that Princess Jeanne was aware of a large quantity of "red mercury," a radioactive substance that could be used to make nuclear bombs. She wanted to make sure this was in the hands of the US government but—the smell gets worse—"funds would be required."

We took notes and thanked the attorney. I sent a note to the First Lady's Office stating that the NSC did not recommend a meeting.

Dennis tracked down the State Department nonproliferation people who had heard of "red mercury," and, as we suspected, it was viewed entirely as a fraudulent initiative, a scam in the vernacular.

I called the attorney to let him know we would not be following up.

About two weeks later, I received a call from the FBI asking if they could visit with Dennis and me. We met in the same room where we met the attorney.

It seems we had been involved in telephone conversations about the purchase of red mercury.

Well, yes, in a sense that was accurate. But we were only involved in the conversation to reject the purchase, not to promote, accept, or endorse it.

The lead FBI agent told us the conversation was referred to in subsequent conversations that had ended up in INTERPOL intercepts. In any event, we walked him through what we did, and he seemed satisfied. To my mind, the INTERPOL point was a bit of a ruse, as INTERPOL has no independent monitoring capabilities as far as I know. The FBI, or someone, was running some sort of intercept program of its own, be it legal or freelance, they were tracking someone and we stumbled into view.

While on the topic of illegitimate issues: months later, a specialist in the Romanian monarchy reported back to the Library of Congress that in the late nineteenth century or early twentieth century, there was indeed a king who had a mistress who had several children out of wedlock and one of them was named Jeanne.

OLLIE AND THE CONTRAS

**Elliott Abrams, myself, Caspar Weinberger, Jackie
Tillman, John Poindexter, Ronald Reagan**

The Reagan Doctrine—that the US would be willing to support anti-communist insurgencies around the world—seemed to grind to a halt in Nicaragua. The Sandinistas had fought their way into power as a leftist but nominally broad-gauged group, ousting the Somoza dictatorship. The initial optimism over their victory increasingly gave way to concern due to their repressive politics and growing alignment with Cuba and the Soviet Union. As the Sandinistas themselves evolved toward dictatorship, the Contras gained support, both within Nicaragua and within the Reagan administration. In the abstract, at least, one would think this an appealing policy, but Congress was ambivalent and slowly cooled on the idea. There were concerns raised about the Contras' human rights record and additional concerns about possible links to the Somoza regime, and there was probably a fair amount of naivete about the increasingly repressive nature of the Sandinistas among some members of Congress. In any event, Congress cut off funding for the Contras although Congress did not specifically prohibit the US from raising funds from other sources. This opened the door for Oliver North, a decorated Marine who led NSC planning for the Contras and was known by the nickname "Ollie."

Ollie had a sense of mission and a sense of theatrics. The organizing principle in his life was to support the Contras, the loose confederation of parties and personalities that were opposed to the Sandinista government in Nicaragua. Ollie's plans for funding the Contras required a lot of adrenaline and a large measure of audacity. Ollie had both, as well as the Hollywood good looks and charm to go with it. He also had such an extraordinary degree of self-confidence that he thought he could navigate the legal and regulatory maze to fund the Contras, or that he would never get caught, or that the ends would justify the means. Maybe some of all of this.

Ollie was youthful, smart, articulate, and an operator. He had no problem taking risks, and he believed in his cause. What might have begun as a logical plan eventually ended as a plan devoid of logic. Step by step, things went wrong. From initial plans to secure third-party funding for the Contras—reasonable enough—the plan degenerated into an arms-for-hostage plan, morally indefensible. Additionally, Ollie seems to have been seduced by the operational element of covert activities and the dramatic elements of secret travel, call signs, disguises, fake passports, assisting the Contras in the field, negotiating with hostages in the Middle East. These were activities that should not be run from the White House, activities for which he had no particular training, and that would be bound to cause controversy even if they had remained within the law. Nowadays, this would be prime fodder for a Netflix series.

Added to this were loose financial controls so that some of the money for the Contras was not accounted for and some ended up in the hands of the nominal facilitators. Nothing wrong with getting paid for services, but people need to be exceedingly careful about propriety and the appearance thereof. When one of the DC contractors bought a sports car from his payment, it couldn't help but send a bad message.

Covert activities can be jeopardized by, well, the kind of people who are drawn to covert activities. There can be an amateurish, even juvenile, sense of derring-do; a bias toward complexity; an unfailing belief in the cause; and a narcotic of danger that seems to attract people of romance and passion. While not intrinsically objectionable, some of these types tend to be more on the margin of competency. The better intelligence professionals are more likely to be plodders: People who pay attention to their environment, who do not draw attention to themselves, and who worship Occam's razor principle of preferring the simplest solution. If your life depends on a chess match, there is nothing wrong with making only one move a day. Better to work with the least exciting person in the room rather than the most exciting. At some point, you realize sports cars don't help you go faster.

Still, there was something beguiling about Ollie, almost roguish. He knew the communists were the bad guys. Heck, we all knew that, but Ollie was prepared to do something about it. That's why people voted for Reagan, wasn't it? That's why we had covert operations, wasn't it?

Like any good rogue, there was a certain amount of blarney, a certain amount of charm, and a lot of dash. One example: I was taking Bob Oakley to see the president. Bob, at the time, was the assistant secretary of state for Narcotics and Law Enforcement, or "Drugs and Thugs" in state parlance. Ollie asked if we could get some presidential cufflinks as a gift for Bob. But there was no particular reason why President Reagan would be giving a gift in the course of a meeting to an individual who was his assistant secretary. It is not as if he were a foreign dignitary. He already worked for the president.

"He's dying of cancer, you know," said Ollie. I was shocked because I was completely unaware of Bob's condition, though Bob had a gaunt look that I had attributed to the demands of the job rather than a medical condition. I quickly talked this over with the president's personal aide, Jim Kuhn, and we agreed that the president should give Bob some cufflinks and do so in a delicate fashion. You can't say, after all, "I hear you are dying of cancer and I might never see you again, so I wanted you to have this little gift." The president, of course, was marvelous, with understated delivery but just a hint that something was going on here beyond merely the presentation of a gift. Again, at times, he seemed to thrive on the emotional dimension of his job as much as the substantive dimension. It was a touching moment, and I carried the warmth of that encounter with me until several weeks later—when I found that none of it was true.

Bob didn't have cancer. He certainly wasn't dying. He looked gaunt and haggard because he *was* gaunt and haggard and probably had been from birth. It was only after reflecting on this encounter some time later that I hit on a more cynical interpretation. Ollie was not trying to hustle a free pair of cufflinks; he was trying to demonstrate to Bob that the president was aware of and supported his (Ollie's) plans even if the president could not say so. The cufflinks were to signify that Ollie met with his approval. So, Ollie was playing me, playing Bob, and playing the president. National security staffer Johnathan Miller said to me after this affair that the great thing about Ollie was that when he screwed you, he did so with such style, you didn't mind being screwed. At that moment, there was a certain truth to that assessment.[44]

Another example: We had a meeting in the Oval Office with the president, National Security Advisor Poindexter, and Ollie. Ollie's beeper went off.

"Well it's not from me," said the president graciously.

"Not from me," said Admiral Poindexter.

"Must be from God," said Ollie. He stepped outside to take the call. Magnificent showmanship and perverse all the same. In one gesture, Ollie one-upped the president and the national

---

[44] Lou Cannon offers an explanation of North's courtship: "North lied to Robert Oakley...telling him that the HAWK missiles had been discovered in a warehouse in Portugal where 'one of his people' was seeking arms for the contras 'and learned that the Israelis had been obtaining arms from the same source for shipment to Iran.' Oakley was also told that one or more U.S. hostages would soon be released in Lebanon. Based on this information, Oakley allowed North to tell the U.S. embassy in Portugal that State was 'aware' of the operation and that the embassy 'could request clearances' for the plane that was to transport the missiles to Iran." Cannon, *President Reagan: The Role of a Lifetime,* 550.

security advisor. One beep says volumes: "I'm not sure what you gentlemen are talking about, but if you don't mind, I will step outside and take this call. You keep chatting, I have work to do." It's not enough to be with the president, you have to trump the president. I found out later that he had his secretary, Fawn Hall, page him deliberately at that moment.[45]

***

You might have a front-row seat for an event and not fully understand it even as you witness it. I was in the Situation ("Sit") Room on another weekend and chatting casually while catching up on work. One of the signal operators showed me a message: "Take the birthday cake to the aquarium." That was the entire message. The message was transmitted through an NSC system that I was not normally supposed to see; even with TSC clearance, I would only be privy to certain codeword operational details—termed "compartmentalized intelligence" on a need-to-know basis. But a combination of weekend watchstanding and probably a mistake on behalf of the operator put it in front of me.

As a reminder that signal operators are not analysts, he commented, "Kind of odd to have a birthday party in an aquarium."

I observed, "It looks like a code to me."

---

[45] In the same spirit, Deputy White House Press Secretary Pete Roussel had gone on a date with actress Jessica Lange. Was it a coincidence that Pete was given the message she called him in the middle of a White House senior staff meeting, and he instructed the message-bearer that he would call Ms. Lange back later? You be the judge.

The operator persisted, "It's not code, it's all in English." And he repeated the message out loud.

"No, not a coded language, but code words. The words stand for something else. It says 'birthday cake' and 'aquarium,' but it actually means something else."

"You mean the birthday party is not in the aquarium?"

"Not only is it not in the aquarium, it is not a birthday party. It is a code."

Only from the newspapers did we later learn that Ollie had indeed taken a birthday cake to identify himself to the captors in Lebanon, a cake being perhaps the clumsiest call sign ever devised, a bit more cumbersome than holding a rolled-up copy of *The Economist* in your left hand.

What had begun as an effort to keep the Contras in the field, and which had enjoyed some success in that regard, turned into an arms-for-hostage scandal, and a financial scandal that threatened to touch the president personally. Bud McFarlane, who had been national security advisor when the program was launched, testified that he briefed the president, who had assented, but there was no written record of any such approval. The president stated he had no memory of any such briefing or approval. Credible third parties, such as Chief of Staff Donald Regan, stated that the topic never arose in any of the NSC briefings of the president in which he participated. The impression given is that McFarlane might have briefed the president, but the discussion was deliberately minimized to the point that it was meaningless to the president, yet still allowed McFarlane, and later Poindexter, to claim presidential support. I never discussed the matter with Poindexter, but the executive secretary did mention almost plaintively, "If only people understood the difference between a planeload of missiles and a shipload." This floated a *de minimis* argument for a policy that never should have been implemented. Finally, in congressional testimony Poindexter stated that he had authorized the diversion of funds and had not told the president.

Ollie's operations evoked Richard Pipes's law of bureaucracy: every institution eventually acts as if it were controlled by its enemies. The scandal consumed much of the administration's political capital and energy over the final two years. Reagan paid the price for it, but as he noted: "I knew Oliver North only slightly when he worked for the National Security Council.... I never met with him privately and never had a one-on-one conversation with him until I called him on his last day at the NSC to wish him well."[46] This was a striking indicator to me because we all had to submit answers to the various investigative bodies in the wake of Iran-Contra, and I remember being somewhat surprised that in one year or so of NSC work, I had met with Reagan roughly three times a week, over 150 times, though many of these were group meetings.

***

Even when military aid was not embroiled in scandal, it still could be controversial. "We have problems with El Salvador," Reagan wrote in his diary during February 1982. "The rebels seem to be winning."[47] By 1985, the situation had improved a

---

[46] Reagan and Lindsey, *An American Life*, 486.
[47] Brands, *Reagan: The Life*, 356. Kindle.

bit due to US political and military assistance, moves that were contentious in the US. I was discussing El Salvador with a Salvadorian colonel. El Salvador was in the early stages of a transition to democracy after years of authoritarian rule. Though the government was democratic, the military was still viewed with some suspicion, and there were still right-wing death squads. The US was providing El Salvador with military support and economic aid as it struggled to combat a communist guerilla movement, which in turn was backed by Nicaragua and Cuba and, its ultimate patron, the Soviet Union.

I put forward a summary of policy: We were willing to help because we saw that a communist takeover of El Salvador would be a disaster for El Salvador and inimical to our interests as well. At the same time, the El Salvador military had to realize we had human rights concerns. These concerns were important in themselves, and they were important for keeping a supportive coalition intact in the US. Americans were simply not going to support a government that was indifferent to human rights abuses.

I thought I made a reasonable point and presented it in a reasonable fashion. The colonel cut me off at the knees. "You Americans are fools," he practically hissed. "Fools," he helpfully repeated, in case I had missed it the first time. "You went into Vietnam with your rules and regulations and you lost. The communists beat you. You simply slink home, and it is a disaster for Vietnam. We cannot lose in El Salvador. We have no place to slink off to. I do not want to be running a restaurant in Northern Virginia like your Vietnam refugees. El Salvador is our home. It is all we have. We have no choice but to fight and to defeat the communists. And you Americans think that because you give us some money, you can tell us what to do. But you yourselves don't know what to do. Keep your money."

I was stung by the vehemence of his remarks. I thought the colonel was off-base substantively, but I had to note his style. I could expect the Salvadorians to be sensitive to criticism, but what prompted his blanket criticism of the US? This was my first experience with what psychiatrists call *hostile dependency,* a relationship in which the dependency of a weaker party on a stronger party breeds not gratitude but hostility. Our aid and our conditions were dehumanizing, even insulting, to the recipient, regardless of whether we were right. Countries, like individuals, need autonomy and the ability to act independently. The fact that El Salvador was so dependent on US support was a bitter pill for this colonel.

***

A second discussion was held on El Salvador, this time with National Security Staffer Peter Rodman who just returned from consultations with the El Salvador military. He related how difficult it was to *teach* someone not to torture: "If they don't accept that up front, I am not sure there is much I can do. So I would tell a class that it is wrong to torture captives, and immediately a hand would shoot up."

"You mean it is wrong to torture innocent suspects."

"No. All suspects. It is wrong to torture any captives."

Another hand. "You mean it is wrong to torture if you might get caught."

"No. It is wrong to torture, period. Whether you might get caught or not."

A murmur went through the classroom. "What if you capture people who had just ambushed your unit and killed some of your buddies? Those guys, surely, you can torture."

"No. That's the point. You can't torture anyone. It is wrong in itself."

Now the murmur continued to grow and there were some statements of disbelief. "How can you say that? The communists torture us every day. Our culture is different from yours. What if the torture helps prevent a bigger disaster?"

There was such a gulf between the students and the teacher that it was almost surrealistic. But the US could not walk away from El Salvador, nor could we accept human rights abuses. There was no choice here except to engage the military and to help them move the right way.[48]

---

[48] "Escalating the Cold War ended up strengthening the role of democratic principle in American foreign policy…. The American people, [Reagan] declared, 'oppose tyranny in whatever form, whether of the left or of the right.'" Sestanovich, *Maximalist: America in the Word from Truman to Obama*, 233.

PRESENTING CREDENTIALS
AND VIP MEETINGS

**The President's Foreign Intelligence Advisory Board:
Albert Wohlstetter, Henry Kissinger, Anne Armstrong
(chair), the president, Leo Cherne. I am taking notes.**

It is an obligation in every nation that new ambassadors present their diplomatic credentials to the head of the host government. This practice also gives the president the option of a brief conversation with each newly appointed ambassador if he desires. I had the assignment of assisting with the presentation of credentials, serving as escort officer. Reagan would have a briefing card before each presentation. Chief of Protocol Lucky Roosevelt would formally introduce the new ambassador to the president for a handshake, a photo, and other remarks as needed. Remarks were usually reserved for when there was a friendship or business at hand, such as a NATO member or an ally like

Australia. Lucky was the perfect person for the protocol. Not only bright and accomplished in her own right, but being married to Archie Roosevelt, a career CIA officer as well as Theodore Roosevelt's grandson, did not hurt. Her formal name was "Selwa," but she had been known since college as "Lucky," a nickname she earned as a bridge player.

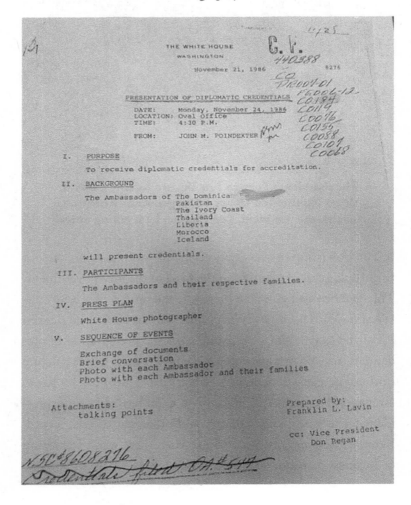

Mechanically, it was a pretty simple activity. The new ambassadors along with their immediate family were "staged" in separate holding rooms in the West Wing and the Executive Mansion and brought to the Oval Office sequentially to be presented to the president. This also allowed for a private Oval Office handshake and a photo, as well as a conversation as desired. *Please remember to remove your White House pass and we will have a nice photograph. Please hand me your handbags. Please let me know if there is any sort of item to be presented or gifted so that we may inform the Secret Service.* Lore held that in times of presidents gone by, a distinguished visitor from an Arab nation caused a bit of a stir when, unannounced, he pulled out some sort of ceremonial sword to present to the president, resulting in a near-tackle from the Secret Service.

There was a new ambassador from Czechoslovakia. Reagan asked me beforehand, "He's just a communist, isn't he?"

"Yes sir. Just a communist," I replied, which I thought was a fair encapsulation of the person's limitations. A bit reductionist, but let's face it, the guy was a pure-bred functionary of the Soviet system and was not a reformer or a dissident or anything of that nature. (Reagan was even more dismissive when asked if he would attend General Secretary Andropov's funeral: "I don't want to honor that prick.")[49]

---

[49] Jack Matlock, Jr., *Reagan and Gorbachev: How the Cold War Ended* (United States: Random House Publishing Group, 2004), 87; Reagan summed up his views on this topic neatly: "Now I knew from firsthand experience how Communists used lies, deceit, violence, or any other tactic that suited them to advance the cause of Soviet expansionism. I knew from the experience of hand-to-hand combat that America faced no more insidious or evil threat than that of Communists." Reagan and Lindsey, *An American Life*, 115.

The new Czech ambassador actually had prepared some brief remarks, clearly rehearsed, unaware that Reagan had already sussed him out. "Mr. President, I hope that the people of our two countries can find ways to improve our relations.... We must live together in peace...have much in common."

Well, our peoples probably have much in common, but not our governments. And after all, you. Are. Just. A. Communist. No, I didn't say it, just thought it. I am certain these were Reagan's thoughts as well as he made this distinction over and over again in the case of totalitarian systems.

Reagan politely half-listened for a minute and broke in with body English first, then an interjection. "Thank you, Mr. Ambassador."

The ambassador didn't break stride. In the Soviet system, if you had the microphone you kept talking, either through resoluteness or obliviousness.

"Mr. President, I hope we can continue this discussion in the course of my tour, and please call on me if there is any way I can be of help."

Reagan repeated himself, "Thank you, Mr. Ambassador." Just a communist.

In the hallway outside the Oval Office, the ambassador looked to me for reassurance. "I thought that went well."

Of course, it had been a fabulous disaster, but I couldn't tell if in the Soviet system he was obliged to say that it went well, or if he actually thought that it went well.

I summoned my diplomatic skills and said, "Well, you made your point."

One time waiting in the West Wing foyer for a dignitary, I, again, was with Chief of Protocol Lucky Roosevelt. A cabinet member breezed through the West Wing for a meeting and greeted us. "How are you? Selwa, how are you?"

She winced ever so slightly at the use of her formal name and ventured to correct him. "'Lucky,' John, I'm 'Lucky.'"

The secretary does not miss a beat. "You sure are, Selwa. You have the best job in town."

***

The incoming ambassador of Papua New Guinea had a question for me. "May I bring my girlfriend to the presentation of credentials?"

"Well, no, we really have to restrict the event to family members only."

"But we are close. Very close."

"I understand, but it is restricted to family members only."

Stretching the rules of diplomatic candor, he related: "But if I can take her into the Oval Office, I am fairly certain she will go to bed with me."

With that comment, of course, this idea was completely dead. The White House cannot facilitate assignations for the ambassador, at least not wittingly.

"Yes, yes, but rules are rules. I don't think I can help you."

The ambassador was soon involved in a drunk driving accident and was recalled. We leave this anecdote without knowing how far he eventually got with his girlfriend, only with the small comfort that the White House was not a party to his efforts.

161

Manfred Wörner was defense minister of Germany and, more to the point, he was tapped to be the next secretary general of NATO. A brief meeting with the president would help set the right tone. A president would not normally meet with a defense minister, and there was a little grumbling about the propriety of such a meeting, so a short "photo op" was arranged for the White House photographer. The two had a nice handshake, and then a sit-down for the photo. A friendly chat with a few supportive words from the president, and the entire event was less than five minutes. I escorted the minister back across the hall to the Roosevelt Room and Wörner made an observation. "Why don't we just hold here for a few minutes?" Perceiving a question on my part, he explained, "I have a stand-up press discussion outside the West Wing. I cannot go out there just five minutes after I went in." I nodded at his insight and signaled the steward for some beverages. The minister and I enjoyed small talk for a few minutes. "Now we can go out," he proclaimed. Perception is reality.

For those who thought Reagan was just going by the script or that his faculties faded in his second term, he could surprise you. Gorbachev released one of the more prominent dissidents, Natan Sharansky, who departed the Soviet Union for Israel but wanted to pay his respects to Reagan for carrying the torch for dissidents. As Lou Cannon noted, Reagan "needed no prompting to present Gorbachev with lists of imprisoned dissidents..."[50]

I took him into the Oval Office and the president welcomed him: "Anatoly..." then he paused. "That's not right, is it? It's not Anatoly—isn't it Natan?"

---

[50] Cannon, *President Reagan: The Role Of A Lifetime*, 404.

Sharansky was gracious and said, "Either one is ok. Anatoly is the original Russian name, and Natan is the Westernized version."

Reagan dug deeper, "But last time we met you were not Anatoly."

"I usually go by Natan," Sharansky stated.

"Well, Natan it is," affirmed Reagan. The Great Communicator strikes again.

WASHINGTON, D.C. 20506

September 17, 1986

MEMORANDUM FOR AL KEEL
ROD McDANIEL

FROM: FRANK LAVIN

SUBJECT: Shevardnadze Meeting, Friday, September 19
              Eduard

Due to the sensitivity of this meeting and Admiral Poindexter's
absence, I would like to fill you in on a few of the mechanics
we are currently planning.

I.   Annotated Agenda

A.   Prebrief: The prebrief will take place in the Oval
Office from 11:00 - 11:30. Participants will be worked out w
Ty Cobb and forwarded in his briefing memo. At the end of the
prebrief Secretary Shultz will join Ambassador Roosevelt in
West lobby to greet Shevardnadze. The rest of the American
(except for the President) will proceed to the Cabinet Room.

B.   Arrival: Shevardnadze and his party (as of now Du
Karpov, Bessmertnykh and interpreter) will arrive escorted
Secret Service and protocol officers at the Southwest gate
approximately 11:25. They will enter through the West Bas
and take the West stairwell to the West Lobby. After Amba
Roosevelt and Secretary Shultz greet them in the West Lobb
will proceed to the Roosevelt Room where Shevardnadze will
the Guest Book. This signing is standard protocol.

C.   Meeting: At 11:30 the Soviet party will enter t
Cabinet Room and receive pro forma greetings (handshakes
the American party. The President will enter, greet the
party and then begin the meeting. It is envisioned that
meeting will not last longer than 30 minutes, but there
other events on the President's calendar until 1:15, if
meeting does run over.

D.   Departure: At the conclusion of the meeting,
party will be escorted out the same way it entered. Th
there will be no opportunity for Shevardnadze to appea
press on White House grounds.   *SIGN*

**Illustrative planning document, this for
the Soviet foreign minister**

CHAPTER 9

GORBACHEV AND REYKJAVIK: THINGS FALL APART

I had a break late on the first day of the summit, and I ducked into the cafeteria for whatever might be available. Near the summit site, there was a sort of cafeteria for use by both the Americans and the Soviets. Not surprisingly, the place was empty. It was around 3 p.m., so there was no meal service, but the juice machine was working. In the seating area, there was one person sitting and reading a book, a guy probably in his early thirties. He waved and said good afternoon with a slight accent, and I said good afternoon as well.

"Do you have a minute?" he asked, and waved me over. I walked the few feet to where he was sitting. "I'm Sergei," he said, "with the Soviet delegation." I introduced myself. He said he was with the supplies department, to make sure the delegation had all the equipment they needed, and to simplify matters, I told him I was with the administrative section.

"I have a question for you," said Sergei in an affable manner and he opened the English-language paperback he was reading. "What does this mean, 'to let the cat out of the bag'?"

"Well, it means to disclose a secret or a surprise," I ventured.

"I know that from the context," explained Sergei, "but it is such an unusual expression, where does it come from? Is there a secret cat in mythology or American history?"

"It is an unusual expression, isn't it?" I had read somewhere a conjecture which did not fully answer the question. "I believe the cat in this expression is the cat o' nine tails, and letting the cat out of the bag refers to taking the whip out of storage so that it can be used." But I was not completely sure.

Sergei nodded. Even with my explanation, it was not clear why that would become an expression for revealing a secret.

We chatted for a few minutes more, then I had to scoot.

The next day I was back in the cafeteria, again taking a break for a glass of juice. Sergei was sitting in the same place, reading a book. I had come in a side entrance and was somewhat masked by a curtain, so rather than yell hello, I thought I would wait until I had walked to the main seating area.

Before I could get to that area and greet Sergei, another person had come in through the main entrance. He was an American, part of the military contingent. I recognized him, though I did not know his name. I thought I would observe.

Sergei waved hello and the GI waved back. Sergei beckoned over and they introduced themselves to each other.

"I have a question for you," said Sergei in an affable manner and he opened the English-language paperback he was reading. "What does this mean 'to let the cat out of the bag'?"

I froze. It took me a minute to understand what was happening. At first, I thought he was just asking the same question to two different people. Then the penny dropped. He was always in the cafeteria. He was always just waiting. He was always asking a friendly question to whichever American wandered in.

***

A key foreign policy decision a president has to make is whether it is better to be a minute early or to be a minute late? Do you put the policies in place before a problem emerges, or do you wait until the problem is upon us before you act?

For most of US history, the preference was to be a minute late. The United States had no international aspirations, nor did we believe we had any particular enemies, and we had the good fortune of several thousand miles of ocean to keep trouble away. That theory held up reasonably well until December 7, 1941, and ever since then presidents have decided that we are better off being a minute early, devoting resources to military treaties and mutual defense organizations, to training and working with like-minded nations, and to supporting policies that underpin our alliance network.

Although this internationalist approach to foreign policy was dominant for most of the post-World War II era, it began to fade under President Obama and declined more sharply under President Trump. Maintaining a strong defense is expensive, and it might invite the US to be more internationally active than was needed, even to the point of invading other countries or provoking others to attack us—so both Obama and Trump worked to reduce US defense relationships.

Reagan, however, believed in being a minute early. The core lesson of World War II was that the US needed to maintain a level of preparedness and find ways to work with other nations. This philosophy drove much of his foreign policy decision-making.

THE PORTUGUESE PRIME MINISTER

**The US side is the author, NSC aide Peter Sommer,
and US ambassador Frank Shakespeare.**

President Reagan hosted Portuguese Prime Minister Anibal Cavaco Silva for an official visit.[51] We needed to review the usual foreign policy issues and a range of security issues with Portugal as a NATO member. We also wanted to show support for Portugal's peaceful transition from military dictatorship to

---

[51] Cavaco Silva had a long career in Portuguese public life, eventually serving as president.

democracy, which had unfolded in the "Carnation Revolution" of 1974. Cavaco Silva was indeed a welcomed guest to the White House.

One small challenge was that he came during a long-planned renovation of Blair House, the official US government guest house. This did not materially affect the visit as the State Department Protocol Office usually makes use of the Madison Hotel, which can allow the visiting delegation to make use of an entire floor or more if necessary. The elevator and stairwells are designed to allow for the security of the visiting dignitary and to make sure there are no disruptions.

But a disruption there was. The very first full day Cavaco Silva was visiting, he received an emergency message. Actually, his military aide got the message directly from Lisbon. It was the "Military Household" calling, the prime minister's own military office that runs the liaison with the Defense Ministry.

"What is it?" the aide asked.

"You called us," said Lisbon.

"No, no one here has called the Military Household. We received a call from the hotline."

Indeed, a special communications line had been installed in the PM's suite at the Madison to allow for emergency contact. No one from the PM's delegation had made a call, yet the Lisbon side showed that a call had been made. In fact, the logs showed the call was made at the time when the prime minister and his delegation were participating in meetings at the State Department.

The conclusion was that there might be faulty wiring, or some other sort of defect, and the Portuguese embassy sent a communications technician to run tests on the special phone line, but the results did not reveal any problems.

Both the Americans and the Portuguese dismissed this event as a fluke, with relief there was no plane crash or terrorist attack in Portugal. Everyone's attention turned back to the business of Washington, where Portugal was participating in a series of useful consultations, capped by a White House dinner.

On the second day, as the rhythm of the visit was in full swing and the mood was upbeat, it happened again. Lisbon called Washington with the same message: *How can we help the prime minister?* Again, Washington replied to Lisbon with the same response: *No one from the PM's party has called Lisbon.* Now there was a mild sense of frustration.

Oddly, each call took place around the same time, between 10 and 11 a.m. Washington time. The PM's chief of staff had a solution. He directed the military aide to park himself in the PM's suite the next day as soon as the PM departed. He was to watch the phone, keeping particularly alert in the 10 to 11 a.m. window in case there was a third disruption.

The military aide was parked. He took his seat a few feet from the PM's desk in the hotel. As he took his position, he made a test call on the hotline to Lisbon and verified that the phone worked and all was in order. Then he busied himself with his papers and notes from the previous two days.

A little after 10 am, there was a knock on the door with an announcement, "cleaning." Almost simultaneously the room key turned in the lock and a cleaning lady entered. The aide nodded to greet her and beckoned her to continue with her work. And she busied herself around the room, straightening and dusting. She turned to the desk with a feather duster. Then she picked up the phone receiver to dust the phone properly as well. And she replaced it in the receiver a few seconds later. The military aide smiled.

AUSTRIA STATE VISIT

Helene von Damm was a naturalized American of Austrian heritage, but most noted for having served on the president's gubernatorial staff and later as the head of presidential personnel. It was no surprise that she ended up as US Ambassador to Austria. Nor was it a surprise that Austrian Chancellor Franz Vranitzky was invited for a state visit, including a state dinner. Per the usual practice, we took the Austrian protocol chief through the West Wing, discussing the presidential meetings, the other meetings and activities, and the state dinner.

The discussions and show-and-tell went well with no real issues or problems. At the end, the protocol chief stated that he had one final request.

"When it comes to musical selections, be it for the state dinner or the military band during the honor guard, we have one request."

"Yes?"

"Please, no 'Edelweiss.'"

"'Edelweiss'? From *The Sound of Music*?"

"Yes."

I could not understand what the issue might be. Was there some sort of political or historical point here? Were the Austrians overly sensitive of the Nazi past? "What's the point? What is objectionable about 'Edelweiss'?"

"It is not Austrian."

"No?"

"No. It has nothing to do with Austria. It is not an Austrian folk song. It is Rodgers and Hammerstein. Americans frequently play it for Austrian guests to the dismay of our entire party."

MOTHER TERESA

I was duty officer one weekend in the Sit Room. We received a phone call from the US ambassador to Sudan.

After introductions, the ambassador described his problem: "I have Mother Teresa here with me, and she wants to speak with the president."

As this was not a sentence I had been expecting, I repeated it to make sure I understood it. This was not as out of the blue as one might suppose as Reagan had hosted Mother Teresa at the White House in 1985 where he awarded her the Presidential Medal of Freedom. and the two of them apparently hit it off.

"You have Mother Teresa with you, and she wants to speak to the president."

"*Yes.*" He seemed pleased that I was able to repeat the sentence. In that case, I thought I had better say it again.

"You have Mother Teresa with you, and she wants to speak to the president."

He said *yes* again, but he seemed less pleased. Now there seemed to be an edge in his voice. I decided not to say it a third time.

"Can you give me a sense of the nature of the call?"

"She is concerned about poor people in Sudan."

"Poor people in Sudan?" (Again, I repeat the previous sentence.)

"Yes, people are starving here. There is an enormous famine. She wants the president to do something about it. She'd like to speak with him."

"All right, let me look into it. I'll talk with Camp David. But you'll need to verify that she really is Mother Teresa."

"What do you mean?"

"How do you know the woman really is Mother Teresa?" I asked.

"Well, I don't know. She sure looks like Mother Teresa."

"Well, you will need to verify her identity."

"How the heck can I do that? She doesn't exactly carry a driver's license."

"You figure it out. You're the ambassador."

"Look here. This is silly. What are the odds of a Mother Teresa look-alike tromping around the Sudan desert?"

"I agree the odds are slim. On the other hand, if you were a Mother Teresa look-alike and you wanted to make a prank call to the president, this is exactly how you would do it. Just figure out some way to firmly establish her identity. I'll call Camp David."

I called the president's personal aide, Jim Kuhn, who was with the president over the weekend. We quickly agreed that since the US had a range of disaster relief programs under way in Sudan, there was no particular need to interrupt the president for this phone call. However, the president would extend an invitation to meet with Mother Teresa when she visits Washington again.

I called our ambassador back.

"She is Mother Teresa. We figured it out. She is Mother Teresa."

"That's good news. Now let me tell you what we have worked out from this end," and I relayed our decision to put forward an invitation in lieu of a phone call. He seemed generally mollified, and after discussing this with Mother Teresa, he relayed that she was comfortable with it as well.

And I never did find out how the ambassador established that the woman was indeed Mother Teresa.

GORBACHEV

Mikhail Gorbachev represented a special sort of challenge to the Reagan administration. His rule carried all the traditional strengths of the Soviet system: enormous military power and an ideology that still resonated with some constituencies even as the Soviet economy was wheezing. In addition, Gorbachev was the first Soviet leader since Lenin who had a sense of public relations and who could deal with the media. He also had at least a limited sense of the shortcomings of the Soviet system and he launched the *Perestroika* and *Glasnost* campaigns in an effort to improve things at home. Although these reform movements led to nothing but the unintended collapse of the Soviet system, in his early days Gorbachev managed to capture a mood of optimism. It was the first time since Eisenhower that the Soviet leader was younger than the American president. This presented quite a contrast with recent images of Soviet leadership as the three previous ones (Brezhnev, Andropov, and Kirilenko) all died in office, following a repeated pattern of visible physical deterioration; guarded media appearances; and contradictory, minimalist, or dissembling statements regarding their health. Reagan related that he wanted to negotiate, but joked, "[T]hey keep dying on me."[52]

This was a rare moment in which the Soviets appeared to have the initiative. Gorbachev stood for a hopeful future. The Cold War was the most important foreign policy issue in the world, and nuclear weapons were the most important element of that Cold War struggle. And now the two leaders were to meet in Reykjavik to discuss this issue.

Reykjavik was a spontaneous decision. Although there had been exchanges of substantive letters between Reagan and Gorbachev over the preceding months, the dates and locale of a meeting were decided without premeditation. There were only ten days from the announcement to the October 11th and 12th meeting, making it as much of a come-as-you-are event as a summit. But sometimes lengthy preparation does not improve outcomes. Unlike other senior-level meetings, no position papers or proposals were exchanged beforehand. Gorbachev had proposed to meet Reagan in either London or Iceland, and Reagan selected Iceland.

I was on the US delegation in Reykjavik, working on the planning and coordination, while Ty Cobb, the NSC director for Soviet, European, and Canadian affairs, led the policy process. We worked with the Russians to decide how many sessions there would be between the two leaders, who would participate in each session, and what the agenda would be. Then the secretariat "staffed out" the work to various departments and agencies for their briefing input. Finally, the papers were edited

---

52 Reagan and Lindsey, *An American Life*, 611.

into a coherent format, providing an executive summary, delineating options, and so forth. All this was done while coordinating with the advance team, the communications team, and the press office.

At the initial meeting with the Icelandic Foreign Ministry and both the US and the Soviet sides, the Foreign Ministry tone was generous and accommodating, but they did have one request: *We are happy to host you here. Whatever we can do to help the visit. But please make sure that your leader does not arrive between noon and 1 p.m. on Monday because this day is the opening of our parliament, and our prime minister must attend. She will not be able to go to the airport to greet your president (or general secretary) if you land during that time.* A simple enough request, and a more than reasonable one considering they were our hosts, and we were the guests. We arranged it so that Air Force One landed according to their rules.

Our planning meetings with the Soviets were not adversarial, but they were cumbersome. We would put forward proposals that we would consider quite routine, even basic. The Soviets would be unable to respond. For example, the American side would propose that there be four sessions: 10 a.m. and 2:30 p.m. on Tuesday, with that schedule repeating on Wednesday. The Soviets would respond that they would have to get instructions from Moscow. We would propose that each session last ninety minutes, and the Soviets would say that they would have to get instructions from Moscow. We would propose that each side host a lunch for the other side (Iceland having graciously offered to host a joint dinner for the two delegations), and the Soviets would respond that they would have to get instructions from Moscow. On and on it went, with White House staffers in their twenties and thirties having full negotiating authority to plan the summit, and their Soviet senior staffers in their fifties and sixties having essentially no authority.

Stories arose within the US side about earlier Soviet behavior. During the Strategic Arms Limitations Talks (SALT), the Soviet negotiator asked the US negotiators to cease mentioning specific numbers of weapons, which would normally be referred to in negotiations. Why? Because other members of the Soviet delegation were unaware of those numbers, and it was classified information. Someone else mentioned that the Soviets were quick to pocket the number two pencils US government negotiators used. We viewed them as the most ordinary pencil available, but for the Soviets it was the best they had seen. The Soviets in Reykjavik were not taking office supplies, from what we could tell, but they were moving slowly, being both prisoners in and custodians of an unforgiving system.

SOVIET CHEATING

The context of US–Soviet relations was not promising. There was a pattern to Soviet military behavior. We would come to an agreement with the Soviets on force placement or exercises. Then, we would subsequently detect some violation of this agreement. We would notify the Soviets, and they would apologize and say it was a one-off incident and it would not happen again. They asked for our data as to what happened, but we could not share it because it might indicate how we capture or process intelligence. There would be no more problems for several months, but then the same problem would repeat. Again, cheating or non-compliant behavior—but the detection was weaker than the first incident. Again, a complaint would be made to the Soviets and again they apologized and said it was a one-off incident. Again, they would ask if we could supply raw data to help them with their investigation and again, we would decline.

Then there would be no more detected violations. Did the violations stop, or did the Soviets just get better? Or did our Signals Intelligence (SIGINT) people decide not to fully inform national decision-makers because we would once again be tipping our hand? I always suspected it was a version of the latter. Cheating persisted, but we were better off not to report it. Only once the behavior hit a threshold similar to previous detection would we complain. Otherwise, we would be showing our hand as to what we could detect.[53]

In any event, there was a widespread view on the US side— universal—that the Soviets were deliberately violating their accords, and they should not be trusted, regardless of Gorbachev's public persona. Off we went to Iceland.

Moving the president is like moving God. We took something like seven hundred US government employees to Iceland. There was Air Force One and crew. The car plane and crew. The press plane and crew. Secret Service. Communications team from the White House Communication Agency. Medical team.

---

[53] My fraternity at Georgetown played a version of this game in which it would spoof the system by calling in erroneous complaints on itself for noise violations, resulting in the dispatch of a DCPD squad car, only to find there was no noise, no party, no gathering of any kind. After a few such calls, the police were sufficiently inured to the complaints as to ignore them, giving us some measure of insurance for when we did host a gathering.

Speechwriters. Senior White House staff. The secretary of state and his team. The National Security Council staffers. USIA people. And secretaries, clerks, drivers, and administrative staff as well. Iceland was so small, Reykjavik was so small; we had to bring in desks, typewriters, office supplies, and even toilet paper. And beyond the seven hundred government employees, there were about a thousand members of the press.

The Soviet system was even more bureaucratic. For unclear reasons, Soviet leadership violated the one request which had been made from the start and landed so as to interrupt the opening of parliament, to the consternation of all Iceland's leadership.

I flew out initially on the pre-advance team for our planning meetings with the Soviets, and to visit sites in Reykjavik, a city of about ninety thousand people. The point of the pre-advance was to make a general site survey that could help in overall design of the trip. The advance trip and advance planning had to do with facilitating execution of a trip or "presidential movement." For example, if we already know the president is going to speak at Ohio State University, we just need to find the best setting on campus, a holding room, arrangements for the media, lighting, and then plan all of the orchestration of the event—warm-up music, marching band, cheerleaders, staging, introduction, national anthem, prayers, balloon drop, and additional matters. That's advance work. Should we go to Ohio State or are there better venues in Columbus for our message? That's the pre-advance.

We eventually settled on Hofdi House, the official reception house of the City of Reykjavik, as the locale for the meetings. I went back for two days in DC and then back to Reykjavik on the car plane, a C-5A Galaxy in which rubber netting was slung for seats, perfectly adequate for the five-hour flight.

Gorbachev had shrewdly positioned himself as close to the anti-nuclear movement (breathtaking when you think about the Soviet's numerical advantage in nuclear missiles) by supporting a nuclear freeze in Europe. This played to the hopes of the left in Europe, those simply fatigued by the Cold War, as well as the unquestioning anti-American constituencies.

For his part, Reagan had also pursued various nuclear initiatives, somewhat at variance with his hard-line reputation of the time. In 1981, Reagan had proposed eliminating all intermediate range missiles (the "Zero Option"), and in 1982, he proposed reducing strategic nuclear warheads by one-third. Each of these initiatives represented a significant departure from conventional arms control, which had traditionally only focused on limiting future growth of these systems. "Reagan armed to disarm," noted NSC senior staffer Henry Nau.

Until Reykjavik, Soviet leaders dismissed these ideas as one-sided and insincere. Yet, Gorbachev's opening proposal in Reykjavik included a 50 percent reduction in strategic offensive arms, complete elimination of all intermediate-range missiles, and extending the 1972 ABM Treaty for ten years.

Not surprisingly, Reagan embraced the negotiations with enthusiasm, delighted to see Moscow's willingness to consider many of our most ambitious suggestions.

Reagan was both more pro-nuclear than his American political opponents and more anti-nuclear than they were. He was pro-nuclear in that he recognized nuclear forces were a necessary evil, and as bad as nuclear weapons were, the failure to maintain a robust nuclear deterrence made a bad situation worse. Reagan was also anti-nuclear in that he was skeptical about the premise of the US deterrent strategy: Mutual Assured Destruction, or MAD. MAD meant that we would be able to destroy the Soviet Union if they attacked the US. Reagan saw it as fatalistic and downside-oriented. *I will try to kill you, if you try to kill me* is not the way to go through life. Reagan viewed the Strategic Defense Initiative as the path away from MAD.

Ty Cobb summed it up:

> The negotiations were complex, animated and highly substantive, and Gorbachev proved to be intelligent, knowledgeable, and facile. Reagan held firm in his principles. No more unverifiable treaties ('Trust but verify' he loved to say in Russian), no more agreements codifying Soviet superiority in arms on the European continent, no more tolerating Moscow's refusal to grant its citizens basic human rights, and— perhaps most importantly to the President— no more reliance on *offensive* nuclear missiles to provide for our security.[54]

Gorbachev matched some of Reagan's earlier ideas, proposing not a nuclear freeze but an actual reduction in nuclear weapons. Gorbachev offered to eliminate all strategic forces, not just

---

[54] Cobb, unpublished paper. "Reykjavik: Turning Point of the Cold War" p.3 , July 2020

ballistic missiles. Reagan then countered that it would be fine with him if they could agree to eliminate *all* nuclear weapons. Gorbachev agreed, but there was a catch: the US would have to abandon the SDI program. Technically, Gorbachev proposed that SDI be confined to the laboratory, but that eliminated any field-testing and any large-scale production—keeping it a dream. Reagan again counter-proposed, offering to share SDI technology with the Soviets. Instead of Mutual Assured Destruction, both countries would now have *Mutual Assured Defense*. Gorbachev seemed to agree, but again stipulated that SDI be confined to the laboratory. Nothing doing, said Reagan, we are going ahead with SDI development.

The talks sort of fell apart, and eventually the Soviet Union did as well. Gorbachev gets credit for what he did *not* do—use force to try to save the Soviet empire. Reagan gets credit for what he *did*—demonstrate the superiority of a free society.

Once the summit started, my workload dropped, rising only if there was a change in the agenda or a new topic arose. Indeed, Steve Sestanovich, the senior director for Soviet affairs, and I finished some paperwork just after midnight the first night of meetings, and we both had that somewhat contented and somewhat empty moment of staff work well done. Neither of us felt like calling it a night, although it was already morning. And someone suggested we go to the largest disco in Reykjavik. It was pretty much what you would expect in terms of large Icelandic discos. Neither of us, it turned out, had much interest in discos of any sort nor did the Icelandic variety exert a special hold over us. So, we had a drink and left. Box ticked.

The upshot of the talks? At the time, they were considered somewhat of a failure in that the two sides did not reach an agreement. But only one year later, at the 1987 Washington Summit, both sides signed the Intermediate-Range Nuclear Forces Treaty for the complete elimination of intermediate-range missiles. Sometimes a deal is not within reach. Sometimes, you can compromise only so much. Sometimes not having a deal is better than having a deal. Sometimes walking away from the table is the shock you need to propel you to a deal.[55]

At the moment of Reagan's departure, Gorbachev asked him almost plaintively, "What more could we have done?"

To which Reagan responded, "You could have said 'Yes.'"[56]

The Soviets sacked their ambassador to Iceland, or in diplomatic parlance, he was "recalled" by the Kremlin. Had he failed to pass on the landing request from Iceland or was he simply taking the fall for a bad decision in Moscow—we never learned. Timing the arrival was probably the only request the Icelandic government had put forward, and quite a reasonable one at that. My conclusion was that the Soviets had a limited feedback mechanism, so that if there were problems or issues, these rarely got relayed to those on top and no adjustment could be made. At one point, someone on top casually stated a preference to land at noon, that was taken as a *diktat*, and when the GOI request was fed into the system, it was never passed up for a reevaluation to be made.

---

55 For example, Reagan walked away from a nominal compromise in 1982, the so-called "walk in the woods" that would have eliminated the not-yet deployed Pershing missiles on the US side but not the SS-20s on the Soviet side.

56 Reagan and Lindsey, *An American Life*, 679.

As for "Sergei," I passed on my strange encounter to a security officer and was told later that "we got a good photo of him." It seems that Sergei really had let the cat out of the bag.

For me personally, the upshot of bouncing back and forth to Iceland for two trips in ten days and scrambling on each end was that I was late in paying my Hechinger (hardware store) credit card bill of perhaps thirty dollars, and for the next several years, it was flagged every time someone ran a security clearance on me. And, I could tell everyone I had gone to the largest disco in Reykjavik, but that arose in conversation less frequently than one might suppose.

Reflecting on the moment, Reagan put it: "At Reykjavik, my hopes for a nuclear-free world soared briefly, then fell during one of the longest, most disappointing—and ultimately angriest—days of my presidency."[57]

But assessments became more positive over time. George Shultz related: "I had a little session with Gorbachev once after he was out of office. He visited me at Stanford. We sat in the backyard and I said to him, 'When you entered office, and when I entered, the Cold War was about as cold as it got, and when we left office it was over. So what do you think was the turning point?' And he didn't hesitate one second. He said, 'Reykjavik.' I said, 'Why do you say that?' He said, 'For the first time, the real leaders got together and really talked about the important subjects.'"[58]

[57] ibid., 675.

[58] George Shultz, "George P. Shultz Oral History," interviewed by Steven Knott, Marc Selverstone, and James S. Young, UVA Miller Center, December 18, 2002, https://millercenter.org/the-presidency/presidential-oral-histories/george-p-shultz-oral-history-secretary-state.

And as the Reykjavik Summit progressed, there were ongoing news reports in the US about material support for the Nicaraguan insurgent guerrilla forces, the Contras. On October 5, as we were still organizing in Reykjavik, the Nicaraguan government shot down a supply plane for the Contras, and captured a US citizen as a crew member, indicating some kind of US support for the mission.

On a personal level, there was some terrible news that took place some two months before Reykjavik. We were a few days away from the due date of our second child, and the baby died. It was a harsh moment, emotionally devastating, and, for Ann, physically draining as well.

I was beat. I was despondent. The death of the baby was a sharp blow. I was trudging through desk work with very little enthusiasm when the phone rang. It was Jim Kuhn, the president's personal aide. "Do you have a minute? The boss wants to see you."

I bounded up the stairs to the Oval Office, trying to collect my thoughts. We were not in the middle of anything I could call to mind that would lead the president to call me in, but with the death I was still a bit behind on paperwork and probably not one hundred percent on top of my job.

We greeted each other, and the president was cheery enough but somehow seemed a bit more somber than usual. "I heard about what happened." He gestured. "I heard how you lost your baby. The same thing happened to us once. It's a terrible thing."

I don't remember how I responded, but we talked for a bit. I was numb from the shock and the fatigue, and I couldn't quite cry. At the same time, the meeting turned me inside out. I was touched and humbled that the president would be so considerate. And I was mystified by his reference to himself because I was not aware of any such incident in his history.

I bumped into Fred Ryan, then the president's scheduler, as I returned to the Sit Room, and he also offered his condolences at the sad news. At that point, I was able to cry. Indeed, I choked a bit and I was not able to stop. I had to hide in my office to compose myself.

Reagan's story is not related in his autobiography, but Morris discusses it. Christine Reagan died in the womb in the final months of Jane Wyman's pregnancy. The next year, the two divorced.[59]

Interestingly, the president's remarks to me were in the first-person plural: "This happened to *us*." Yet there was no reference to Jane Wyman.

BACK TO DC

French President Jacques Chirac was invited for a state visit and that meant a state dinner, the hottest ticket in town. Dionne Warwick graciously consented to provide the evening entertainment through the intercession of Linda Faulkner, White House social secretary. The cultural attaché at the French embassy agreed that it was a lovely choice. For me, the questions were more practical: What would she sing and what about the lyrics? Was there some old 1960s Warwick standard that has one line that could be seen as a slight to France? If there was, that would be tomorrow's headlines. A little quality control came into

---

[59] Morris, Dutch, p 250-253

play. Warwick's manager provided the playlist, and the OEOB Librarian was able the next day to get a book of Warwick's lyrics going back to the Burt Bacharach–Hal David hits of the 1960s. I got to spend a few hours in the OEOB Library. It all checked out. My nightmare was that we could miss a detail, akin to Carter decorating the Japan state dinner with white flowers, when white is the color of mourning.

German Chancellor Helmut Kohl was coming to town. When a friend in the First Lady's Office uttered a sort of negative sigh, I had to ask what was wrong. "Because she will have to sit next to him at dinner and he doesn't speak English." On the substantive front, a rather comprehensive paper had been prepared for a meeting with the German chancellor concerning one of the key NATO issues of the day: Could the US and Germany standardize tank turrets? Even if both countries used different chassis, we would each benefit from standardized turrets and weapons systems. The Pentagon presented the NSC with a lengthy paper discussing the pros and cons of this move—but it arrived only the day before the meeting. The paper might have been two hundred pages long. I struggled with it and struggled some more. I consider myself reasonably literate in matters of foreign policy, but I had no particular background in defense industrial policy, nor in procurement, nor in defense technology, nor certainly in armor. I continued to try to chew through the paper, now the night before the meeting. Finally, after several hours, having made notes, cross-tabs, highlights, underlines, marginal comments, I realized I was not mastering this subject in a late night read. And I went home, frustrated with myself. If it were up to me to solve this issue on the fly, well, we were all in trouble. I reasoned that surely there was someone else in the US system who was grounded in this issue, who had the background and the technical skills, and who could help direct the talks the next day.

The next day at the talks, the discussion was led by… Vice President Bush. He not only had read the paper, but was grounded in the issue and could fluidly converse on the specifics. It was magnificent and maybe even a bit intimidating. Why would a vice president do that? *How* could he have done it?

I mentioned to Col. Sam Watson, deputy national security advisor to the vice president, that it was one of the more impressive displays of policy mastery I had seen, and that I had myself been unable to come to terms with the challenge.

Sam offered a rather gracious explanation. "Don't worry; the vice president gets to take classified material home. You don't. He just read longer than you did."

My conclusion from this episode: Ronald Reagan was good at managing the out-box. George Bush was good at managing the inbox. They made a good team.

***

American businessman Armand Hammer passed away in the summer of 1986. The newspaper obituaries dutifully presented his life story, including the fortune he amassed at Occidental Petroleum and his close relations with the Soviet Union. In part, this stemmed from his father's friendship with Lenin, and in part, this stemmed from his role in selling Russian art in the West that the communists had seized after they came to power. In any event, more than one news account mentioned that he had been a "go-between" between the Soviet Union and the US, and several suggested that he played that role at the behest of the United States government. Interestingly, in my discussions with the Russia hands in government, I could find no confirmation that Hammer had ever played such a role, though people agreed that he had senior-level access in the Soviet Union and that he was one of many people to whom US Soviet experts might occasionally turn for their take on events.

As those accounts ran, we received several inquiries from leading US businessmen who were offering to serve as go-betweens between Moscow and Washington, now that Armand Hammer was no longer around.

"We have a go-between," I would typically explain. "He is called the ambassador. In fact, we have an entire team that serves as a go-between. It's called an embassy."

"What if that doesn't work?" was the rejoinder.

"Well, the Soviets have their ambassador and their embassy as well."

"What if that doesn't work?"

"Well, the State Department has a range of officials who can be dispatched, as does the White House and the NSC."

"What if that doesn't work? Isn't there a need, occasionally, for private communications?"

"Well, there's the hotline."

"Isn't there a need, occasionally, for even more private communications?"

These conversations almost drifted into fantasy. "Mr. Businessman, you are suggesting that if there is no one in our embassy who can carry out their stated function, nor no one in the Soviet Embassy, nor no one in our entire government, and the hotline does not work as well, then perhaps you could help out."

"Yes."

"Fine, on that basis we will take your offer under advisement and be back with you at the appropriate time."

I had a parallel set of encounters with nominally well-meaning Americans after Gorbachev accepted the president's invitation to visit him in Washington. As planning for the visit began to gather speed, I received a letter from a prominent American surgeon saying that lasers could remove the large birthmark on Gorbachev's forehead, and suggesting that President Reagan offer such a service as a present to Gorbachev. The surgeon then stated that he would do the work for free. I politely declined the offer, only to find a similar offer in my mailbox the next day. I politely declined that as well. Over the course of a few weeks, we received a half dozen such offers. It was hard for me to see how it would be helpful for the US President to dwell on a supposed cosmetic problem of his counterpart, a consideration which seemed to be lost to many.

THE MAN WHO COULD NOT BE STOPPED

The G7 Summit was set for Venice, Italy, in 1987, so toward the end of 1986 the White House sent a pre-advance team to Venice. Pre-advance can take place months ahead of advance and is particularly helpful in overseas trips to help set the overall itinerary. What other cities and countries should he visit before or after the Venice trip? Of course, every hand in Europe goes up. Every embassy informs us they would be delighted to host the president. Foreign ministries echo the statement. Even in countries with which there are foreign policy issues or the relationship is not particularly warm, there is a strong demand for the president.

The fact that the entire continent of Europe (well, Western Europe) was open to us was a bit of a challenge. Who did the president need to see from a foreign policy perspective? What events or constituencies would fit with what themes? Was there a trade message in a country? Let's have the president tour a US export success or officiate at a ribbon cutting. Was there a constituency in the US that can be reached through a foreign trip (the three I's of American politics—Ireland, Italy, and Israel)?

We found ourselves off to Venice. The pre-advance consisted of a military aide, communication technician, Secret Service, press advance, the NSC represented by me, and leading us from the White House Advance Office was The-Man-Who-Could-Not-Be-Stopped, TMWCNBS.

TMWCNBS was middle-aged and had started doing advance work in the Nixon White House. He was bright enough, professional, and certainly aggressive. If you had read any history about the lack of congeniality, or even courtesy, as a management characteristic of the Nixon White House, you would have understood much about TMWCNBS's approach to advance work and, perhaps, to life.

That being said, he was disciplined and competent. He knew his business and he knew how to keep the people on top happy—mainly the first lady and the chief of staff. Nobody else need matter. Also, there was a certain value in being aggressive because the White House has its way of doing things, and sometimes you just had to bulldoze the other side. No sense having a two-hour chat to shape a consensus when you know what you want to do. It was logical, if not collegial, to please your superiors and their spouses, and dominate everybody else. It was not necessarily a bad approach, if not the most humane one, and it was more or less acceptable if you knew what you were doing. Even though he exuded all the sincerity of a Christmas card from a law firm, TMWCNBS knew what he was doing.

I was off to Rome on the US Air Force variant of the G5, the Gulfstream jet, along with a good White House crew all led by a hard-working guy who was in his own corner of the Myers-Briggs test. We have a few days of meetings in Rome with protocol officials, foreign ministry types, and US Embassy types. It was all a new experience to me. One thing was clear: TMWCNBS and I were not exactly hitting it off. We did not work closely together in Reykjavik, though—from my memory—we had no real issues there. I always got along with the advance team in general, which to my mind included some of the more talented people of the White House. But he and I were not clicking. At least part of this is my fault in that I can have bad antennae. I was not appropriately deferential, and true to his Nixonian pedigree, this man fairly screamed of insecurity. In one conversation, he was talking about himself, and he mentioned in a calculated-to-appear-uncalculated sort of way, "Yes, when Mike Deaver left, I sort of stepped up to help out. That's when I moved from advance work to general issue management. Plus, I do assignments here and there for the first lady." The remarks were at a minimum grossly exaggerated. Nothing wrong with overstating one's role I suppose. I responded in a modest, if impolitic, fashion by rolling my eyes, which I thought was a mild display of skepticism. I was surprised to be on the receiving end of an intense glare from TMWCNBS. Strike one for me.

Later in Venice, we were at a dinner and I happened to be sitting across from him and an outsider to whom he was again explaining his role. He stated he was the only assistant to the president in the White House. Everyone else was assistant to the president for x or assistant to the president for y, but he was the only person with that simple title.

Again, I foolishly waded into it, saying something dismissive such as: "Yes, you and Bert Lance," referring to Jimmy Carter's disgraced budget director. My point was simply that one's title and rank did not necessarily bear on the quality of one's work or of the individual. A valid interpretation of character but completely at odds with TMWCNBS's message and indeed his entire professional stature, his sense of self, and his philosophy of life. He also took my flippancy as a sign of disrespect, which, of course, it must have been. "What kind of person brags about his White House title?" is a reasonable question. Yet the lesson is, if someone above you in the chain of command is bragging about his title, don't challenge him.

Peggy Noonan reminds us of Leo Rosten's aphorism: "Who is a hero? He who suppresses a wisecrack."[60] I failed that hero test. Strike two.

I am not sure what strike three might have been, or even if there was one. But as the plane returned to the US, our pilot informed us that we would not be able to make Andrews Air

---

[60] Leo Rosten quoted in Noonan, *What I Saw at the Revolution*, 201.

Force Base non-stop because of a bit of a head wind and a bit of a heavy load. We would touch down in New Jersey to refuel. There was nothing terrible or unusual in that. But once we took off again, one of the advance men took the phone to call ahead and say he would be late. I took the phone when he was done to do the same.

TMWCNBS exploded. "You don't need to make that call. You don't need to waste everyone's time," he shouted, ensuring that everyone on the plane could hear.

I was taken aback by the ferocity of his comments and perplexed at the substance. All I was doing was calling ahead.

"Oh like you need to call ahead. Like they need to know by the minute where you are," he continued.

"Well the advance man called ahead and I am just doing the same."

TMWCNBS paused for a split second. "You are right. But that's not the point. That's not the point." He paused to recalibrate his artillery. "What did you contribute on this trip?"

"Pardon me?"

"What did you contribute on this trip? What did you add?"

Not sure where this was going, I started in a tentative fashion. "Well, I represent the NSC in terms of getting a sense..."

"No, that's not what I meant. You didn't add anything. You didn't fit in. If you want to argue about it, I can throw you off the plane right here. But I'll tell you this. You are never working on another trip I'm doing. And I'll tell that to Poindexter as soon as we get back."

He was bitter; he was implacable, and he was theatrical. It was not completely clear to me what was going on, except that he wanted to demonstrate to the entire plane that he was fed up with me, and he wanted to do it in such a public way as to burn all bridges. The plane passengers spent the rest of the hour-long ride in awkward silence, broken by occasional muffled conversation.

In the following days, I was a bit despondent because it was not clear to me how I would function in my job if the head of the advance office had declared me unsuitable. If TMWCNBS did insist to Poindexter that he could not work with me, that could well end my NSC assignment. There was no immediate need to take action because no trips were planned, and we were heading into the holiday season. I had a few weeks or maybe a month to think this through. I thought Poindexter would go to bat for me, probably, but TMWCNBS would likely hold firm since he had his reputation on the line.

At this point, however, the White House was increasingly consumed by the scandal that became known as Iran-Contra. Chief of Staff Donald Regan, one of TMWCNBS's patrons, was teetering. It was clear this scandal was going to take on a broader public dimension. Morale was plummeting. Peter Rodman stood up at an NSC staff meeting. "Take heart," he opined. "I was here during Watergate, and that was much worse." That was an effort to *raise* our morale.

The other members of the advance staff who were on that flight dropped by my office to chat about things and to commiserate. *These sorts of things happen. He's always like that. Don't worry.* Their concern was somewhat reassuring, but I couldn't help but think that perhaps a few people wanted one last look at the corpse before the funeral. There was no utility in worrying, but I also needed a solution.

Poindexter resigned after the diversion of funds was discovered. Ollie North, Fawn Hall, and a few others were out the door as well. Some were directly working with Ollie. Johnathan Miller was director of the White House Office of Administration, and he had cashed some of Ollie's traveler's checks. Out the door. Frank Carlucci was brought in to replace Poindexter. He brought in an interesting professional from the Army to serve as his deputy, a corps commander from Germany, Colin Powell, with whom he had worked in the Nixon White House (ah, so there could be collegiality there as well).

There was considerable turmoil in the NSC because the entire institution, traditionally viewed as the elite of our foreign policy establishment, was in disrepute. Carlucci had an enormous incentive to fire everybody, in that the cleaner the sweep the better the president (and Carlucci) might look. In addition, he had his own people he wanted to bring in. We had a boisterous staff meeting in the OEOB with Ken Adelman, then serving as an advisor to Carlucci, which was sort of a team *un-building* exercise. If there were any doubt that we were damaged goods, Adelman disabused us of this notion. In fairness, he handled a difficult assignment professionally ("…the worst job I ever had in my life…" he noted).[61] Carlucci needed his own team, and the institution had been damaged. Yet the incumbent NSC staff also had a fair point: if we got sacked because of

---

[61] Kenneth Adelman, "Kenneth Adelman Oral History," interviewed by Jeff Chidester, Stephen F. Knott, and Robert Strong, UVA Miller Center, September 30, 2003, https://millercenter.org/the-presidency/presidential-oral-histories/kenneth-adelman-oral-history-director-arms-control-and.

someone else's misdeeds, our individual reputations would be unfairly damaged.

During all of these staff convulsions, resignations, indictments, hearings, firings, accusations, and the hostile media coverage, I found my own morale a bit off as well. Activity slowed down, but did not cease, and we still had to perform our jobs despite a widespread view that we were all about to be fired and, in any event, TMWCNBS would be happy to kick me while I was down.

As for TMWCNBS? There are some lessons here. One is that subordinates have an obligation to get along with seniors, and I failed that test. I lacked the awareness to see that what to me was light-hearted sarcasm was taken to be disrespectful. I was too young to have deduced that truth of the human condition, that bullies tend to be insecure. It would have been simple enough to have offered a complement, as empty as it would have been. Elliot Richardson reminds us, "Washington is really, when you come right down to it, a city of cocker spaniels.... It's a city of people who are more interested in being petted and admired...[62]" For the most part, the fault had to lie with me.

Senior officials also have an obligation to get along with subordinates. This is not simply a courtesy, but good management. Managers need information, advice, and ideas. Once they are viewed as domineering or personally offensive, that information flow stops. TMWCNBS had the enormous advantage of having good professional advance skills, but he had the enormous disadvantage of not connecting well with people other than his

---

[62] Richardson quoted in Smith, *The Power Game*, 125–126.

seniors. He did not frequently make mistakes, but once he did, he had very little ability to correct them.

Indeed, it had been only a few months before my episode with TMWCNBS that he had become personally involved in the Reagan administration's greatest public relations disaster besides Iran-Contra. He organized a trip to a German cemetery where the president could say some kind words about German war dead. Unfortunately, TMWCNBS approved a cemetery at Bitburg at which *Schutzstaffel* officers—SS—were buried, not the sort of people with whom the president wanted to be associated.[63] The result was weeks of bad publicity with several people calling on Reagan not to attend, notably Elie Wiesel, who made a passionate plea at an event in the White House. From that point on, TMWCNBS was known among other nicknames as "The Hero of Bitburg." He left the White House several months after Reykjavik.

Despite TMWCNBS's shortcomings, this was hardly a shining moment for me, illustrating casualness and even a flippancy in interaction that would occasionally get me into trouble. Fortunately, my capacity for getting into trouble was usually exceeded by my capacity for getting out of trouble, this time perhaps barely so.

The end of 1986 was not a happy moment for the Reagan administration. The Iran-Contra scandal broke open in October. Republicans lost eight Senate seats in the midterm

---

[63] The pre-advance was led by Deaver and TMWCNBS, and then reviewed and approved through the entire US government system. In a comment that could only come from the source, Cannon writes that TMWCNBS "alone" seemed to have "gnawing worries." Cannon, *President Reagan: The Role Of A Lifetime,* 509.

elections, giving control of that body back to the Democrats for the first time since 1980, and Reagan went into the hospital for cancer surgery, from which he would take over a month to fully recover, again bringing health issues back front and center. There was unease about the suitability of Don Regan as chief of staff. And the Iran-Contra affair appeared to get worse by the day. More resignations. More allegations. Discussions of impeachment. And the NSC was at the vortex of this. Rumors of firings, mass firings. General suspicion from White House colleagues. The winter of 1986 was the nadir of the Reagan administration.

Work deterioration continued. Marybel Batjer, who had worked with Powell at the Pentagon, was brought in formally to replace me. Yet I was not fired, just shifted out of the West Wing to the OEOB with unclear responsibilities, not a positive sign. Frank Carlucci reached out to Bryce Harlow, a colleague from the Nixon, to provide advice. This allowed me to have some productive discussions with Bryce as he worked with Carlucci to build a new team.

Even the move from the West Wing to fourth floor OEOB brought with it some drama. I was given a desk in a shared office setting, not unusual for the building, and one of the other inhabitants was an Army code clerk assigned to the NSC. I came back from lunch one day to find him sitting at what had been my desk some forty minutes earlier. "I hope you don't mind," he said pleasantly, "but I moved all of your stuff to my old desk so I could work out of here." He motioned to what had formerly been his workspace in the adjoining room. "People say you won't be here much longer anyhow." Even in World War I, people didn't pry the boots off VICTIMS until they were dead.

I was a little taken aback that I would be pushed in such a fashion, and I called my NSC colleague Bob Pearson for advice. "If he just moved your material to his old desk without asking, you need to take his stuff and move it back when *he* is at lunch." Which I did the next day, playing back to him the same false words with the same false smile. *"I hope you don't mind..."* The code clerk seemed equally taken aback by my assertiveness. But an uneasy truce was maintained.

Though Marybel handled her arrival professionally and bore me no animosity—the signs were not positive. At one point, I was one of the most senior NSC staffers not yet fired, and this as a mid-level officer meant the purge had gone pretty deep and the next bull's-eye might be painted on me. It was clear things were going the wrong way and that even if I "survived" my future was not promising.

There was one final episode of TMWCNBS. Apparently, some of his flaws spilled over into his personal life. After the White House, he remarried and was working on Wall Street. There are different versions, but the story goes that he was suspected by his new wife of infidelity. He strenuously denied it and even suggested his wife call him at The Hay-Adams when he went to DC on business because he was simply going to eat dinner in his room. His wife made the call and he was indeed in his room. But this was a resourceful woman. The next day, the story goes, she called The Hay-Adams again and stated she was calling from Montclair General Hospital, the emergency room. "We have a case here that looks like food poisoning and I need you to tell me what he had for dinner last night. They state it was a room service dinner. Please pull up the bill."

"Yes ma'am; I can connect you with room service, and they can relay the orders from last night…. Let's see, the order for room service was *two* lobsters, *two* soups, *two* desserts."

And that was the end of the second marriage.

Perhaps the man who could not be stopped, could be stopped.

A coda to the loss of the baby: Ann and I had spent months saving a bit of money that would be needed for expenses for the new baby. With the death, none of those purchases would be necessary, but neither of us could envision using the money for ourselves. Another tragedy struck when an NSC colleague lost her husband. She was expecting a child, and the NSC took up an informal collection to provide some sort of financial support. Ann and I were able to donate our savings, hopefully relieving a burden for the widow and taking the money off of our hands as well. Somebody would have a crib and a stroller, but it was not to be us.

SOME DOORS OPEN, SOME DOORS CLOSE

The Iran-Contra period was particularly frustrating for the first lady. Bad news seems to hit the political spouse worse than it hits the principal. Ronald Reagan knew that there were ups and downs to politics—to life—and that his term had seen enormous strides forward, this despite setbacks. He also had the celebrity's ability to laugh off criticism and keep focused on the goals. For Nancy Reagan, it was not so easy. Not being directly involved in government, she had to play the role of supportive spouse, which she did dutifully. Of all the bouts of fortune with which the president had to contend, even strained relations with his children, life with Nancy was always a solace. Yet, you sensed that Nancy would wince at criticism of her husband. She was crushed with the bad news of Iran-Contra and the GOP loss of the Senate in November 1986. She felt let down by the White House staff. The fault could not have been Ronnie, it had to be *them*. She was at least partially correct, but she was powerless to do anything about it. I am not surprised she dabbled in astrology as it is the natural response of the helpless—someone who desperately wanted good news for her husband but who lacked the ability to bring it about. She was left with escapist rituals, incantations almost, in the hope that good news would come.

No surprise that her relations with Chief of Staff Don Regan deteriorated. Regan was a smart man, all business, highly effective in his native setting, comfortable with peers, but less comfortable with others. He was a capable chief of staff, but he had lower sensitivities regarding his public role, and he did not cultivate the first lady, an oversight that was not insignificant.

All of these forces came together after Pat Buchanan resigned as White House communications director in early 1987. Pat had long stated his desire to step down after the 1986 midterms, and he made his move after the holidays.

Nancy made her move. Was there anyone in the West Wing who she could work with? Anyone she could trust? She had little faith in Regan, and she found him condescending. She pushed a communications professional, Jack Koehler, to replace Pat. Jack had been born in Germany and emigrated to the US in the 1950s. He was a working journalist and rose through the ranks of AP, ending up in senior management. He had sporadic dealings with the Reagans, so there was a degree of familiarity. All looked good, on paper at least.

I encountered Koehler only once. The Mayor of Berlin Eberhard Diepgen—at that point it was the Mayor of *West* Berlin—was visiting the US, so we set up a meeting with Reagan. Mayors do not usually rise to the level of a presidential meeting; in fact, this was the only one that I could recall, but the enormous symbolic value of a free Berlin was what was at stake and here was a chance to show the US remained firm behind that city, so they had an Oval Office meeting.[64] We had the normal contingent—Frank Carlucci as national security advisor, and two or three staffers plus the president—with equivalent participation from the German side.

As was usual, I was with the greeting party as the mayor arrived at the West Wing, and we went into the Roosevelt Room, immediately across the hall from the Oval Office, to use it as a staging room. This allowed participants from both sides to congregate and exchange greetings before meeting with the president, saving a bit of time. Occasionally, outsiders wandered into this staging area, be it known or unknown to the organizers, opportunistic or permissive. This was largely unobjectionable, and it could help break the ice while we waited for the all-clear signal from Jim Kuhn.

Indeed, on this occasion, Jack Koehler mentioned to me that he wanted to meet Diepgen, and he joined the party in the Roosevelt Room. Completely acceptable as he was senior staff

---

64 When Reagan decided to provide relief to Harley-Davidson by sanctioning motorcycle imports, I helped manage the order to target only the Japanese bikes and to leave the German bikes off the sanction list, as BMW made its bikes in Berlin.

and not a bad idea for him to say hello. Not only was Koehler an immigrant from Germany, he started professionally working for AP in Berlin and Bonn, so he had more than a casual reason to be there, plus it would be for a minute.

Sure enough, in a minute, Kuhn gave the signal, and I asked for the mayor and his party to proceed across the hall, with the rest of the party following. I noticed, to my surprise, that Koehler got to the end of the line to enter the Oval Office. He was not on the list, and he was not invited. I wasn't sure what he was thinking, but I had a strict rule about the president: nobody crashes the party. I inserted myself in front of Koehler, who was the last person in line, and as I entered the Oval Office, I closed the door on him. Right. In. His. Face. A bit harsh, but as we were in the presence of the mayor, there was no way to have a conversation with Koehler or ask his views on the matter. The Secret Service agent at the door checked with me and asked if that was it. "That's it," I said.

People were getting their handshake photo with the president, I was helping everyone to their assigned seats, and the navy stewards were pouring coffee. And, what do you know, the office door opened up, and…it was Jack Koehler. Well, son of a gun, I had to give the guy points for persistence. He just sort of talked his way in. I jumped in, with an old advance man trick. "Mr. Koehler, right this way." I embraced him from the side, had him in a bit of a grip, and we walked in a circle, right back to the Oval Office door, and I pushed him out. "Wait right here, and I will be back for you." That was somewhat of a white lie but usually did the trick.

Finally, everyone was seated and the meeting was about to start, and from the staff door—the one that accesses the secretary's and Jim's office—in pops Koehler again. This was the third attempt to crash. I was flummoxed. This guy apparently would not respond to anything except a direct order from the president. I didn't know what to do at that point. This guy would not give up. Impressive, in a perverse sort of way. I was at a loss as to what to do at that point short of using a taser.

I crouched down next to Carlucci who was at the end of the couch. "I don't know what to do about Koehler. He sort of invited himself. I kicked him out, but he came back in."

"Oh, Frank," said the national security advisor, "I forgot to tell you. Koehler had asked me if he could sit in, and I told him it would be OK."

I sat Koehler down in a side chair and tried to look as nonplussed as possible. Koehler, to his credit, did not make a fuss at having been chucked out of a presidential meeting twice and having to climb his way back in.

In about a week, Koehler was out. It was revealed that when he was about ten years old, he had joined the *Deutsche Jungvolk*, the pro-Nazi organization for youth ages ten to fourteen. There was never any indication that Koehler was pro-Nazi or that he did anything different than most other persons of his age group. Indeed, his life post-1945 had been dedicated to freedom of the press. Nonetheless, he graciously resigned when the story came out, stating he did not want to cause the administration any embarrassment.

More consequentially, Don Regan was also out. Howard Baker had replaced him as chief of staff at the end of February, and Koehler's departure meant Baker's longtime assistant, Tommy Griscom, could become the White House communications director. Another very capable longtime Baker aide, John Tuck, played a central role in keeping the West Wing running smoothly. In all, it was an effective, professional team. And Baker knew from decades of public life one fact above all else: spouses matter. Specifically, first ladies matter, and wives are not just adornments. Baker's then-wife, Joy, was the daughter of longtime Senate Minority Leader Everett Dirksen. No fool, Ev. No fool, Joy. And no fool, Nancy.

Soon enough, Carlucci was out, but for a good reason—he went to the Pentagon to serve as defense secretary on the heels of former Texas Senator John Tower's failed nomination.

I was out, too. Frank Donatelli joined the White House as assistant to the president, responsible for political and intergovernmental affairs. He asked me to be his deputy for the political side, with the rather elaborate title of deputy assistant to the president, and director, Office of Political Affairs. I leapt at the opportunity. I was out and back in simultaneously.

CHAPTER 10

THE FIRST LADY

**In the receiving line at the state dinner for
French President Jacques Chirac**

The first lady of the United States (FLOTUS) had a reputation
for being difficult, but I thought that was inaccurate. I never
experienced any such behavior. However, Nancy Reagan was
particular in what she wanted, and she was protective of her
husband. She was skeptical of certain members of her staff, but
I never found her to be unpleasant. There was a reasonably simple "Yes, Minister" approach to the first family. It was just not

that difficult to keep them happy. Always set a positive tone, signal that you understand the request, and you would move it ahead. Most of what they wanted, say 90 percent, was about things you were going to do anyway, or relatively simple, or predictable, or feasible, or at least not harmful.

The remaining ten percent of what they wanted might be unnecessary or even counter-productive, but it was usually easy enough to address through a back-channel discussion, be it with the FLOTUS Chief of Staff Jack Courtemanche or with her Social Secretary Linda Faulkner or Deputy Cathy Fenton—three solid professionals who kept the East Wing running and did so with an upbeat, diligent approach. These were the FLOTUS-whisperers who could have a reasonable conversation with Nancy Reagan and walk through the trade-offs in a particular decision as to why it might not be a good idea. Her main intervention was on matters of schedule. I am not referring here to the astrology-driven interventions, but a more human desire to keep a heavy schedule for a president "of a certain age" in check. White House staffers typically overloaded the schedule, competing with each other to get their own programs on the calendar, and it was not surprising or even unwelcome that the first lady would challenge this tendency.

The conventional view of Nancy Reagan as first lady was: *be careful.* Word was she could be arbitrary and forceful. There was no appeals process. However, it quickly became apparent that this conventional view was largely inaccurate. There were certain matters on which she was indeed very particular, but, if approached in the right way, she tended to be responsive. In fact, the First Lady's Office was easy to work with. You could explore ideas, discuss alternatives, and smoothly arrive at solutions. Nobody was looking for a quarrel; everybody just wanted to get the job done and part of the job was to keep the first lady happy. She was a woman of reason and willing to entertain options, even though her preferences usually won out.

In some respects, Nancy Reagan got a bad rap, and, in some respects, she brought problems on herself. Her husband was a populist of modest (actually, poor) background. Nancy Reagan came from money—at least after her mother remarried—and was viewed as an elitist (or she grew into that role). Ronald Reagan liked Hollywood, but he never let Hollywood change him. You didn't always get that impression with Nancy Reagan. There is nothing wrong with wealth, or a celebrity lifestyle, and there is part of us that might even envy it, but a word of warning is in order as well. If your love of the finer things is perceived as disdain for the everyday things, watch out. Ronald Reagan enjoyed the better things, as many of us would, but he had plenty of simple everyday tastes as well and that did not change as his fame grew. He never went over the top—no champagne and no caviar lifestyle. Nancy, however, had more expensive tastes. When it came to receiving designer gowns as gifts, she exposed herself to criticism. Nancy offered the defense that the gowns were loaned, and she always intended to return them. Even when she was perfectly innocent, such as when she replaced thirty-year old White House china using private funds, there would be a desire by some to portray her in a bad light.

If you ask what drove Nancy Reagan, what kind of person she was, what her goals were, I think the answer is a simple one: to help her husband. She devoted essentially her entire married life—her entire adult life—to helping him, rearranging her career, her home, and her life in the process. It was an extraordinary sacrifice, not uncommon among women of that generation or political spouses in general. It requires subordinating one's identity to one's spouse, suffering all of the insults and criticisms of the husband and sharing only indirectly in the joys and triumphs. Nancy Reagan did a superb job in this respect and deserves high praise for her success. As she said, "for as long as I can remember, I have wanted to belong to somebody, and to have somebody belong to me. I never wanted to go it alone."[65] I saw some flavor of this occasionally at my family gatherings. Ann's father was in Congress and Ann's mother was the political spouse, although in her case, she worked full-time as a chemical engineer. It meant a series of sacrifices on her behalf, but this is not uncommon in a marriage in which one person has a highly demanding or public position, and the other partner must strive to make it work.

In this sense, criticism over the occasional desire of Nancy Reagan for fine china and fine dresses seems a bit mean-spirited. Serving as first lady brought with it a substantial burden; let her at least enjoy some benefits. Compared to modern-day celebrities and affluent individuals, the first lady's indulgences seemed quite limited, even quaint.

Along the same lines, I thought that her "Just Say No to Drugs" campaign was under-appreciated. Somewhat in the same vein as her husband's depiction of the Soviet Union as an "evil empire," Nancy Reagan's exhortation was bracing for its honesty and impact. Drug use had a certain cachet in some

---

[65]   Reagan and Novak, *My Turn*, location 601. Kindle.

circles. It was sometimes viewed as "liberating" or "mind-expanding" or perhaps a wealthy person's indulgence, or a bohemian affectation, and all of this obscured the enormous destruction it wrought, particularly upon poorer people and in minority communities. As a matter of first principles, Nancy Reagan stood up and said, "Just say no," observing that drugs could be life- and soul-destroying. At least by stigmatizing the problem, she made it easier for parents, educators, public officials, and health professionals to deal with it.

The impact of "Just Say No" went beyond influence and tone-setting. With a push from the first lady, the White House organized a conference of US ambassadors in September 1986 from major drug-producing, trafficking, and consuming countries, pulling them together with Justice Department and State Department officials, and, yes, the first lady, to explore how we could better coordinate anti-drug efforts in the multiple countries of assignment. She went on to give an address at the United Nations, the first first lady to do so.

Finally, among her contributions we have to note her honesty in dealing with cancer and her mastectomy. Betty Ford had done this earlier, but Nancy Reagan rose to the moment as well. You can cover up a problem, or run from a problem, or you can put the problem on the table. Not only was Nancy Reagan's transparency with a serious medical issue useful in itself, but it helped raise awareness of breast cancer and encourage people to take breast exams.

The first lady had a constituency of one. In my years in government, rarely did someone come to see the president who did not want something. Every meeting was a transaction. The first lady was the only person in the president's world whose clear desire was his happiness and well-being. Remember, this first lady entered his world at a low moment, after his divorce. She lifted him up then, and she lifted him up every day. The actor Jimmy Stewart, a close friend of both Reagans, opined that Ronald Reagan would have won an Oscar if he had married Nancy Reagan earlier.[66] She was his closest advisor.

Her interventions were not random. She was interested in quality control. Were we doing the right thing? She wanted to know the reason, the background. Presidential advance person Shelby Scarbrough noted, "She looked at events through a different lens."

If you combine this legitimate, even commendable, concern with the fact that she did not know much of the White House staff personally by the second term, and that she might at times be over-protective, then you're going to have moments of disagreement, even perhaps friction. The most celebrated of these moments was with the dismissal of Donald Regan, a talented man who performed well as treasury secretary but was not suited for his subsequent job of chief of staff. Nancy Reagan saw that bit of truth before most of us, and she worked to have him removed. Good for her.

Add to that story some unflattering personal anecdotes, such as her occasional reliance on an astrologer, it was easy to paint a portrait of a slightly deranged Lady Macbeth. And unfortunately, in some people's eyes, that was what she became. That portrait is unwarranted and undeserved.

---

[66] Cannon, *President Reagan: The Role Of A Lifetime*, 442.

To my mind, her motivation was well-founded and her instincts were sound. Political spouses have a special place in my heart because of the unsung work they undertake, and I think history will treat Nancy Reagan more kindly than some of the contemporary press did. Every president—every person—needs a best friend. and if we are lucky in life that role will be played by the spouse. Ronald Reagan was lucky in life.

Nancy Reagan explained her guardian role: "Ronnie tends only to think well of people. While that's a fine quality in a friend, it can get you into trouble in politics."[67]

Ronald Reagan saw Nancy in the same role as *minister of Ronald Reagan affairs*, the minister with a constituency of one, when he wrote: "I believe, in general, people are inherently good and expect the best of them. Nancy sees the goodness in people but also has an extra instinct that allows her to see flaws if any are there."[68]

Michael Reagan illustrated this point more colorfully: "Dad looks at half a glass of water and says, 'Look at this! It's half full.' Nancy is always trying to figure out: 'Who stole the other half from my husband?'"[69]

---

[67] Reagan and Novak. *My Turn*, location 1028. Kindle.
[68] Reagan and Lindsey, *An American Life*, 124.
[69] Michael Reagan quoted in Baker and Glasser, *The Man Who Ran Washington: The Life and Times of James A. Baker III*, 131.

CHAPTER 11

1987–89 OFFICE OF POLITICAL AFFAIRS

From left: Myself, Joan Sutherland, Greta Terrell,
Frank Donatelli, Judith Butler, Lisa Stoltenberg, Mark
Neuman, President Reagan, Carlyle Gregory, Becky
Sullivan, Kathy Lovin, Margaret Alexander, Jean Bell,
Mary Wylie, Boots Thompson, Tom Thoren

Frank Donatelli rejoined the White House in February 1987 as assistant to the president for political and intergovernmental affairs. As the title suggests, he oversaw two offices: the Office of Intergovernmental Affairs, responsible for administration relations with non-federal government offices such as governors and mayors, and the Office of Political Affairs, responsible for relations with party organizations, political groups, and candidates. Frank had two deputies, one for each office, and I served as the deputy responsible for the Office of Political Affairs (OPA).

I served almost two years as OPA director, from February 1987 to January 1989, with three responsibilities. The first was to manage the president's political activities. We were responsible for whatever the president did to help Republican candidates: Senate, House, gubernatorial, and even state legislative candidates. We had a number of programs for those candidates, including fundraisers, endorsements, commercials, rallies, and any kind of presidential interaction. For most of 1988, it also meant helping Ronald Reagan help George Bush (discussed in Chapter 11).

Our second responsibility was to represent the political seat at the table for all White House decisions; this did have an impact on the presidential campaign later on. For normal White House decisions such as presidential scheduling, legislative agenda, and speech-writing, we would be the political voice. The political effect of a decision was rarely the deciding factor, but particularly in the months leading up to the election, the timing of events and the weight given to various issues became important.

Our third role was representing the president to the political community. The president could not sit down with every congressional candidate, party official, political professional, or political writer, so it fell to us to put forward his views and interact with these groups as the president would.

I inherited a good office from my predecessor, Haley Barbour. But one by one, the old staffers moved on, mainly because White House hours are so grueling that it is difficult to keep up the pace after a few years. Additionally, most staffers will get job offers from the private sector or elsewhere in government. The more talented people move on, and the weaker performers tend to remain. Within a few months, I had built up my own team with Carlyle Gregory as my deputy; Judith Butler, Becky Sullivan, Tom Thoren, and Mark Neuman as regional directors; and a terrific group of assistants and interns, Francis Dietz, Frank Kelly, Greta Terrell, Chad Walldorf, Kathy Lovin, Scott Coffina, Margaret Alexander, and Boots Thompson.[70] Enormously capable, they were highly motivated, had a strong sense of mission, and could navigate the egos and factions of various candidates, campaigns, and political groups.[71]

One word of caution: Politics produces wonderful people, and also crazy people. You will meet some of the brightest

---

[70] Margaret Alexander's husband, Don, had served as commissioner of the Internal Revenue Service, crossing swords with Richard Nixon for ending the practice of using the IRS to target political opponents of the president.

[71] After a few years in the White House, good people tend to move on and weaker people tend to hang on. To that tenacity of mediocrity, add the fact that everyone has a history, a political pedigree, or a friend. Everyone in the White House is there for a reason, even if it not for the reason of competence, and it becomes clear that it is not easy to fire anyone. It is far easier to shuffle the person or to hand them off to someone else, a bit of guile that developed into an art form as offices sought to shed these hangers-on. In a move to block the hangers-on, Chase Untermeyer, who led the 1988 Bush transition, issued a directive banning any appointee from the Reagan White House from holding the same position in the Bush administration.

strategists, colorful field organizers, and funniest communications people in the world. Be wary, not of political operatives, but of people who are exclusively political operatives. If someone has no identity or passions outside of politics, they are more likely to be less well-rounded and less interesting. Worse, they are more likely to lack the ordinary human experiences in which the policies they advocate would take place. And since ideology is their only identity, they are prisoners of that ideology, unable to find common bonds with people with whom they might have a policy disagreement. We should all be guided by principles, but one of those principles should be to respect different points of view.

THE CHALLENGES OF 1987

1987 was an embattled time for the White House, particularly early in the year. The administration was only slowly recovering from Iran-Contra and the loss of the Senate. In his July congressional testimony, Admiral Poindexter finally nailed shut the question of possible presidential involvement: "I made the decision," Poindexter said. "I felt I had the authority to do it. I thought it was a good idea. I was convinced that the President would, in the end, think it was a good idea. But I did not want him to be associated with the decision.... I made a very deliberate decision not to ask the president so that I could insulate him from the decision and provide some future deniability for the president if it ever leaked out."[72]

---

[72] *Hearings of the Iran-Contra Investigation Before the Joint Congressional Committee* (1987) (testimony of John Poindexter, former national security advisor of the United States).

This allowed the administration to move from defense to offense and turn to a number of important initiatives as it entered the final two years. Chief among these were support for the Contras in Nicaragua, and the nomination of Robert Bork for the Supreme Court. I had the sense that both these goals were slipping away, and I confided my fears to Howard Baker's aide, John Tuck.

John was categorical: the two most important issues we faced were the Bork confirmation and keeping the Contras afloat. Both of these would be decided in the Senate. This was Baker's core strength, given his years in the Senate. We were not going to let these votes go down.

I was somewhat mollified by his confidence, but I could sense the ground shifting nonetheless. The opponents of Bork were doing something that had never before been tried in American history: running a political campaign against a judicial nominee. This meant the nomination would become a political football—with television ads, rallies, letter-writing campaigns, and a general deterioration of the debate. Baker was counting on a Senate of an earlier time, in which Senators could consider their constitutional obligations in a detached, rarefied atmosphere, and courtesies and relationships would help carry the day. Alas for Baker, and for Bork, those days had passed. The process had shifted from an inside game to an outside game.

A telemarketing firm approached us. They had devised something they claimed had never been done before, the ability to have a computer make phone calls to a list of phone numbers. No more phone banks. No more callbacks. No more paper tally sheets. Just fire up the mainframe and turn it loose. That, in fact, was what they wanted to do. Was there an issue where we could demonstrate its effectiveness? They would be happy to let us try it for free.

An interesting idea, but the White House itself would not likely be able to make use of this technology. However, there was an independent political organization, the National Conservative Political Action Committee (NCPAC), where I had done some college work (see Chapter 2), that was supporting Bork and might be able to make use of it.

A quick call to Maiselle Shortley at NCPAC and it was arranged.[73] NCPAC would supply the computer company with a magnetic tape of the phone number of every registered Republican in Pennsylvania, the home state of GOP Senator Arlen Specter, a key swing vote needed for the nomination. We helped them find an audio tape of Reagan's weekly radio address in which he called for Bork's confirmation. Bingo, a taped script was put together which went something like this: "Stand by for a message from President Ronald Reagan." A brief pause, then the president spoke: "We need Judge Bork on the Supreme Court. Please tell your senators to support this nomination." Back to voiceover: "Call Senator Arlen Specter today at xxx-xxxx and ask him to support the president by backing Judge Bork. Please call Arlen Specter at xxx-xxxx. The president needs your help."

The effect was electric. Although computer-generated phone calls are today commonplace, at the time it was a first. Never in American history had people received a phone call

---

[73] Maiselle's brother, Terry Dolan, who had passed away, had established NCPAC in the 1970s. Her other brother, Tony, was White House chief speechwriter.

with a direct request from the president to take action. Specter's office was flooded with calls, perhaps several hundred thousand. People were angry. His lines were tied up. Specter was angry.

White House Communications Director Tommy Griscom called me in. "Did you do this?"

"Well, we knew about it, and we facilitated it, but we sure didn't do it."

"I can tell Specter we had nothing to do with it?"

"We didn't do it," I repeated, avoiding a direct answer but remaining technically honest.

"You didn't do it."

Unfortunately, Bork went down to defeat in the Senate, 42–58, with Specter joining five other Republicans voting against. The bad news didn't stop there. The administration attempted a bounce-back strategy of nominating Doug Ginsburg to the Court, and just as we were getting in gear, his nomination was withdrawn because of past incidents of recreational marijuana use, which overshadowed his record as a highly-accomplished jurist. Worse than these two defeats, perhaps, was the mutation of the judicial confirmation process into a domestic political exercise, guaranteeing future nominees would be subject to similar stunts, trivialities, and grandstanding.

The second initiative saw a better outcome, although the Contras saw their funding halted. The Sandinista government agreed to elections in 1990, and Contra-supported Violeta Chamorro won a handsome victory, 55 percent to 41 percent.

```
  GOVT RM 87 OEOB
  THE WHITE HOUSE           Western  Mailgram
  DC 20500 30PM             Union

1-155601U303034 10/30/87 ICS WA08186          PDVA
  00037 MLTN VA 10/30/87 JN74460




  YOU ARE INVITED TO A WHITE HOUSE BRIEFING WITH PRESIDENT
  REAGAN ON FRIDAY, NOVEMBER 6TH. THE PRESIDENT WILL DISCUSS
  HIS NOMINATION OF JUSTICE DOUGLAS GINSBURG TO THE SUPREME
  COURT. PLEASE ARRIVE AT THE PENNSYLVANIA AVENUE ENTRANCE TO
  THE OLD EXECUTIVE OFFICE BUILDING AT NOON. THE BRIEFING IN
  ROOM 450 WILL CONCLUDE AT 2:00 P.M. TO CONFIRM YOUR ATTENDANCE
  PLEASE CALL MARGARET ALEXANDER AT (202) 456-2245 BY TUESDAY,
  NOVEMBER 3RD AND PROVIDE YOUR SOCIAL SECURITY NUMBER AND
  BIRTHDATE.

     FRANK DONATELLI
     ASSISTANT TO THE PRESIDENT FOR
     POLITICAL AND INTERGOVERNMENTAL AFFAIRS

  20:05 EST

  MGMCOMP
```

Ever seen a souvenir ticket for the Titanic? Here is an invite for a Ginsburg event for his doomed Supreme Court nomination.

As 1987 drew to a close, the political season began to heat up, and our mission shifted from supporting the president's agenda to supporting candidates. We had different approaches for Senate candidates, congressional candidates, and the presidential nominee.

Given that it was the final two years of the president's tenure, Reagan already had campaigned as president in three sets of races since his 1980 election. He had a firm sense of what steps he would take and what he would not take. This was fair, in that one can only ask a president to do so much, and regardless, demand for his time would vastly exceed the supply.

The *magic wand theory* (see Chapter 7) of the presidency held that a personal intervention by the president—be it an endorsement, a television ad, or most important, a visit—would exert magical powers over the electorate. But the president could not take a poor candidate and make him a good candidate. He could not take a bad fit for a state and make him a good fit. A roaring success of a rally couldn't make up for four years of passivity. If the swing voters in a particular race happened not to have a high opinion of the president, then a visit by him might not make sense at all. This was all logical enough, but the contrary view, the *magic wand* view—that a visit by the president was a universal fix—held wide sway. It seemed there wasn't a state party chair, or a Senate candidate, or a fundraiser, or a member of Congress who did not, on some level, subscribe to this theory.

More realistically, rather than subscribe to the magic wand theory, we had a White House formula. The president would sign one fundraising letter per year for each of the three party committees (RNC, NRSC, and NRCC). He would do two events for each party committee per year.

SENATE CANDIDATES

By the same formula, candidates for Senate would get video footage with the president, discussing matters at his desk and walking together on the portico between the West Wing and the Residence. Select candidates for Senate would also get a presidential visit, a fundraiser in the candidate's state, and even a Washington event.

For some candidates, like New Jersey Senate candidate Pete Dawkins, the Heisman Trophy winner, we had magnificent events like bringing fellow Heisman Trophy winners into the Oval Office to present the president with a football they had all signed. Admittedly, few people running for Senate had Dawkins's lengthy record of accomplishment, from graduating from West Point, to earning multiple combat decorations, to becoming the youngest general in the Army. We had a large rally in New Jersey as well as fundraisers. Dawkins still got beat by incumbent Frank Lautenberg, 45–52.

For some candidates like Congressman Trent Lott of Mississippi, we were able to have large Washington events, and he didn't need the help. Lott beat Congressman Wayne Dowdy 54–46.

For other candidates like Maryland's Alan Keyes, a combative nature seemed to overwhelm his undeniable intelligence and oratorical strength, making it difficult for any help to make the difference. Preternaturally belligerent, Keyes managed to start an argument at the White House as we were preparing to bring him into the Oval Office for a video shoot. A man of many skills, perhaps his greatest skill was the ability to make goodwill evaporate. Keyes earned 38 percent of the vote to incumbent Paul Sarbanes's 62 percent.[74]

We had strong candidates like George Voinovich of Ohio who still lost, and we had weaker candidates like incumbent Nevada Senator Chic Hecht who almost won. You play with the cards you are dealt.

We supported a strong Senate nominee in Massachusetts, which led to the one time the president got annoyed at me, as far as I know. It was my fault. I committed the greatest sin one could possibly commit. I stepped on his line.

Joe Malone was the Massachusetts state treasurer and the Republican nominee against longtime Senator Ted Kennedy. No one, least of all Joe, was under any illusion that Kennedy could be beaten, but it could be a fun campaign, and Joe would get his name out if he did a good job. We were trying to do what we could to help, and we finally were able to schedule a time for Reagan to do some TV commercials with Joe. The only problem was that the date was just after Joe's wedding when he was

---

[74] At the meeting before we went into the Oval Office, Donatelli made an offhand comment to Keyes, along the lines of, "It will take a lot of events to cover the state effectively." Keyes erupted in anger and stated, "Don't tell me how to change my diapers." The sentence does not parse. It does not work literally. It does not work metaphorically. We could assume that what he meant to say was "don't tell me what to do" and "don't treat me like a baby who needs his diapers changed," but by conflating the two thoughts, he ended up with a mystifying, if pugnacious, comment. Fitting for a mystifying, if pugnacious, candidate. Keyes threatened to take his complaints to Reagan directly when they met. Donatelli cautioned him that if he went into the Oval Office with a chip on his shoulder, he was bound to have an unproductive meeting. The fever broke and Keyes calmed down. "He was a cauldron," Donatelli noted. After losing in 1988, Keyes later ran for Senate in Illinois, where he had never lived, against Barack Obama, and got 27 percent of the vote, losing all but ten counties out of 102. (Trump carried all but twelve of 102 counties.)

to be on his honeymoon. Because of the president's schedule and travels, if we did not film the spots that day, we might not be able to film them again for a month or two.

I called Joe. We had gone to school together though we had not really known each other. His plan was to go from Boston to the Caribbean for his honeymoon. I suggested he come down to Washington for a day, bring his bride to meet the president, and then leave directly from Washington for his honeymoon. He thought that would work.

I prepared the briefing paper and brought in Joe and Linda, the newlyweds. Of course, the most interesting fact about the entire event was that Joe had been married the day before. This was a perfect Reaganesque moment. I introduced them, and the president gave a warm greeting. They started discussing the race. We talked about things in general as the technicians set up the lights for the shoot. The conversation started to drift, and we were getting ready to start shooting. The president still had not mentioned the wedding. There had been two or three breaks in the conversation where it could have been introduced. Did not read his briefing paper, or had it slipped his mind?

"Let's go make some commercials," said the president, and they started to move.

I decided to jump in. "Mr. President, today is also special for another reason. Joe and Linda were just married yesterday, and today is the first day of their honeymoon."

"I know," said the president, with an edge in his voice that I had never heard before. Emphasis on "know," and the word was drawn out just a few milliseconds. A smooth, rich, "I knoooooowwwwww."

I instantly realized to my horror that I had blown it. He had not forgotten the wedding reference. He knew that point was the key element of the meeting. He had a special time when to bring it up, and he was just waiting, waiting, waiting, and I had stumbled.

His words to me were quite gentle, but it was clear what he meant. I had transgressed. Not shown bad manners, but transgressed in a metaphysical sort of way. He owned the event, and my clumsiness took it away from him.

Luckily, Ronald Reagan never carried a grudge, and my misstep did not damage a pretty positive relationship. On the broader topic of the campaign, Joe got shellacked 34–65 percent.

We saw a more effective display of Reagan's involvement in the case of Conrad Burns, a first-time candidate in the Reagan-friendly state of Montana, where the Reagan TV ad, the Reagan visit, and Reagan fundraiser might just have put him over the top. Burns knocked off incumbent Senator John Melcher 52–48. We saw it in the increasingly Republican state of Florida, where Congressman Connie Mack beat Congressman Buddy MacKay for Lawton Chiles's seat, with 50.4 percent. Beyond Reagan visits, we sent out cabinet members and other dignitaries, organizing surrogate events, media events, fundraisers, and rallies.

Reagan would not do candidate recruitment. He would not pitch. I ended up in discussions with then-failed mayoral candidate Rudy Giuliani about taking on Daniel Patrick Moynihan in his reelection to the Senate, but I never got beyond discussions with his assistant, Denny White. I spoke with former Navy Secretary John Lehman about running for Senate against Chuck Robb in Virginia, but to no avail. To be fair to Giuliani and Lehman, each would have been underdogs in these respective contests.

The result of all this was that the Democrats picked up one Senate seat in 1988, increasing their majority from fifty-four to fifty-five.

TODD AND HIS PROBLEMS

I received a call from Larry Harlow in the Office of Legislative Affairs, the office responsible for coordination with Congress. I have a lot of respect for Larry and OLA, and he also happens to be the son of Bryce Harlow, who had been helpful to me as the NSC was falling apart (see Chapter 8).

Larry asked me to take a call from former Senator Roger Jepsen, one of those defeated for reelection in the 1986 midterms. Jepsen was polite and professional, and he sought nothing for himself. He wanted me to interview someone for a job, Todd. He explained that Todd's father had been supportive back in Iowa, having served successfully in the state legislature. I told the senator that I had a small office and did not have any openings. The senator was practical and asked if I wouldn't mind seeing him anyway—*perhaps you can give him some pointers or talk about careers in Washington.* This seemed like a reasonable courtesy, and my office made an appointment for Todd.

When Todd arrived for the appointment, I received a call from the Secret Service. They were verifying who I was and if Todd had an appointment with me. Yes, I confirmed that he did. "We have a little problem," the agent told me. "Mr. B has been arrested for assault with a knife in a bar in Virginia and is currently out on bail awaiting trial. We would not normally let people with this background in the building."

A bizarre story, but at least it ended the job discussion, I should think. The agent said, "Here is Mr. B" and handed the phone over.

We exchanged greetings. "Todd, I hear there is some bad news out there."

"Yessir, but I can explain."

"Look, look, I'm not the court. You need to explain it to them, not me."

"I'm innocent and I can prove it."

"That's fine, but you need to tell the judge, not me. My advice is to get the best lawyer you can and spare no effort in clearing your name. If it is all a mistake, you need to get into this and clean it up."

"Right, right. I'm doing this."

"Then it doesn't make sense for us to sit down right now, does it?"

"What do you mean?" he asked.

"Well, you can't work here—so there is no sense even exploring it."

"Can't you just hand me papers and assignments over the guard desk?"

"No, that's not practical. We cannot just hand you material in the morning and pick it up at the end of the day. We really need people who can work together on a team."

"Right, right. I see. Well, I'd like to be on your team."

"What you need to do first is clear your name. Then we can sit down and see what might make sense."

We had a cordial chat, given the circumstances. I never did find out what happened in his court case. But there was a disturbing story about him several years later in the *Washington Post* in which he was named as a leading distributor of neo-Nazi and white supremacist heavy metal music. Sometime in that journey, he began working as an FBI informant in that movement, so he at least had a latent spark of humanity in him or a survival instinct.

CONGRESSIONAL CANDIDATES

Senate candidates got videotape and congressional candidates got a photo. We lined all Republican congressional challengers up in the Indian Treaty Room, placed the president in a chair, and one-by-one had them sit in an adjoining chair, to give each of them a side-by-side photo with the president. Given the large number of candidates, our support in congressional races was largely directed institutionally through the National Republican Congressional Campaign Committee. Reagan made no appearances on behalf of individual congressional candidates, but we would have them on the dais at a presidential event, and they would be mentioned in the president's remarks.

We developed a program to help endangered incumbent members of Congress. What resources could we deliver? What boost could we provide their campaigns? We identified the five or ten most threatened incumbents and met them individually. They could be divided into two groups: those who were basically competent but who were in unfavorable districts, and those who were basically incompetent. The people in the first category could be helped. The people in the second category were difficult to help. Most of them would dispute that they were in trouble. Most of them lacked the self-awareness to think through the nature of their problems and correct them. It stands to reason that if you were fully aware of your shortcomings, you would correct them, so obliviousness goes together with mediocrity. The GOP's own Dunning-Kruger club, composed of those lacking awareness of their own weaknesses.[75]

Reagan was steadfast in his adherence to the eleventh commandment: thou shall not speak ill of a fellow Republican. This meant no involvement in Republican primaries. No tilting the field, no picking winners. Ironically, given Reagan's adherence to this aphorism Stu Spencer once mentioned to me, "We made that whole thing up." As he explained it, Reagan was entering the 1966 Republican gubernatorial primary as an outsider, potentially vulnerable to criticism over his limited (nonexistent) government background. So the Reagan campaign conjured up the eleventh commandment as a mechanism to devalue and inhibit such criticism. "We never expected him [Reagan] to actually believe it, not to mention live by it."

The tactic worked; Reagan's 1966 primary opponent George Christopher did not run a negative campaign. Reagan internalized the eleventh commandment message, and it was accepted as law in the Reagan White House. It was so rigid that I had to think twice before putting my name on a host committee in a contested Republican primary in Mississippi in which the opponent, Mike Gunn, had an unsavory history of affiliations, having

---

[75] Weaknesses in the GOP field went beyond professional mediocrity. In a replay of the unsettling Todd affair, the Secret Service called me before the photos with the congressional candidates. How important was it that the president met a particular candidate from New Jersey who was scheduled for a photo op? He had multiple convictions for violent assaults. I pulled him from the event.

done fundraising for the former Ku Klux Klan leader David Duke. Even my modest involvement brought a reprimand on the grounds that I should only be acting on behalf of the president (see the Liberty Lobby incident in Chapter 3). The irony here was that Reagan would be appalled to know there were candidates with Klan connections. Several years later, Gunn's career came to an end when the *Los Angeles Times* revealed the affiliation with David Duke. Bad enough in itself, but it arguably crossed a legal line because Duke was running for federal office (US Senate from Louisiana), and Gunn's failure to declare compensation from Duke possibly constituted an FEC violation.

The result of the congressional races was that Democrats picked up two seats, increasing their margin to 260 to 175.

***

A Republican congressman who was a strong Reagan backer recommended someone to us for employment who had worked in his congressional campaign, then gone on to work as a fieldman for the state Republican Party. I explained we had no openings, and the candidate enthusiastically offered to be a one dollar a year man—essentially doing the job for free.

He checked out well in the interview process and his references also checked out. When he was going through the clearance process, a friend of mine from the Secret Service dropped by my office. This was a pleasant surprise, I noted, because no meeting had been scheduled. The agent commented that he did not want a meeting on my schedule (which would have made it part of an official government record).

"Not supposed to share this with you, but the person had a lawsuit a few years ago on sexual harassment, and it was settled out of court. Part of the settlement was to seal the papers, so it is all a secret. So this conversation never happened."

"How bad was it? Was it a dirty joke?"

"No, it was bad. Not just a bad joke."

"Oh, that's bad. It was an action on his part, not just words."

"Yeah, not just words."

"Oh, that's bad. What do you suggest?"

"There's something else. He had a separate harassment law-suit against him two years earlier."

"Same person?"

"Different person, but same type of incident."

"Not just a rude comment, but a serious incident?"

"A serious incident."

"This is terrible. We can't let this person in the White House."

"That is the right response."

I had to pull the plug on this person right away, but I could not disclose the basis for the decision. I could not tell the congressman the reason why. The agent was violating all sorts of protocols and perhaps even the law in relating what he did, much to his credit.

***

As important as the Senate, House, and other campaigns were, none of them were as important as the 1988 presidential race. Reagan knew that the impact of his presidency could be limited if he were to be followed by a president who did not share his views. This simple fact shaped much of our 1988 activity.

CHAPTER 12

THE 1988
PRESIDENTIAL RACE

In US politics, not everyone who wins deserves to win, but pretty much everyone who loses deserves to lose. I use "deserve" not in a moral sense, but as a practical political construct. There was something about the losing campaign or candidate that did not fit with the voters. Michael Dukakis was not a bad man and in many ways he had a successful career, but by the end of the 1988 campaign, it was clear that he richly deserved to lose. He failed to put forward a vision that appealed to a majority of Americans, and he failed to display a personality that allowed Americans to feel comfortable with him. The other story of the 1988 campaign is that step-by-step, George Bush was able to win the confidence of American voters. He deserved to win.

As the presidential race was heating up, one of my first steps was to call the campaign manager of each Republican presidential candidate for a general discussion. Lee Atwater (Bush's campaign manager), Bill Lacy (Dole's), and Ed Rollins (Kemp's) had each been director of the Political Office. So, for Bush,

Dole, and Kemp, I was dealing with people I knew. That left the Pete DuPont, Al Haig, and Pat Robertson folks with whom I was meeting for the first time. We went through a series of discussions to let people know that we were representing the president, he was neutral, we wanted to do whatever we could to help the Republican nominee, and we would deal with all candidates on a basis of equality during the primary. I maintained a weekly roundtable meeting with the campaigns and the party committees throughout the election cycle.

The campaigns all behaved in a professional fashion, and they knew that Ronald Reagan was not going to endorse a candidate because he felt it was a matter of propriety and that it was undemocratic for an elected leader to play an active role in choosing his successor. Reagan had a strong personal attachment to George Bush and professionally had grown to respect him. He also had a lot of respect for Bob Dole and Dole's support in the Senate. He also had known Jack Kemp, who had worked for Reagan on his gubernatorial staff.

In early 1987, it is fair to say that a plurality, if not a majority, of the Reagan team was behind Bush, and deservedly so. I was in that group, though I had some reservations, and I found Jack Kemp appealing, at least in the abstract. Yet, White House staff was sworn to neutrality, and it was generally observed.

All of the Republican presidential candidates, even the darker horses, were running as pro-Reagan candidates. No one was running to repudiate him. There was not a programmatic or an ideological basis for taking sides in the fight, and there was not a basis derived from personal relationships for taking sides in the primary, and above all there was the president's stated preference that it was unbecoming for an elected leader to start throwing his weight around in a democratic process to pick his successor. To cap off this outreach process, Reagan was to host a meeting with all of the Republican candidates. It was set for October 17—Black Monday—the day the US stock market dropped over 22 percent, and the meeting was scrapped.

Bob Dole gave a strong early performance and won the Iowa Caucuses and went on to win South Dakota, Minnesota, and Wyoming, in addition to his home state of Kansas. But Bush had broader support. By Super Tuesday on March 8, it was clear Dole was no longer competitive. Kemp never got traction, and did not win a single primary. By the April 19 New York primary, he was already out of the race. Bush won almost every other state, including a sweep of the South (thanks, Lee Atwater), and that ended the race. We rapidly shifted to general election mode. At that point, the best uses of the president's time were to promote party unity, work in fundraising, and convince "Reagan Democrats" that Vice President Bush was an acceptable successor.

Reagan was enthusiastic in helping Bush. They had developed good chemistry over eight years. What began as a marriage of convenience, evolved into genuine warmth. Years later, watching Bush choke up as he delivered his eulogy at Reagan's funeral demonstrated those deep feelings. On a political level, Reagan had seen his work as governor washed away when Jerry Brown replaced him. He did not want to see eight years of hard work eroded again.

The endorsement was trickier than one might expect. It appeared simple, to have a popular incumbent president support his vice president as successor. Indeed, Bush's victory would be the first time a sitting vice president succeeded his president since Martin Van Buren succeeded Andrew Jackson in 1836.[76] This suggests that American voters have a penchant for change, and they like to see incumbents turned out from time to time. Similarly, administrations can end on a down-note. It can be difficult to keep up the pace of activity and recruitment of talent after eight years.

This made two contributions from the White House vital to the Bush effort. First, we needed enough success to get Reagan's overall approval numbers back up. It would be unlikely his own vice president could win if Reagan himself was unpopular. Second, we needed to position Reagan as anti-establishment. On one hand, Reagan had been an outsider in US politics longer than he had been an insider. On the other hand, Reagan was finishing eight years as president, a position from which it would be a challenge to label himself anti-establishment. Yet he pulled it off. One of his signature applause lines from his address to the GOP National Convention in New Orleans was, "We are the change," a line he used repeatedly at campaign stops.

As to personal popularity, Reagan began 1987 with discussions of impeachment and his approval at its low point, and he ended 1988 as the most popular president since Eisenhower. Iran-Contra was put to bed, Reagan had a successful summit in Moscow, and a modest wave of nostalgia over the eight years seemed to set the tone for these final months.

---

[76] President-elect Bush, the day after the election: "I also want to thank Martin Van Buren for paving the way—it's been a long time, Marty!"

From the Bush point of view, the endorsement was also a thoughtful process. For one, the American voters jealously guard their rights and do not like to be told for whom to vote. An endorsement had to have a light touch. Second, an endorsement risks smothering the recipient. A new president has to stand on his own two feet, and being defined by, helped by, endorsed by one's predecessor risks devaluing the identity of the candidate. On one hand, the vice president has to be able to state from his own experience that the president did a superb job and the vice president will keep a good thing going. On the other hand, the vice president must also say, "I am my own person. I will make my own decisions. I will lead our nation in the next phase of the journey." A bit of a high wire act, potentially. Only fifteen of the fifty-one vice presidents in US history have become presidents, and nine of them moved up through death or resignation.

Despite being well-known, Bush lacked an independent political identity when he announced his campaign for president, for the simple reason that it is impossible for a sitting vice president to have an identity separate from a sitting president. He had to undertake the journey of re-introducing himself to the American public.

When Bush announced his campaign, *Newsweek* even ran a cover story with the theme that Bush might not be up to the job of president because he was (wait for it) polite and (worse) he had an accommodating personality. The caption of the cover story: "Fighting the Wimp Factor."

Bush's secret weapon: he knew all of this. George H.W. Bush was as self-aware a person as you could find, and he knew he was benefiting from the successes of the Reagan administration even as he knew he had to establish his own identity. He could not repudiate any of the Reagan agenda (and if you asked him, he did not want to do so), but he needed his own agenda. Still, with the Misery Index of economic distress (combining the unemployment and inflation rate) averaging 19.6 percent in the year Reagan was elected, it was now down to a 9.9 percent average for 1988, a tad off a 50 percent drop. Bush had the wind at his back.

Bush, to his enormous credit, had served Ronald Reagan loyally as vice president and had worked hard at cultivating Reagan's conservative constituency with considerable, but not complete, success. Additionally, he had the stature of his office and the time to undertake party chores almost without restriction. He spent much of the midterm 1986 cycle traveling the country for fundraisers and other activities for local party leadership and candidates.

One example of this attention to detail: Lee Atwater took me to lunch. It was the fall of 1987, and Lee, longtime friend and Reagan hand, was now Bush's campaign manager. I had known Lee well over the years, since he was active in Karl Rove's leadership of the College Republicans, so it was an easy, friendly conversation. Remember from Chapter 3 that Lee helped me move from volunteer to paid staff in the White House. After a few minutes of catching up, Lee got to the point.

"I have your assignment. Jack Kemp will formally be declaring for president at the end of the month. We will have a majority of the Republican Congressmen from New York announce shortly thereafter that they are for George Bush."

I was surprised to hear this. A majority of Kemp's congressional peers from his home state will openly support Vice President Bush?

"Yes," said Lee. "Your assignment is to secure the endorsement of George Wortley for George Bush so we can announce his name on the list as well."

There are a few things you need to know about George Wortley. First, he was a wonderful guy. Second, he was my father-in-law, and we always had a positive relationship. Third, he was a member of Congress, representing the Syracuse area. (Chapter 2 explains how I worked with Roger Stone in George's 1980 primary to withdraw a misleading Reagan endorsement).

I took Lee's logic, that an endorsement of NY state GOP congressmen for Bush would certainly be a punch in the nose for Kemp, but there were a few problems.

What was not a problem was that I was for George Bush and I was happy to help. Plus, Lee helped me out over the years, so I was more than inclined to respond to his request.

The problems were two-fold. First, George Wortley was close to Jack Kemp. They collaborated on a lot of issues. They were essentially upstate NY neighbors. Most importantly, George Wortley had a tough primary in 1982 when redistricting had thrown him in with another GOP congressman, and Jack Kemp had endorsed him and campaigned for him. George Wortley seemed unlikely to endorse George Bush.

The real problem, though, was the relationship. One of the reasons I had a great relationship with my father-in-law is because I had a lot of respect for him, and I would never try to abuse the relationship or make use of his office for my gain. He had his professional identity, and I had mine. It would not have been appropriate to violate that and ask my father-in-law to do something he did not want to do. It was not realistic for me to do this.

I made these points and Lee was unconvinced. "Well, that is your assignment," said Lee. It is a bit unfair, I protested.

"Yeah, it might be a bit unfair," replied Lee, not without some sympathy, "but I am running a presidential race here, and you need to do your bit."

"I don't think I can do it," I protested.

"You need to do it."

I mumbled something.

Lee said, "I am putting this down as a done deal and thank you for delivering George." The "delivering" made me wince as it was the one thing I could-not-would-not do.

I got home and confessed all this to my wife. I could not ask George to help on this. Ann was helpful: "Well, you could ask. That would be ok."

"I have to tell you, I feel uncomfortable even asking. I would never ask a political favor from your dad."

"Yes, but at least you can tell Lee that you tried."

I was uncomfortable about the whole matter. It was a question of propriety. It was just inappropriate for a son-in-law to be asking a father-in-law this kind of question.

I had a day or two to think about this because George Wortley was taking us to Sunday brunch at the Cosmos Club, a venerable fixture in DC. Sunday came, and we walked past the wall of photos of members who were Nobel laureates, past the wall of members who had won Pulitzer Prizes, past the display of members who were on US postage stamps, past the display of members who were on foreign postage stamps.

Normally, I might have enjoyed this combination of ego and history, but at the moment I was obsessed with my mission. I did not see any way out, having more-or-less promised Lee that I would pursue this. Or Lee had this down as a promise.

At the same time, I had more-or-less promised myself I would not pursue this. In any event, George was not going to budge. He was a pretty good friend of Jack's. All I would do would be to irritate my father-in-law, irritate Lee, and irritate myself for getting in the middle.

Ann reminded me there was nothing wrong with asking.

We were having a nice brunch, and I was waiting until the end, when tummies would be full and people were upbeat and chatty. My mouth was actually dry. I was not sure how I was going to phrase this. I was waiting for a pause in the conversation.

George bent toward me, a signal I should do the same. He looked me in the eye and said *sotto voce*: "I am going to endorse Bush."

"What? Really? But you are friends with Kemp." I instantly kicked myself for arguing against my own position.

"I know that, and Jack is a good guy. But Bush is the guy for this job."

"I think you are right, George. I think you are right." A wave of relief washed over me.

I excused myself to visit the men's room. I vectored to find a phone and connect with Lee through the White House switchboard. Mission accomplished, though without any actual work on my part.

With more New York Republican members endorsing Bush than Kemp, Lee had his message: those who know Kemp the best were not supporting him.

After brunch, I asked Ann if I was a terrible person.

"How are you terrible? You didn't even broach the topic with my dad."

"I know, that was dumb luck. But the real luck was George was for Bush in any event. But am I a terrible person for taking advantage of this?"

"No, you were going to be blamed if he went for Kemp, so you might as well get the credit for him going for Bush."

I squeezed her hand.

***

One more Kemp story: I was with Jim Baker to Ohio for a surrogate event, and we were returning to DC on a chartered G5 after a successful day's work. Baker asked, "Well, who does George Bush pick as his running mate?"

Nice to be asked, and I flattered myself to think his question was more than a parlor game. Was I feeling a bit guilty because I supported Bush over Kemp? In any event, I answered unhesitatingly, "Kemp."

I reflected later that I failed the test. Not that Kemp was the wrong answer, though he was. Any answer was the wrong answer. Rather than offer one's likes and dislikes of a particular figure, the rational approach would be to respond to the question by establishing a set of criteria, form a consensus around the criteria, and then determine who matched the criteria. We all have our favorites. We all have our biases. So the right answer was to avoid simply listing one's favorite, and focus instead on the analytical framework to get the best answer. Process before substance. How the answer is structured reveals more than the answer itself. Only those who are already committed or fall short in analysis would list a favorite. I fell short.

Later, Bush aide Chase Untermeyer helped me think through Jack Kemp. "You don't like Jack Kemp. You like the *idea* of Jack Kemp. You like what he stands for. But Kemp as vice president would not work." Well put, Chase.[77] Kemp was an appealing proponent of economic prosperity and social mobility, but one who could also be challenging to work with.

***

Fundraising was not difficult, though execution involved a great deal of work. But the fact is that the Republican base was delighted with Reagan, and they regularly rallied to his side. They did not need a great deal of coaching to believe that Bush would be a good president and Dukakis would be a disaster.

Convincing the Reagan Democrats required more work, but over time Vice President Bush carried almost all of the traditional Democratic constituencies that Reagan had twice carried: northern ethnic Catholic voters and southern conservative Democrats. These were groups that called themselves Democrats for historical reasons, but who philosophically had little in common with Dukakis, as he was solidly on the left of his party.

---

[77] Kemp is described as "a supremely ambitious figure who got on Jim Baker's nerves by weighing in on matters far afield of his area of responsibility." Baker and Glasser, *The Man Who Ran Washington*, 460.

THE SUMMER OF DUKAKIS

Super Tuesday—March 8—was the largest primary day, built around nine Southern states. It was promoted by moderate Democrats to give them a voice in the Democratic primaries, and it became the centerpiece of Tennessee Senator Al Gore's 1988 campaign. OPA Associate Director Tom Thoren put together a Republican turnout plan for Super Tuesday, complemented by similar activity by Haley Barbour in a private capacity. The result: this was the first time in US history that GOP turnout on Super Tuesday was greater than Democratic turnout, and it prefigured the consolidation of the GOP vote in the South. Gore's performance was respectable on Super Tuesday, winning five states. But the Dukakis team was shrewdly able to add some non-Southern states to the mix (Massachusetts, Washington, Rhode Island, and Maryland). Dukakis ended up winning seven states that day. Gore did not win any primaries after March 8.

As the primaries drew to a close and summer approached, Dukakis looked strong. He enjoyed the typical bounce a candidate enjoys as a nomination is wrapped up. He touted the *Massachusetts Miracle* as his home state enjoyed a strong economy. He positioned himself as a technocrat, not a liberal. After he was nominated at the Democratic convention in Atlanta, he surged to a 17 percent lead over Bush, leading 55–38 percent.[78]

---

[78] "Dukakis Lead Widens, According to New Poll." *The New York Times*, July 26, 1988. https://www.nytimes.com/1988/07/26/us/dukakis-lead-widens-according-to-new-poll.html.

On top of this, the Bush campaign was facing financial constraints. In 1988, the spending cap imposed by the Federal Election Commission for presidential candidates during the primary campaign was $20.05 million, and by the end of June, Bush had spent close to $20 million, mandating almost a complete shut-down of activity for the remaining six weeks until the GOP convention, when federal funds for the general election would be released. In contrast, the Dukakis campaign had only spent $18 million by the end of June and had a convention one month earlier. This allowed Dukakis to dominate advertising and campaign events for much of the summer.[79] However, that advantage eventually turned into a disadvantage for Dukakis. Both candidates received $46 million upon nomination, and with an earlier convention, Dukakis had to make that money last one month longer than Bush did.

Howard Baker stepped down as chief of staff on July 1 and was replaced by his deputy, Ken Duberstein. Few could match Baker's knowledge of Washington or attention to the Hill, but Ken came pretty close. "Sentence commuted to time served," said Baker with a smile in my last meeting with him.

This period between the Democratic convention and the Republican convention in New Orleans was a bit of a low point in the Political Office. We were well aware that Dukakis's artificial surge was cresting, that his record had not been sufficiently challenged, that he had many weaknesses that could be brought to the surface, that the *Massachusetts Miracle* was less than might meet the eye, and that the Democratic primary field had been

---

[79] Chad Walldorf, "What I Saw After the Revolution: The Reagan White House and the 1988 Campaign," (unpublished paper), May, 1991 p, 87.

pretty weak. There was little doubt in my mind that Dukakis was riding an artificial wave of support that would recede with the advent of the Republican convention.

Lee Atwater made a simple point: we could not control the narrative until the Republican convention. At that point, we would be able to counteract the positive image of Dukakis, but we were going to be behind him until then. It was a long six weeks.

Much of the Republican rank and file was not as optimistic. *Why is Bush behind? What is going on? What do you do in the Political Office, anyway? Let's get Reagan out there. Wave the magic wand. Wave the magic wand.*

Amidst this anxiety, I spoke to the Republican Party of Ohio Central Committee about how the campaign was going. I was generally successful in explaining that things were on track and we had a plan for getting back in the lead. I assuaged the leadership—all except for one member of the Central Committee who asked several questions in an accusatory tone and displayed general discontent with the state of the campaign. This was understandable except for the fact that there was an AP reporter covering the event, and he wrote it up along the lines of "Ohio Republican leadership attacks White House campaign support," or words to that effect. Adding to my consternation, that Central Committee member called me at the White House a day or two later when that story came out, giving me the opportunity to observe that he was a knucklehead, and he was being unhelpful to the president by pushing these kinds of comments in front of the press. His point was that I essentially worked for him, since I was a staff person and he was elected party leadership. This led me to observe that he was not just a knucklehead but an arrogant and counter-productive knucklehead. Rarely is it constructive to take note of idiocy, but it can be therapeutic. I then called up Bob Bennett, the able Ohio GOP chairman to insist that this man not be included in any presidential events we run in Ohio. Indeed, we had him escorted from the room at a subsequent event.

***

One more story from the summer of Dukakis: it began with Dick Wirthlin, who had served as the president's pollster since his 1966 gubernatorial race. Genial and professional, Dick was an enormous asset to the Reagan presidency. He continued to brief the president weekly on poll numbers, immediately after which the numbers were given to OPA and me. After one briefing, I gave my friend in the British embassy the polling data, and it went back to London. Margaret Thatcher and Her Majesty's Government were getting the briefing material for the president more-or-less within twenty-four hours of the president getting it.[80]

The data was all private polling data and not US government material. The Brits could keep a secret. *And we're all friends, aren't we?*

---

[80] I was also helping a bit on NORAID, meaning the Irish Northern Aid Committee, nominally a charitable relief organization but widely viewed to be supporting the IRA. Indeed, the US courts delicately found it to be providing support "other than relief..." Support from NORAID had a certain appeal in some circles, and we worked to make sure that US elected officials did not unwittingly support this organization, mainly by informing them of the president's opposition and of the US court's findings.

Sometimes friendships have political utility. During this summer of Dukakis, a member of the royal family, let's call him Brian, wrote Dukakis an effusive note of praise, which was clumsy enough by itself, and certainly displayed bad judgment. It had been over two hundred years since we in the colonies looked to the royals for political advice. Worse, if it were to get out, it would be a mild embarrassment for Bush, undercutting his claim to international leadership, and another day or two of positive news cycles for Dukakis, that he was the golden boy.

My friend in the British embassy intercepted the letter, and it was never delivered. Brits are not just good at keeping our secrets; they could bottle up their own secrets as well. Keeping the polling channel open turned out to be more than a courtesy.

At the Republican convention, Vice President Bush was superb. As mentioned, a sitting vice president labors under an unspoken, almost lethal, constraint: he is forbidden by custom from having an independent political persona. Indeed, a vice president's *only* public responsibility is to support the president. Akin to the first lady, he has a constituency of one. What the vice president might say in private to the president is his business, but if that vice president ever were to make a comment in public that differed from his boss by a fraction of an inch, that difference would make headlines across the nation. A successful vice president must loyally subordinate his political identity. The problem then becomes that the American public has no sense of who he is; they know him only as an advocate for his boss. Even when he announces for president, a sitting vice president has little latitude in establishing an identity because he cannot repudiate the administration he is currently serving.

Only at the moment of his national party convention, as the vice president formally assumes the role of party nominee, is it acceptable for a vice president to define himself as not just an advocate for the incumbent. He has to perform twin goals that can be in some tension: reaffirm the success of the current administration, but offer a path of his own.

George Bush carried it off. "Read my lips: no new taxes." This ultimately ill-fated pledge defined the moment. Bush seized the high ground and established himself as a worthy steward of the Reagan legacy. He was assertive without being impolite. There were other places in his speech where he marked out his identity, holding out the prospect of his being a "kinder, gentler" president. It was a rhetorical and a political success.

The Republican base firmed up behind Bush and he leapt ahead of Dukakis. By September, Bush was ahead 49–41.[81] Some of Dukakis's more exotic political moves came to the forefront. As governor, he had signed a proclamation in favor of witchcraft. He refused to require the Pledge of Allegiance in schools. He was soft on defense and wrong on taxes. Most notably, and controversially, he supported a furlough program in which convicted felons in Massachusetts state prisons were given weekend passes to return home, even convicted murderers. This story made it to the front pages with the case of one Willie Horton, who was in prison for murder, released under Dukakis's program, and who went on to commit rape and

---

[81] The numbers suggest a Reagan impact. In the Aug NYT/CBS poll, Bush was sixteen points behind Dukakis and was supported by only 56 percent of those who approved of Reagan. By the Sept NYT/CBS poll, where Bush had an eight-point lead, he was now supported by 75 percent of those who approved of Reagan. *The New York Times*, September 20, 1988.

assault while on furlough. Capitalizing on the egregious nature of these crimes, an independent political action committee produced an anti-Dukakis ad based around this incident.

This was a high-octane cocktail of sex, murder, and inevitably, race (Horton was Black), and Dukakis bungled the response magnificently. At various times, he argued that the program was originally established by a Republican, that George Bush had favored a similar program in Texas, that the attacks on Horton were racist, and that the attacks were not independent but orchestrated by Bush. He never explained or defended the actions, but directed all of his efforts in attempts to impugn the criticism. Yet, by only criticizing the critics and by avoiding a substantive defense of his program, Dukakis essentially validated the criticism. The "you did it too" argument allowed Dukakis to reach the two-wrongs-make-a-right voter and to lose everyone else.

THE POWER OF INCUMBENCY

Vice President Bush had a set of advantages that offset Dukakis's strengths of novelty and finance, chiefly the power of incumbency and the ability to win media attention, to act presidential, and to even to help shape the lines of policy discussion—all important elements of the craft of politics.

As far back as December 1987, when Gorbachev had his Washington Summit with Reagan, Bush was able to have breakfast with him at the Russian embassy, leaving his then-rival Bob

Dole to crack that he was "surprised Bush didn't invite Gorbachev to Iowa for a fundraiser."[82]

And in June of 1988, when the agricultural sector was suffering from a drought, Bush could spend a day with farmers, accompanied by Agriculture Secretary Richard Lyng and Illinois Governor Jim Thompson.

In September 1988, Bush attended the destruction of US missiles as required by the INF Treaty, a useful signal that Reagan's "peace through strength" approach to defense was bearing fruit.

On October 3, Bush was at Edwards Air Force Base to greet the Space Shuttle discovery as its astronauts returned, the first mission since the tragic Challenger disaster.

And on October 20, Bush filled in for Reagan as he swore in Lauro Cavazos as secretary of education, a tip to Bush's earlier promise to appoint a Hispanic person to the cabinet.

None of these events might have been significant by themselves, but collectively they made it easier to envision Bush as president, since he was already performing aspects of the job.

FINAL WEEKS

Bush came out of the convention with a nice lead, creating a buoyant mood in the White House. We needed to carry out our plans, fend off attacks, and not get distracted by secondary issues or internal dissension. But if we could exercise discipline

---

[82] Gerald M. Boyd, "Summit Aftermath; Gorbachev Visit Called Boon to Bush," *The New York Times*, December 12, 1988.

over the final few months, we felt increasingly confident that Bush would win.

The last few months of the campaign were seven-days-a-week affairs, and long days at that. As we neared the finish line, the tempo increased. The amount of campaign information and data increased. The amount of anxiety increased. The ability to make decisions and think rationally decreased. Fatigue set in. We began to operate on reflex. Stay on message. Stay on message. Stay on message. We were ahead. We just needed to make rational planning decisions against long-established operating criteria. Don't mess up. Vice President Bush understood the importance of remaining disciplined under pressure and "Don't Worry, Be Happy" became his unofficial campaign song.

The seduction of the magic wand exerted a stronger hold on decision-making as the election drew near. We were a few points behind in a state? Send the president. The other candidate was outspending us on TV? Send the president. General political anxiety, low self-esteem, or simply bored? Send the president. Given the finite number of days and trips, the challenge was to allocate the president's time in an effective fashion.

Every datum, every comment, every new ad flooded into the White House. The chore was how to sort through these data points to adjust the campaign. Fortunately, the Bush campaign and the White House each had mature decision-making systems. I had a weekly coordinating meeting with the even-keeled and meticulous David Bates from the Office of the Vice President and high energy and strong follow-through Ed Rogers, Lee Atwater's deputy at the campaign. Similarly, the Political Office had weekly phone consultations with all fifty Republican state chairs, so there was a system in place. I needed to get on the road to see for myself.

I made a series of campaign trips, going on the road about two days a week to speak to groups. These trips were paid for by the Republican National Committee or some other party organization because we couldn't use government funds.

I headed to the West Coast to give some talks and meet with donors. I called on Gil Glazer in LA. Gil grew up in the Great Depression, graduating from high school in Knoxville during 1938. His dad was a welder, and Gil had joined the family business and served in the Navy in WWII. The welding business grew into a steel fabricating business and became quite successful, allowing Gil to branch out into real estate, including shopping mall development in Los Angeles. Gil had been active in Republican circles, so it was worth a call in the course of a California trip.

Gil was affable and welcoming and he told me straight up, "I gave $50,000 to George Bush and $50,000 to Bob Dole and $50,000 to Al Gore." I responded that the parallel donations to Bush and Dole pretty much made sense, given his long-standing Republican orientation, but what explained his support of Al Gore?

"Actually, I gave the donation to Gore first," said Gil. He told his story. Gil had gotten to know Gore's father, Al Gore, Sr., when the latter was the congressman from Knoxville, and after the war, Gil was working for the Haganah (the pre-independence paramilitary organization), procuring military surplus for the Israeli underground as they prepared for independence. He happened to bump into Gore, Sr., who was making a congressional tour of Europe, and Gil shared his problem: the US Army had surplus mortars on Cyprus and Israel needed them, but he could not shake them loose. "Let me fix that," said Gore, and he did. He was able to procure the mortars as surplus and get them to Israel.

"What do I owe you?" asked Gil. "Not a thing," said Gore, "but one day I might come to you for a favor." Forty years later, the senior Gore did call Gil for the favor. Gil gave Al Gore, Jr., $50,000, but he felt bad about it because he did not support Gore, so he gave the same amount to Bush and Dole as well.

***

Back in DC, I was on C-SPAN, taking calls from viewers. One viewer, in the guise of asking about media fairness, alleged that Michael Dukakis "may well have been treated for a mental affliction." It was as if a ghost had arisen from the grave to pitch me the easiest, sweetest question ever offered on a talk show. If you dig out an old tape of this interview from C-SPAN, you will note I had to move my mug to my mouth to mask my momentary laughter.[83]

I dismissed the allegations. *Let's keep the discussion on the issues, please. It is not a matter of Dukakis's mental ability; it is a matter of his views on policy. Thank you.*

---

[83] https://www.c-span.org/video/?4555-1/call-frank-levin

ELECTION EVE 1988

As Election Day approached, Reagan had already held seven different rallies in California, speaking before a total of sixty thousand people.[84] But polls showed Dukakis within a point or two in that state, and Reagan felt he needed to make one final push. Reagan told Donatelli: "You know, I can live with the fact if we lost California, but I couldn't live with myself if we lost it by a point or two and I didn't make this final trip."[85]

The magic wand does not always work, but in support of his own vice president, it certainly did. Reagan did twelve fundraisers for Bush (or state committees) and twenty-three rally events, not the work of someone with only passing interest in the outcome.[86] Reagan made a round-trip 4,640 mile flight on the final day of the campaign, traveling a total of eleven hours and speaking to crowds estimated at eight thousand in Long Beach and ten thousand in San Diego. His speeches were among the more sentimental of the final campaign swing. At the first stop in Long Beach, he told the crowd, "This is my last campaign and seeing all of you...it's like closing a circle, like sailing into the harbor after a long and wonderful voyage to be greeted by old beloved friends."

At his final campaign stop in San Diego, he said: "This is a special moment for me in a special place and, yes, with special people.... So if I could ask you one last time, tomorrow, when

---

[84] Walldorf, "What I Saw After the Revolution," (unpublished paper), 143. (May 1991)

[85] ibid., 145.

[86] ibid., 28–29.

mountains greet the dawn, will you go out there and win one for the Gipper?"

The *Washington Post* noted that "Bush carried California by less than 300,000 votes but picked up a 170,000-vote majority in San3 Diego County and a 300,000-vote majority in Orange County, the GOP strongholds where Reagan tried to boost the turnout."[87]

Reagan returned to the White House in somewhat dramatic fashion on election eve. There was a certain poignancy to the moment because he had just completed his final campaign swing as president. We wanted a rousing welcome home for the Gipper. Our office staff, volunteers, and interns made signs to welcome the president. We knew that Reagan enjoyed greeting well-wishers as he came off Marine One to return to the White House.

I mischievously posed a question to the Political Office: Who can come up with a sign that will draw Reagan over? People tried some of the obvious choices, and signs were made up that read "Four More Years," and "I (heart) Reagan." "Reaganites for Bush" was my favorite guess, because it encapsulated the message Reagan had been delivering on the trail: if you liked Reagan, you'll like Bush. All of these slogans were well-intentioned, predictable, and some even trite. Still, they all sort of worked. Reagan came over and shared a few words of good cheer to a rousing greeting staff and supporters. This had been the Gipper's final campaign swing as president. The journey was over.

---

[87] Lou Cannon, "President Reagan, passing the torch..." *Washington Post*, November 10, 1988, A48.

The sign that won, the sign that pulled Reagan over was not a political pitch but a tug of the heart. It was created by the intern Scott Coffina and it read simply, "Will you be my Grampa?" Reagan immediately responded to the human appeal and, perhaps, the chance to play a role. He came over and gave Scott a hug. For Reagan, the emotional dimension of the job—the ability to make someone feel better about themselves—was at least as important as the substantive dimension.

George Bush won a handsome victory, beating Michael Dukakis 53–46 percent and doing even better in the Electoral College, 426–111. Bush deserved to win and Ronald Reagan and his team could feel justly proud of their support. We were leaving the White House with our heads held high. Not only had we done our duty to help George Bush, but we had advanced a policy agenda over eight years that left the United States better at home and abroad.

Not just growth for the country, but growth for me as well. To mature a bit while still retaining a sense of the absurd. To maintain personal integrity in a bureaucratic system, pushing against the Klan and sexual assault. To help substantively to keep the Reagan policy agenda on track. To try to be a good friend and a listener to people who needed help. To work within the give and take of a team, keeping collegiality and wit front and center. These building blocks of my career were first formed and tested under Ronald Reagan.

The 1988 election was the end of my journey with Reagan as well. Although we were in office through the 1989 inauguration of President Bush, and I was able to stay in some contact after he left office, there was no longer the close working relationship or the sense of mission. Five years after he left office, even the limited contact ended with Reagan's announcement he was afflicted with Alzheimer's disease and would cease public appearances. As John Updike reminds us, the other "regrettable think about death is the ceasing of your own brand of magic."

CHAPTER 13

SEARCHING FOR JUPITER: EXPLAINING RONALD REAGAN

Now we are at the end of our journey, with the central question illuminated but not fully answered: Who was Ronald Reagan? "The secret to Ronald Reagan is that there really is no secret," wrote Nancy Reagan. "He is exactly the man he appears to be. The Ronald Reagan you see in public is the same Ronald Reagan I live with."[88] I think this is an accurate assessment, but it means only that Reagan was unaffected or unpretentious, still leaving the answer incomplete.

To his political opponents, Reagan was easy to ridicule as a buffoon. But if you had spent any time with him, you would realize how inaccurate that characterization was. In working with Reagan across eight years, I saw many layers and facets, all carefully guarded by a genial public persona and honed over years in the public eye. After a while I got the sense that the

---

[88] Reagan and Novak, *My Turn*, location 1718. Kindle.

public image he projected had at some point fused with his own vision of himself. He played a role, and he became the role he played. He had his lines, and he wasn't going to deviate. Reagan was on stage, and you were the audience. This is not to say that his message was not heartfelt. Reagan was reading, writing, and talking about his ideas on individual freedom and US-Soviet relations long before he played any public role. He cared deeply about ideas. My conclusion: Although his critics said he was detached, Reagan was so sure of his ideas and self-confident about his strengths and weaknesses that he stayed above the fray, not because he was acting but because he was guiding. If ever a president said what he was going to do, and then did it, it was Ronald Reagan. Yet even this consistency of message and goal does not fully explain the individual.

Edmund Morris, who wrote the best and the worst book about Reagan (same book), likened the search to understanding Reagan to searching for the planet Jupiter. The early astronomers could not see Jupiter, but they knew it existed because of the gravitational field it created.[89] True enough, we can understand Reagan's impact more readily than we can understand him.

This gave Reagan a sense of the ineffable. Morris wrote: "All men have their stories, tumbled like stones in the current of telling, until they are polished into something less (or more) than autobiography."[90] After spending a lot of time with Reagan, I didn't always find it easy to discern what was the truth, what was the truth as he remembered it, to what extent he realized he was sticking to his version of the truth, or to what extent

---

[89] Morris, *Dutch*, 243.
[90] ibid., 112.

it even mattered. When Reagan had two feet of his intestine removed in 1985 after cancer was detected, he stated: "I didn't have cancer. I had something inside of me that had cancer in it, and *it* was removed."[91] A rather creative approach to a medical issue, but I suspect Reagan actually believed what he was saying. Was it Joseph Conrad who told us that each man must be true to his own myths?

Reagan constructed that public persona and only rarely, very rarely, let you have a glimpse of what was behind it. Nancy Reagan wrote: "There's a wall around him. He lets me come closer than anyone else, but there are times when even I feel that barrier."[92] Lou Cannon concluded: "Ronald Reagan was humanly accessible to people who had never met him and impenetrable to those who tried to know him well."[93]

Some say this insularity is typical of children of an alcoholic parent. Longtime Reagan confidant Judge Clark knew Reagan as well as anyone, having served as his chief of staff while governor, then in Washington as national security advisor and interior secretary. He discussed how such children behave: "Some become resentful, but most simply want tranquility in their lives. Trusting others is a challenge. They can't deal with people one on one. They don't want to hear bad news. They need a happy ending to every story. If there is no happy ending, they delete the story from their memory."[94]

---

[91] Cannon, *President Reagan: The Role Of A Lifetime*, 198.
[92] Reagan and Novak, *My Turn*, location 106. Kindle.
[93] Cannon, *President Reagan: The Role Of A Lifetime*, 141.
[94] William Clark, Jr., quoted in Thomas C. Reed, *The Reagan Enigma* (California: Figueroa Press, 2014), 221.

Policy aide Annelise Anderson expanded on this: "[T]he successful child of an alcoholic is very perceptive about people and they say, like [Bill] Clinton, they can walk into a room and in a little while they know exactly how everybody feels, where the tension is…I think the other thing children of alcoholics learn is to keep their own counsel, and I think this he [Reagan] does. If you perceive that that person thinks something different, you just be quiet until things change. You don't say, 'Let's talk about that. I don't agree with you,' because that's too dangerous. And so you learn to be this way and you think, *I will always be a nice kid*."[95]

Did this guarded public persona also have something to do with years as a celebrity? As a movie star, you live on fame, you generate fame, you seek fame, but fame has a cost—the public wants to connect with you and wants a conversation with you. People believe because they saw your movie, they have the right to discuss it with you, even to critique it with you.

We all like to cultivate friendships, but that pleasure is not permitted to a movie star, or a governor, or a president. You cannot discern how rational, friendly, or helpful someone is going to be unless you invest time in building a relationship. But there are too many people asking too many questions to make that investment, so you develop a high-speed, high-volume approach. Everybody gets a smile, that's cost-free. Everybody gets a joke, that's cost-free. Everybody gets a sympathetic ear and a friendly comment, cost-free as well. Then it is a friendly

95 Annelise Anderson, "Annelise Anderson Oral History," interviewed by Stephen F. Knott, Marc Selverstone, and James S. Young, https://millercenter.org/the-presidency/presidential-oral-histories/annelise-anderson-oral-history-associate-director-office.

goodbye and you are on to the next event. "There was a kind of splendid isolation about the man," wrote his director of personnel, Helene von Damm.[96]

We think of friendships as an open-ended upward slope. The more we invest, the more time we spend together, the more we enjoy each other's company, the better our friendship. Not so with presidents. Their public role more or less precludes this scenario. They cannot connect with people on an open-ended basis. There is a plateau at which the relationship is optimized.

Maureen Reagan once advised me to always show a bit of your teeth for photos because it looked like you were smiling (somehow it made me feel as if I were snarling) and always hold your hands just below chin-level when applauding so the cameras will pick it up. Ronald Reagan could always show a bit of teeth, always throw his head back with a knowing smile. He could do it multiple times in a row. Was he actually happy or was he acting? Did it matter?

Reagan always was presented as unassuming and genial with that friendly smile and a warm handshake. But there was a certain sadness to the geniality. It was a defensive mechanism. Friendly with everyone, but friends with no one.

One NSC colleague advised not to misjudge the president's friendliness. As he put it, and he meant everyone including the chief of staff, "We're all hired hands on the ranch." The president made little effort to learn staff names, even for people he worked with daily. It was said that Darman delivered papers to the Oval Office and spoke with Reagan daily, but even after a

---

[96] von Damm, *At Reagan's Side*, 224.

year, Reagan did not know his name. The president knew very well who Darman was, but names did not matter much.

Reagan liked to use humor. There was the meta-point and the particular point. The meta-point was that we were all friends. We tell jokes to friends, to people we like, to people we trust. So this was a friendly dinner. It was not an economics lecture. It was not a harangue. It was just a group of friends swapping stories.

The particular point is that every joke has a ring of truth to it. Market economics work. The Soviet Union does not work. You are better off going through life as an optimist.

Reagan would tell the story about an official trip he took to Mexico as governor. He gave what he thought was a reasonably good address but received only tepid applause and polite titters at the laugh lines. Then a man stood up after him to give a talk—it was not completely clear who this man was as he was not really introduced—and this man's talk received hearty applause along with occasional hearty laughter. Reagan, though not understanding the speech, thought he'd better join in the spirit and he commenced laughing and applauding along with the rest of the audience. His host leaned over to him to explain, this man was the translator and he was simply reading the translated version of Reagan's original speech. Reagan told this story with a chuckle, meaning he was laughing at his own misplaced laughter. And as he told the story, you would begin to laugh as well. The Möbius strip.

Reagan had no problem poking fun at himself, but to say that Reagan was not introspective would be an understatement of high order. He cultivated an absence of introspection with an

almost Zen-like perfection of obliviousness. He brought confidence, optimism, but little ego into the discussion. As Clark
noted, some people can delete unhappy thoughts from their
memory.

Here's how Reagan presents one particular encounter in
his autobiography. He has invited House Speaker (and political
adversary) Tip O'Neill to the White House: "...[A]nd Tip said
'You know, I have been in and out of this place for twenty-seven
years and I have never seen it look as beautiful as this.'"[97]

A gracious statement from a man who led the opposition
to Reagan in Congress. Here is how former Secretary of State
George Shultz relates the same scene. In his depiction, it is not
a social occasion, but O'Neill is coming by the White House to
convey his unhappiness at the US invasion of Grenada:

> The Democrats, particularly Tip O'Neill, were
> cool...'Mr. President, I have been informed
> but not consulted,' O'Neill said. With that,
> he stomped out of the family quarters of the
> White House. A couple of minutes later, as we
> were standing around talking, Tip came back.
> 'Mr. President,' he said, 'I just want to say that
> I've been coming to these family quarters for
> a great many years, and I've never seen them
> in such wonderful shape. You and Nancy have

---

[97] Reagan and Lindsey, *An American Life*, 250.

made them look and feel like a real home.'
Then he turned and left.[98]

What is related by Reagan as a compliment might be more
accurately termed a compliment-*cum*-apologia. Tip's criticisms
don't fit with the narrative and Reagan cut that part of the scene
from the reel.[99]

Look at how Reagan describes his 1968 campaign: "Running for President [in 1968] was the last thing on my mind...I
wasn't interested."[100] Yet 1968 campaign manager Tom Reed
notes: "I had met with Reagan over one hundred times in the
company of others to discuss this project...I accompanied Reagan on dozens of politically funded flights on a chartered Jet
Commander to meet with backers in our intended primary
states.... When Lyndon Johnson withdrew from, and Bobby
Kennedy entered the Democratic contest in March 1968, we
moved up to a chartered 727 jet to accommodate over 40 members of the traveling press."[101] Again, that scene is deleted.

Third, what about a failed marriage? Does that not prompt
any thoughts? Reagan's autobiography runs over seven hundred
pages, but he devotes precisely two sentences in those pages to
his first marriage: "The same year I made the Knute Rockne

---

[98] George Shultz, *Turmoil and Triumph: My Years As Secretary of State* (New York:
Scribner, 1993), 335.
[99] Nancy Reagan describes the moment second-hand, presumably from her
husband's retelling: "Around that same time, Ronnie convened a meeting of
the congressional leadership in the Yellow Oval Room. After the group had
left, Tip O'Neill came back up on the elevator to give Ronnie a message:
'Please tell Nancy that I've never, ever, seen the White House look this
beautiful!'" Reagan, *My Turn*. Kindle. Location 454
[100] Reagan and Lindsey, *An American Life*, 176–77.
[101] Wyman quoted in Reed, *The Reagan Enigma*, 179.

movie, I married Jane Wyman, another contract player at Warners. Our marriage produced two wonderful children, Maureen and Michael, but it didn't work out and in 1948 we were divorced."[102]

This is a skilled, practiced desire to avoid reflection, a normal enough reaction in many respects, even understandable. But at some point is it worth thinking about setbacks in life and what might have been done differently, what lessons were learned? Indeed, isn't that the point of an autobiography? But Reagan was simply not interested in introspection, at least not negative introspection. Why wallow in bad news? If you need to project optimism, you have to be optimistic. And to do that over several decades, through several careers, it means to some extent simply focusing on the good news and ignoring the bad news. A useful tactic in many respects, but it doesn't make for a good book.

There is no discussion of how people drift apart after the initial romance fades. No discussion about how Reagan's career was leveling off while Wyman's was still advancing. Wyman was nominated for an Academy Award for Best Actress in 1946 for *The Yearling*, and in 1948, she went on to win that award for *Johnny Belinda*. And by that point Reagan's career was no longer moving ahead. As Wyman explains: "We parted company because I was doing well in motion pictures. He had moved on, into politics and speech-making."[103] No discussion of the loss of the baby *in utero* and the wrenching effect that must have had. No discussion of how the trauma of divorce might have made

---

[102] Reagan and Lindsey, *An American Life*, 192.
[103] Reed, *The Reagan Enigma*, 20.

him as determined as possible to be a good husband to Nancy. No discussion of how a divorce affected his relationship with his first two children. No discussion of the stigma of a divorce at that time in the United States. How did it affect Reagan's appeal or his marketability? Even sixteen years later, divorce in public life was sufficiently controversial that Nelson Rockefeller's became a political issue as he campaigned for the 1964 Republican presidential nomination in the California primary, with the campaign against him—Barry Goldwater's—championed by Ronald Reagan. No discussion. That scene is cut.

This type of forgetfulness or historical rewriting can be maddening. But on a different level, it can also be a source of strength. Political life, like movie life, is full of insults, indignities, and shortcomings. You have to develop a thick skin and remain focused on your goal. There will always be someone who is criticizing your work or your politics. You cannot stop and engage every critic. O'Neill was unhappy. But then, O'Neill opposed most of what Reagan stood for. Is it worth reacting to O'Neill's reaction? Or is it best just to slough it off as if it never happened. The 1968 campaign was a bit of an experiment. Why use that to define your political identity?

Is this approach in part due to an actor's habits? Actors remember forward not backward. Yesterday is in the can. Nothing can be done about it. Need to learn tomorrow's lines. There will always be another call for "Action!"

And yet, and yet. Jane Wyman's shadow fell over the White House. I returned from a trip with the president. It was either the weekend or after hours at night, but after bidding farewell, I had to drop by my office for some follow-up activity. The president was going back to the residential quarters of the White House wrapping up the day. At that time, there were no VCRs or taping mechanisms, and all the TVs in the White House complex were run through the same centralized playback system. The evening news was played back at certain times and if you wanted something at other times, you had to call WHCA, the estimable White House Communications Agency that ran that one-size-fits-all playback mechanism. I turned the TV to the channel to watch the news playback and *Falcon Crest*—the Jane Wyman TV vehicle—was playing. Somebody was clearly taking advantage of the after-hour nature to catch up on their soap operas. I called WHCA to ask if they could play the evening news. "Sorry Mr. Lavin, the playlist for the evening is under the direction of the Usher's Office." In other words, the usher of the residence; either the president or the first lady had asked for it to be shown.

And how smart was Reagan? Smarter than you might think, though I suspect he was more wise than he was smart. Not that he wasn't intelligent or well-read—he was both. He was also a bit detached. His view of the presidency was that he was to offer leadership and not management, which was the right call. When he honed in on something important, such as negotiations with the Soviets, he could go toe-to-toe with anyone on the US team, or anyone on the Soviet side. And he did. Ed Meese sums it up: "One of the most astonishing things to me is to read the numerous accounts of the Reagan era that portray the president as an essentially passive figure, somehow disengaged, ignorant of the facts, or incapable of leading. This is a totally false depiction of the Ronald Reagan I knew and worked with…" [104]

One example after Reykjavik: Early in the day after we returned, Poindexter gathered the NSC team to review the draft speech that the arms control staff had done for the president's TV speech to the nation that evening. It also turned out that the president had his own draft—five single-spaced legal sheets in longhand that he had written up on his return. No cross-outs, no inserts, just page after page of presidential handwriting. Well, the staff groaned at this. (NSC Senior Director Stephen Sestanovich recollects that the president's presentation was significantly sharper and clearer.) Poindexter agreed to take the staff text to the president and see if he would agree to it, since the experts insisted they had the better statement of the detailed arms-control substance. Not long after, he returned, looking kind of deflated. No dice. The president liked his own better. He was willing to use part of the staff draft to finish out his own, which had broken off about two-thirds of the way through. But otherwise, stick with his draft. This was not somebody lost in the fog.

Another example, this from surgery: Reagan needed a polyp removed and when he came out of general anesthetic after having the procedure, he picked up the conversation with Don Regan exactly where he left it twelve hours before, discussing Bob Dole and budget issues. [105] Reagan had a secret weapon, several actually: he had a high degree of self-awareness and he was devoid of intellectual pretension. He had no problem sur-

---

[104] Meese, *With Reagan*, 14.
[105] Brands, *Reagan: The Life*, 496.

rounding himself with talent and then delegating. And he had a compass. He knew where he wanted to go. Just as important, he was willing to stake his political career on his beliefs and put in the hard work to get there.

I remember a story from 1985. Over exchange rate concerns, Treasury Secretary Jim Baker met with his foreign counterparts at the Plaza Hotel in New York City for the eponymous accord to push down the value of the dollar, thus boosting exports. How did we reach the Plaza Accord? A friend from the NSC related that on briefing Reagan on international monetary policy, we might as well have used sock puppets. The friend feigned a squeaky cartoon voice as he mimicked two such puppets in conversation. "Mr. Dollar is mad at Mr. Yen, so he is going to ask Mr. Deutsche Mark to help out. Mr. Deutsche Mark said OK, so now all three of us will meet at the Plaza Hotel and promise to be friends." A cheap shot, but we get the point.

We can imagine Bill Clinton pulling together his Treasury Department team and the NSC team and spending four hours on Saturday chewing through a briefing, one that would start late and be interrupted by phone calls and let's have lunch brought in and "Y'know I was on a panel with the Japanese finance minister at Davos" and "I have another story to tell you." And Clinton ends up exactly where Reagan ended up. Indeed, the four-hour meeting did take place under Reagan, but since Reagan was not there, the four-hour meeting was ninety minutes. Reagan, to his credit or discredit, did not need to be part of it. Clinton, to his credit or discredit, needed to bathe in the interagency process. *I harmonize policy options, therefore I am. Cool waters, wash over me.*

In the same vein, Colin Powell told me about one of his first meetings with Reagan after he became national security advisor. Powell had entered the NSC as Frank Carlucci's deputy and then replaced Carlucci when the latter became defense secretary. Powell had a good relationship with Reagan, but had only been working at the White House for a few months before he moved to the top national security job.

Soon after he assumed the role, Powell was faced with a NATO issue (the exact nature of which is lost to time). It seemed a bit complicated and it involved some trade-offs. Powell was not exactly sure what Reagan would like to do in this sort of instance, so he went down the hall and to the Oval Office to see the president, Powell being one of the two of three aides to have "walk-in privileges."

Powell took a minute to explain the issue to Reagan and paused. Reagan also paused and drew in his breath. "Y'know it's a funny thing," he said, as he motioned to the window. "I put some nuts out there yesterday for the squirrels, and I don't think the squirrels have touched a single one of them."

At first, Powell was taken aback. Did Reagan not hear what he had just said, or did he not care? Almost as instantly he realized the truth. What Reagan was saying to him was—*don't bring me problems; bring me solutions. You wouldn't be here unless I had confidence in your judgment. So please come back to me with your recommendation and summarize the trade-offs and we can make a decision.*

But how would Jimmy Carter have dealt with the same message? Likely he would have set up an NSC process and worked through a series of presentations from the joint chiefs, pulling in the US ambassador to NATO on the secure line, a much more elaborate process and not necessarily ending up with the right decision in any event.

Carter needed to wallow. Clinton liked to chew. Maybe for them the process was as important as the outcome. But Reagan had a destination. If you knew where you were trying to go, it was simpler to decide on a course of action. Carter liked to show that he could master the details of government arcana. Clinton liked to show he was the smartest guy in the room. Reagan didn't even need to be in the room.

The wrong way to act as president is to appoint yourself as the Supreme Court for every decision. The right way is to set the goals and select the people and let them make the decision. The buck stops with the president, as Harry Truman noted, so the president owns the decision and the outcome. But the process of decision-making should be left to those with expertise.

This type of light management could be taken to extremes. Reagan brought his old governor's chair with him to the Oval Office. It was a barrel chair, which he enjoyed for comfort and nostalgia perhaps, but the chair was fixed; it could not elevate or lower. Soon after he took office, his secretary saw he was sitting askew at his desk (the Hayes/Resolute desk), with his legs not under it. When challenged, he somewhat sheepishly stated that his legs did not fit under the desk. She said, "Mr. President, we can fix that." The White House carpentry shop constructed a three-inch wooden platform to be inserted under the desk, thereby giving him enough space to fit his legs under and sit straight.

In the same vein, you could follow the NSC's work with the three-by-five cards that were prepared for Reagan to use for foreign policy events. What was put on those cards was what went out—straight from the president. This put an enormous burden on the NSC—indeed all of the White House staff —to know what the president's policy and objectives were. As long as the words were reasonably consistent with the president's policies, there would be no problem. But there were occasions that some details of policy turned out to not be to the president's liking. In such circumstances, Reagan just skipped over those words. There was no pushback, no correction, and no presidential complaint. He just did not speak to the particular point, and it was up to the staffer to figure out why the point had dropped.

Indeed, delegating to others might have been more difficult as his tenure went on. It was striking in the second term that almost all of his longtime associates had left the White House: Baker, Meese, Deaver, Nofziger, and Clark. He was alone. "The first failure of Reagan's second term was that he made no effort whatsoever to keep intact the team that had performed so well for him," surmised Cannon.[106]

The Reagan presidency has exerted a hold over American political life for over a generation, establishing a reference point for both supporters and detractors. Bill Clinton, in his 1996 State of the Union address, offered, "The era of big government is over." Even today as we pass four decades from his election, Reagan's views of America's international role, the welfare state, and tax rates continue to shape the political debate. Reagan was one of the few candidates in history to

---

[106] Cannon, *President Reagan: The Role Of A Lifetime*, 495.

begin as the protest candidate and end up as the establishment candidate, a testament to the transformational impact he had on the Republican Party.

Was he conservative? In some fundamental ways, he was. He believed in the importance of liberty, the importance of market economics, he held skepticism about the role of government, and he was pro-life. But in some ways he was not. He was not a Puritan regarding Hollywood lifestyles ("Go ahead and count," Nancy Reagan wrote in her memoir, referring to the birth of their first child, Patti, seven and a half months after the wedding[107]), and he placed fiscal restraint below other priorities. Was he in some respects a conservative Democrat? George Will notes that "in 1981 he began doing for the welfare state what FDR did for capitalism; saving it by tempering its excesses."[108] Yes, he was a traditionalist in many ways and a populist, with enormous respect for the average American along with a bit of skepticism about the chattering class.

British political philosopher Roger Scruton offered a definition of conservatism that would fit in many respects with Reagan, in sharp contrast, for example, with those who rioted on January 6:

> Conservatism starts from a sentiment that all
> mature people can readily share: the sentiment
> that good things are easily destroyed, but not
> easily created. This is especially true of the

---

[107] Reagan, *My Turn*, location 1708. Kindle.
[108] Will quoted in Hayward, *The Age of Reagan: The Conservative Counterrevolution*, 674.

good things that come to us as collective assets: peace, freedom, law, civility, public spirit, the security of property and family life, in all of which we depend on the cooperation of others while having no means singlehandedly to obtain it. In respect of such things, the work of destruction is quick, easy and exhilarating; the work of creation slow, laborious and dull. That is one of the lessons of the twentieth century. It is also one reason why conservatives suffer such a disadvantage when it comes to public opinion. Their position is true but boring, that of their opponents exciting but false.[109]

But this is not a complete explanation. For Reagan, stability and order in a society a were not just an end, but also a means to a greater end, to allow society to change. Reagan saw individual liberty as the organizing principle of society, and that civility and community were not just goals in themselves, but they were also reassurance during times of change. A proper government recognized that society was dynamic, always changing, and people wanted structure and continuity amidst that change. The role of government was not to be backward-looking or to lock in a certain *status quo*, but to provide the architecture that would allow society to adapt in an acceptable fashion.

Reagan also had the serenity, self-confidence, and self-awareness that came from knowing his own weak points

---

[109] Roger Scruton, *How to Be a Conservative* (United Kingdom: Bloomsbury Publishing, 2014)., page viii

and not being troubled by them. He was not an intellectual, but he liked ideas. He was not an academic, but he liked books. He liked stories. He was confident in his faith, a happy Midwestern Christianity that sustained him in difficult times and instructed him to love his neighbors. He liked movies. He liked horses. He avoided denigrating others, even political opponents. As Margaret Thatcher eulogized, he firmly believed in "the great cause of cheering us all up."

Was Reagan a hero? Disraeli said that every politician must understand himself and understand his times. Reagan understood his times. He fit the moment. Reagan understood himself in the sense of self-awareness. He knew what he didn't know. He didn't mind if Jim Baker handled the Plaza Accord or if people made fun of his limited knowledge of exchange rates because he knew a handful of essential truths. He did not just hold that democracy and liberty required a defense; he held that totalitarian systems required defeat. He stood for the promise of America, the promise of inclusion: that you can be from any background and there is still opportunity for you in this country. The promise of mobility: that you can make something of yourself. The promise of optimism: that tomorrow can be a better day. That promise of creativity and experimentation: that America loves the innovator, the disrupter, the risk-taker, the Lone Ranger. Ever the optimist, Reagan fit Michael Oakeshott's definition of one who prefers "present laughter to utopian bliss." Was Reagan a hero? To me, I suppose, he sort of was.

CHAPTER 14

AFTERWORDS

The assault on the US Capitol on January 6, 2021 stood in such sharp contrast with Ronald Reagan's approach to government that it convinced me this book was necessary. Much has been written about Reagan's leadership style, including parts of this book, but let me review six approaches to leadership that the fortieth president embraced and (with one exception) the forty-fifth president seemed to disregard:

1. *Tone matters.* Be careful of personal conduct. People who regularly denigrate or abuse other people raise questions as to their fitness for office. In the policy world, communication is usually not an end in itself, but a means to an end. The goal of communication is to help shape a consensus, and using communication to demean others makes it harder for some to support you. Reagan occasionally found support from opposition leaders like House Speaker Tip O'Neill. Trump ended up with nothing from House Speaker Nancy

Pelosi who openly ridiculed him during his State of the Union address.

2. ***Inclusivity matters.*** The advantage of a political philosophy is that a political party becomes a universal party. The Republican Party was founded on a set of ideas rather than a group identity, so people from any background should be welcome. A leader should spend time with constituencies that might not be a traditional fit. Reagan's outreach was universal, shaped by his radio and movie experience. You need to talk with everyone you can. Trump's approach was insular. The point of a Trump rally wasn't outreach; it was a form of narcissism, designed to speak only to those already in agreement.

3. ***International leadership matters.*** We value alliances and collaboration—not because we are naive or because it is an act of charity. We undertake a leadership role because America is safer and more prosperous when we build alliances. Our two great international successes of the past century, World War II and the Cold War, depended on America's ability to lead a coalition. Reagan set the stage for the North American Free Trade Agreement (NAFTA) with his call for a "North American Accord." Trump lost international support when he withdrew from the Trans-Pacific Partnership and when he publicly denigrated our NATO allies.

4. ***Economic growth matters.*** Whatever problems we face, from racial disparity to the environment, will be that much easier to tackle with economic growth. To give Trump credit, he was able to preside over three years of

growth. This is arguably the one area where there is an overlap between Reagan's worldview and Trump's.

5. ***Values matter.*** The first rule of a president should be to act like a president. Behave in a way that makes it easy for people to like you, to want to respect you, and to follow you. Reagan knew he was leading a great nation and reached an approval high of 68 percent according to the Gallup poll. Trump merely asserted greatness and reached an approval high of 49 percent[110].

6. ***Defeats matter.*** Reagan actually received more votes in the 1976 Republican primaries than did his rival, President Gerald Ford, but the distribution of these votes allowed Ford to be awarded more delegates. Reagan was gracious in defeat, endorsing Ford from the convention podium and campaigning for him in the general election. Accepting defeat showed a level of maturity that allowed Reagan to unify the GOP when he went on to win the nomination four years later. Trump's bitterness at defeat and his sustained efforts to overturn an election reflect, to put it mildly, a lack of maturity and a willingness to hurt both the Republican Party and our national interest in pursuit of his personal benefit.

We want our presidents to change America, to change the world, and ultimately to change us. Sometimes, in some ways, changes can be made. These are changes that come with the tide of history and not changes for us as individuals. Much of what

---

[110] https://news.gallup.com/interactives/507569/presidential-job-approval-center.aspx

is important to us—the transcendental need to love someone and to be loved, the ability to find satisfaction at work or some purpose in life, and the joy of a happy family—are outside the scope of government. But we continue to project our hopes onto a president, or our heroic image of a president. Berthold Brecht tells us, "Unhappy the land that has no heroes."[111] We disdain the technocratic approaches, we find day-to-day management to be boring, and we seek a higher purpose in our leaders, so we are destined to be disappointed. "The regularity of disillusionment follows as the night follows the day," writes political scientist James David Barber. "Instead of miracles come halting progress and/or crashed hopes, as the President discovers how short a distance his independent powers can take him.... As the country runs through that cycle of uplift and downfall again and again, the force of the story wanes and skepticism sets in."[112] If the twin requirements of leadership are to articulate a vision and to create a consensus for action, Reagan showed himself to be one of the more superb leaders of our era.

On Ronald Reagan's last morning in office, January 20 1989, his National Security Advisor, Colin Powell, gave his final report on the state of the world. Powell said simply, "The world is quiet today, Mr. President." President Reagan called those the best words ever heard in the Oval Office[113].

---

[111] Bertolt Brecht, *Galileo* (United States: Grove Press, 1994).

[112] James David Barber, *The Pulse of Politics: Electing Presidents in the Media Age* (New York: W. W. Norton, 1980), 318.

[113] Cannon, p3

BIBLIOGRAPHY

Baker, James A. III, *Work Hard, Study...and Keep out of politics*, G.P. Putnam, 2006

Baker, Peter and Susan Glasser. *The Man Who Ran Washington: The Life and Times of James A. Baker III*. United States: Knopf Doubleday Publishing Group, 2020.

Bayless, James L. *Washington on Wry Heritage Histories*, 2017

Brands, H.W. *Reagan: The Life*. New York: Knopf Doubleday Publishing Group, 2015. Kindle.

Buckley, William F., *The Reagan I knew*. Basic Books, 2009

Cannon, Lou. *President Reagan: The Role Of A Lifetime*. United States: PublicAffairs, 2008.

Haig, Alexander M., Jr. *Caveat: Realism, Reagan and Foreign Policy*, New York: MacMillan, 1984.

Haldeman, H. R. H. R. *Haldeman to Richard Nixon*, June 20, 1967.

Darman, Jonathan, *Landslide*, Random House 2014

Fallows, James. "'My Friends': Communications and a 'National Family.'" Our Towns, May 8, 2021. https://www.our-townsfoundation.org/my-friends-communications-and-a-national-family/.

Hayward, Steven F. *The Age of Reagan: The Conservative Counterrevolution*. United Kingdom: Random House Publishing Group, 2009.

Lavin, Frank. "More Than a 'Great Communicator.'" *The Wall Street Journal*, June 8, 2004.

Matlock, Jack, Jr. *Reagan and Gorbachev: How the Cold War Ended.* United States: Random House Publishing Group, 2004.

Meese, Edwin, III. *With Reagan: The Inside Story.* Washington, DC: Regnery Publishing, 2015.

Memo Regarding Prime Minister Thatcher Visit in Coordination Office, NSC Records, RAC Box 13.

Morris, Edmund. *Dutch: A Memoir of Ronald Reagan.* United Kingdom: Random House Publishing Group, 2011.

Noonan, Peggy. *What I Saw at the Revolution: A Political Life in the Reagan Era.* New York: Random House, 2003. Reprint.

Reagan, Nancy, and William Novak. *My Turn: The Memoirs of Nancy Reagan.* New York: Random House, 2011. Kindle.

Reagan, Ronald and Robert Lindsey. *An American Life.* United States: Simon & Schuster, 1990.

Reagan, Ronald. "Remarks at a Republican Campaign Rally in San Diego, California." Transcript of speech delivered at San Diego Convention and Performing Arts Center, California, November 7, 1988. https://www.reaganlibrary.gov/archives/speech/remarks-republican-campaign-rally-san-diego-california#:~:text=America%20represents%20something%20universal%20in,and%20not%20become%20a%20Frenchman.

Reagan, Ronald. "Remarks and a Question-and-Answer Session With Area Junior High School Students." Transcript of speech delivered at the State Dining Room at the White House, Washington, DC, November 14, 1988. https://www.reaganlibrary.gov/archives/speech/remarks-and-question-and-answer-session-area-junior-high-school-students.

Reed, Thomas. *The Reagan Enigma.* California: Figueroa Press, 2014.

Regan, Don - for the recordHarcourt, Brace, Jovanovich, 1988

Robinson, Peter. *How Ronald Reagan Changed My Life.* New York: Harper Perennial, 2004.

Rowland, Robert C. "Principle, Pragmatism, and Authenticity in Reagan's Rhetoric." Paper presented at Ronald Reagan Centennial Symposium, University of Southern California, February 2011.

Sestanovich, Stephen. *Maximalist: America in the World from Truman to Obama.* New York: Knopf Doubleday Publishing Group, 2014.

Shirley, Craig Reagan's Revolution (the 1976 campaign)

Shirley, Craig Reagan Rising (1978-1980)

Shirley, Craig Rendezvous with Destiny (1980 campaign)

Shultz, George. *Turmoil and Triumph: My Years As Secretary of State.* New York: Scribner, 1993.

Smith, Hedrick. *The Power Game: How Washington Works.* New York: Random House, 1988. Kindle.

Untermeyer, Chase *When Things Went Right.* Texas A&M University Press, 2013

von Damm, Helene. *At Reagan's Side: Twenty Years in the Political Mainstream.* New York: Knopf Doubleday Publishing Group, 1988.

Wirthlin, Richard, and Wynton C. Hall. *The Greatest Communicator: What Ronald Reagan Taught Me About Politics, Leadership, and Life.* Milwaukee, Wisconsin: Trade Paper Press, 2005.

ORAL HISTORIES

Adelman, Kenneth. "Kenneth Adelman Oral History." By Jeff Chidester, Stephen F. Knott, and Robert Strong. UVA Miller Center, September 30, 2003. https://millercenter.org/the-presidency/presidential-oral-histories/kenneth-adelman-oral-history-director-arms-control-and.

Anderson, Annelise. "Annelise Anderson Oral History." By Stephen F. Knott, Marc Selverstone, and James S. Young. UVA Miller Center, December 17, 2002. https://millercenter.org/the-presidency/presidential-oral-histories/annelise-anderson-oral-history-associate-director-office.

Deaver, Michael. "Michael Deaver Oral History." By James S. Young, Steven Knott, Russell L. Riley, Charles O. Jones, and Edwin Hargrove. UVA Miller Center, September 12, 2002. https://millercenter.org/the-presidency/presidential-oral-histories/michael-deaver-oral-history-deputy-chief-staff.

Shultz, George. "George P. Shultz Oral History." By Steven Knott, Marc Selverstone, and James S. Young, UVA Miller Center, December 18, 2002. https://millercenter.org/the-presidency/presidential-oral-histories/george-p-shultz-oral-history-secretary-state.

UNPUBLISHED WORKS

Cobb, Ty. "Reykjavik: Turning Point of the Cold War". Unpublished paper. July 2020.

Walldorf, Chad. "What I Saw After the Revolution: The Reagan White House and the 1988 Campaign." Unpublished paper.

INDEX

A

Abe, Shintaro 130
abortion 17
Abrams, Elliot 146
Acland, Antony 134
Adelman, Ken 196
administration office. *See* Office of
    Administration
administration policy 82, 127
    Central America 82, 96
administrations. *See also* Carter
    administration; Reagan admin-
    istration
    Bush 99
    Eisenhower 58
    Johnson 114
The Advance Man 18
African-American community 81
agencies
    Agency for International
        Development 3
    Central Intelligence Agency
        (CIA) 126
    United States Information
        Agency 52–53, 179
    White House Communica-
        tion Agency 178, 270
Agnew, Spiro T. 78

Agriculture Department. *See* De-
    partment of Agriculture
agriculture secretary 252
Ahearn, Rick 56, 109
Air Force 48
Air Force One 101, 110, 113–
    114, 176
Air Force Two 56
Alexander, Grover Cleveland 91
Alexander, Margaret 214, 216
Alzheimer's disease 259
ambassadors 171
    Austria 171
    Sudan 172
American Friends Service Com-
    mittee 14
Anderson, Annelise 263
Anderson, John 27, 60
Andrews Air Force Base 56
Andropov, Yuri 159, 174
anti-Semitism 63
aristocrats 44
Armstrong, Anne 157
assistant secretary 48, 62
    of commerce 99
    of state 149
assistant to the president 126,
    193, 206, 215
    for communications 108

associate director 45, 81, 245
of presidential personnel 49
The Atlantic 122–123
attorney general 24–25, 71, 82
Atwater, Lee
Bush campaign 233–235,
239–241, 247
Office of Political Affairs
47–48, 50
Austen, Jane 4
authoritarian regimes 16, 121
Autry, Gene 36

B
Bacharach, Burt 187
Baker, Howard 27, 218
chief of staff 74, 134,
205–206, 246
Baker, James A. IV 25–26
Baker, James A. III 243, 275
chief delegate hunter 25
chief of staff 70–78
1978 Texas attorney general
race 24–26 71, 76, 82
Reagan administration 54
treasury secretary 272
troika of power 70–78
West Wing 98
Barber, James David 282
Barbour, Haley 216, 245
Bates, David 253
Batjer, Marybel 199–200
Bell, Jean 214
Benavidez, Roy 57
Bennett, Arnold 2
Bennett, Bob 248
Berlin, Isaiah 27
Black, Charles A. Jr. 45
Black Monday 235
Blair House 169

BLS (Bureau of Labor Statistics)
47
Boards and Commissions 58
Booth, John Wilkes 120
Bork, Robert 218
The Boys on the Bus 18
BP (British Petroleum) 99
Bradley, Mel 100
Brady, Jim 56
Brecht, Berthold, 282
Breger, Marshall 100
Brezhnev, Leonid 174
British embassy 134
British Petroleum (BP) 99
Brown, Jerry 235
Buchanan, Pat 202
Buckalew, Judi 100
Bundestag 138
Bureau of Labor Statistics (BLS)
47
Burnham, Daniel 66
Burns, Conrad 226
Bush administration 99
Bush, George H.W. 1, 130
Germany 138
1980 campaign 25, 27
1988 campaign 47, 237–
238, 246, 252–253
1988 presidential race
233–236, 258
Reagan administration 56,
94, 188
Republican convention 249
business community 80
Butler, Judith 214, 216
Byzantine Empire 16
Grand Strategy 16

C
Camp David 129–134

Cannon, Lou 36, 162, 262, 275
Canton, Ohio 9–10
Capitalism and Freedom 16
capitulation 139
Carlisle, Belinda 45
Carlucci, Frank 196, 199, 203, 206
  defense secretary 273
Carnation Revolution 169
Carter Administration 22–23, 48, 81, 126
  "Crisis of Confidence" speech 23
  "malaise" speech 23
Carter, Jimmy 193, 273–274
  1980 election 75,
  1976 election 21, 30, 78
  Pershing II deployment 137
Catholics 96
  northern ethnic 96
Catoctin Mountains, MA 133
Cattlemen's Association 102
Cavaco Silva, Anibal 168–169
Cavazos, Lauro 252
CBO (Congressional Budget Office) 47
CEA (Council of Economic Advisors) 47
Central Intelligence Agency (CIA) 126
Challenger Space Shuttle disaster 252
Chamber, Whitaker 16
Chamorro, Violeta 220
Charen, Mona 100
Cherne, Leo 157
Chew, David 132
chief delegate hunter 25
chief of congressional affairs 58

chief of protocol 157, 161, 171
chief of staff 95, 132, 262, 264
  briefings 152
  first lady 202
  Iran-Contra affair 195, 198–202, 217, 206
  objections 74
  removal 205, 212, 246
  White House 82, 191
Chiles, Lawton 226
Chirac, Jacques 186
Christopher, George 72, 230
  1966 Republican gubernatorial primary 72, 230
Churchill, Winston 17
CIA (Central Intelligence Agency) 126
Cicconi, Jim 26, 76
civilian federal workforce 43
Clark, Bill 71
Clark, Judge 262
Clements, Bill 24, 26
Cleveland, Gaines 28
Cobb, Ty 175, 181
  National Security Council (NSC) director 175
Coffina, Scott 216, 258
Cold War 28, 121, 137
  foreign policy 96–97, 175
  nuclear freeze 180
  Reykjavik summit 175–185
College Republican Student Fieldman School 15
Commentary magazine 15, 115
Commissions and Boards 58
Committee on the Present Danger 16
communism 2, 16, 121
  movements 22

Communist Party USA 45
Connally, John 27
Congress. *See* United States Congress
Congressional Budget Office (CBO) 47
congressional candidates 229–232
congressional liaison 58
congressional page 14
The Conscience of a Conservative 12, 16
conservative philosophy 12
    economic 26
    foreign 26
    social 26
constituencies 80–81
    African-American community 81
    business community 80
    ethnic groups 81
    farmers 81
    Hispanic community 80–81
    Jewish community 81
    leadership groups 81
    religious groups 81
    veterans' organizations 81
    women 81
Constitution. *See* United States Constitution
Contras 146–147, 152, 185, 218. *See also* Sandinistas
Cooksey, Sherrie 98
Corporation for Public Broadcasting (CPB) 58
Council of Economic Advisors (CEA) 47, 102
counselor to the president 70
Courtemanche, Jack 208

CPB (Corporation for Public Broadcasting) 58
Craigie, Walter 24–25
Crane, Phil 27
"The Cremation of Sam McGee" poem 79
C-SPAN 255
Cuba and communism 46
Czolgosz, Leon 120

D

Darman, Richard 40, 76–78, 132, 264–265
David, Hal 187
Davis, Patti 141
Dawkins, Pete 223
    Heisman Trophy 223
    West Point 223
Day, Doris 91
Deaver, Mike 38, 53, 192, 275
    presidential events 102–103, 107
    Reagan's communications 38
    troika of power 70–78
defense
    department 48
    industrial policy 187
    minister 162
    ministry 169
    policy 81
    technology 187
Delahanty, Tom 56
DelGiorno, Peter 30–31
democracy 17
Democrats 18, 44
    Reagan 109, 235
    southern traditional 96
Democratic National Convention (DNC) 13, 245
departments

Agriculture 122
Health and Human Services
62
Justice 211
Treasury 272
Department of State 95, 107,
144, 211
Advance Office 126
Protocol Office 126, 169
deputy chief of staff 70
defense secretary 206, 273
deputy assistant 206
deputy defense secretary 24
deputy director 52, 82
deputy executive secretary 120,
124
deputy national security advisor
188
deputy press secretary 26
deputy secretary of agriculture 53
détente 22
Dickens, Charles 30
"Dictatorships and Double Standards" article 15–16, 121
Diepgen, Eberhard 203
Dietz, Francis 216
diktat 183
diplomatic credentials 157–159
director 82, 105, 123, 196
of personnel 264
of the Political Office 233
Dirksen, Everett 206
Disraeli, Benjamin 278
DNC (Democratic National Convention) 13, 245
Dolan, Tony 108
Dole, Bob 251–252, 254, 271
1980 Republican primaries
27

1988 presidential race
233–235
Donatelli, Frank 26, 100, 206,
256
1978 Texas attorney general
race 24
Office of Political Affairs
214–215
Office of Public Liaison
(OPL) 82–83, 93, 98
Dowdy, Wayne 223
Duberstein, Ken 246
Dukakis, Michael 115, 233,
244–249
Massachusetts Miracle
245–246
1988 election 258
political moves 250–251
Duke, David 231
DuPont, Pete 234
Dutch: A Memoir of Ronald Reagan
261

E
Economic Club of New York 34
economic policy 43, 80
economics, supply side 27
The Economist 152
Edelweiss 171
Edwards Air Force Base 252
Eisenhower administration 58
election day 31
1988 256–258
elections 75
status quo 75
change 75
Electoral College xi, 258
Elliot, Ben 108
El Salvador 154
transition to democracy 154

embassies 134
    British 134, 248
    French 186
    Portuguese 169
    Russian 251
    Soviet 190
    United States (U.S.) 142,
       192
Emma 4
Epilepsy Foundation 91–92
Escalante, Jaime 90
escort officer 157
ethnic groups 81
evil empire 2, 28
executive assistant 76
executive director 59
executive secretary 49, 120, 152
executive secretary of the NSC
    123, 126

F
Fallows, James 35
farmers 81
Faulkner, Linda 186, 208
FBI (Federal Bureau of Investiga-
    tion) 47, 144
*Fear and Loathing on the Cam-
    paign Trail* 18
FEC (Federal Election Commis-
    sion) 231, 246
Federal Bureau of Investigation
    (FBI) 47, 144
Federal Election Commission
    (FEC) 231, 246
Federal Trade Commission (FTC)
    122
Fenton, Cathy 208
Ferraro, Geraldine 84
Fireside Chats 34

First Lady of the United States
    (FLOTUS) 207–213. *See also*
    Reagan, Nancy
    chief of staff 208
Foley, Todd 100
Ford, Betty 211
Ford Motors 8
foreign ministry 176
    Icelandic 176
foreign policy 14, 43, 74, 191
    advisor 25
    Cold War 96–97, 175
    idealism 120
    realism 120
Foster, Gary 109
French embassy 186
Friedman, Milton 16
FTC (Federal Trade Commission)
    122

G
Gallup poll 281
Garcia, Jerry 17
Garfield, James A. 119
George Washington Hospital 56
Georgetown University 11, 16,
    23, 46
    college Republicans 15–16,
       29, 50
    School of Foreign Service 11
Gergen, David 76, 106
Germond, Jack 18
GI Bill 9
Gilder, Josh 108
Ginsburg, Doug 220
Giuliani, Rudy 226
glad-hander 25
Glazer, Gil 254–255
    Haganah 254
Glenn, John 95

Godson, Baron 46
    House of Lords 45
Godson, Dean 45
Goldwater, Barry 12, 73, 269
GOP (Grand Old Party) 15, 230
    National Convention 236
Gorbachev, Mikhail 74, 162,
    174–175
        Glasnost campaign 174
        Perestroika campaign 174
        Soviet cheating 178–182
        Washington Summitt 251
Gore, Al Jr. 245, 254–255
Gore, Al Sr. 254–255
governor 110, 235, 250, 262
government jobs and roles. *See
also* assistant to the president;
chief of staff; national security
advisor
        agriculture secretary 252
        assistant secretary 48, 62
        assistant secretary of com-
        merce 99
        assistant secretary of state
        149
        associate director 45, 81,
        245
        associate director of presi-
        dential personnel 49
        attorney general 24–25, 71
        budget director 73, 122,
        193
        chief delegate hunter 25
        chief of congressional affairs
        58
        chief of protocol 157, 161,
        171
        congressional liaison 58
        congressional page 14

counselor to the president
    70
deputy chief of staff 70
defense secretary 206, 273
deputy assistant 206
deputy defense secretary 24
deputy director 52, 82
deputy executive secretary
    120, 124
deputy national security
    advisor 188
deputy press secretary 26
deputy secretary of agricul-
    ture 53
director 82, 105, 123, 196
director of personnel 264
director of the Political
    Office 233
escort officer 157
executive assistant 76
executive director 59
executive secretary 49, 120,
    152
executive secretary of the
    NSC 123, 126
FLOTUS chief of staff 208
foreign policy advisor 25
governor 110, 235, 250,
    262
interior secretary 262
lieutenant governor 24
Navy secretary 46, 226
NSC director 144, 175
Office of Political Affairs
    (OPA) director 215
press secretary 56
regional political director
    31, 47
secretary general 162

secretary of education 252
secretary of state 56, 74, 134, 179
senior director 182
social secretary 186, 208
special assistant 26
staff secretary 76–78, 107, 123, 132
treasury secretary 212, 272
White House communications director 202, 206, 220
Grand Old Party. *See* GOP (Grand Old Party)
The Grapes of Wrath 12, 14
Great Britain, 1
Great Depression 10, 34–37, 254
The Great Liberator 1
Gregory, Carlyle 214, 216
Greider, William 122
Griffith, Lanny 59–60
Griscom, Tommy 206, 220
G7 Summit 190
Guiteau, Charles 120
Gunn, Mike 230

H
Haig, Al 56, 78, 234
Haldeman, Bob 105–107
Haldeman, H. R. 105
Hall, Fawn 151, 196
Hammer, Armand 188–189
"Happy Days Are Here Again" (song) 37
Harlow, Bryce 58, 199, 227
Harlow, Larry 227
Health and Human Services. *See* Department of Health and Human Services
health policy 100

Hecht, Chic 224
Heisenberg principle 87
Heisman Trophy 223
Heritage Foundation 15
Hewitt, Hugh 29
Hicks, Chris 122–123
Hildebrand, Joanne 109
Hinckley, John 110, 112
Hispanic community 80–81
Hitler, Adolf 37
Hofdi House, Reykjavik 179
Holmes, Mycroft 77
Holmes, Sherlock 77
Hooley, Jim 109
hostile dependency 155
Horton, Willie 250
House, Edward 25
Humphrey, Hubert 12, 109
Hurd, Douglas 136
Hurston, Zora Neale 7
Hussein (King) 128

I
IBM Selectric II 49
incumbents 113
    Congressional candidates 229
    1975 campaign 19
    NSC staff 196
    president 21, 113, 235, 250
    Senate candidates 223–224, 226
Indian Treaty Room 229
INF (Intermediate-Range Nuclear Forces) Treaty 252
interior secretary 262
Intermediate-Range Nuclear Forces (INF) Treaty 252

The International Criminal Police
Organization (INTERPOL)
145
international monetary policy 272
interoffice review 77
INTERPOL (The International
Criminal Police Organization)
145
Iran-Contra affair 195, 198–202,
217, 236
Iron Curtain 96

J
Jacobi, Mary Jo 99
British Petroleum (BP) 99
Shell 99
Japanese Foreign Ministry 128
Jeanne (Princess) 143–144
Jepsen, Roger 227
Jewish community 81
Johnny Belinda 268
Johnson administration 114
Johnson, Willa 51–54
Joint Base Andrews 56. *See* An-
drews Air Force Base

Judge, Clark 108

Justice Department 211

K
Kama River truck plant 8–9
Karski, Jan 16
Kelly, Frank 216
Kelly, Jim 130
Kemp, Jack 233–235, 239–244
Kennedy, John F. 119
Kennedy, Ted 23, 115, 224
Keyes, Alan 223–224
Khachigian, Ken 108
Kirilenko, Andrei 174

Kirkpatrick, Jeane 46
Kissinger, Henry 12, 157
Koehler, Jack 202–205
Deutsche Jungvolk 205
Kohl, Helmut 137, 187
Kojelis, Linas 100
Kremlin 183
Ku Klux Klan 231
Kuhn, Jim
Oval Office 87, 203–204
personal aide 134, 149, 173,
185

L
Lacy, Bill 233
Lady Macbeth 212
Lance, Bert 193
Laqueur, Walter 16
Lautenberg, Frank 223
Lavin, Abby 100
Lavin, Ann 100, 185, 241–242
Lavin, Frank 8–32, 80
law of bureaucracy 153
leadership groups 81
Legislative Affairs Office 85, 227
Lehman, John 46, 226
Lenin, Vladimir 174, 188
Liberty Lobby 62–64
Library of Congress 144–145
lieutenant governor 24
Lincoln, Abraham 17, 118–119
Littlefair, Andrew 109
Los Angeles Times 231
Lott, Trent 223
Lovin, Kathy 214, 216
Luttwak, Edward 16
Grand Strategy of the Byz-
antine Empire 16
MX basing systems 16
Lyng, Richard 252

M

Mack, Connie 226

MacKay, Buddy 226

MAD. *See* mutual assured destruction

Madison Hotel 269

Malone, Joe 224–225

Mansfield, Mike 130

Marine One 135, 257

market economics 16, 276

Marshall, George 58

Maseng, Mari 109

Mason, James 45

Mason, Morgan 45

mass media 36–37

Massachusetts Miracle 245–246

Master Sergeant 57

McCarthy, Tim 56

McFarlane, Bud 152

McGovern, George 12–13

McKinley, William 119

McPherson, Peter 3

Meese, Ed 53–54, 82, 270–271
    counselor to the president
        69–78
    White House 275

Meese, Ursula 53

Melcher, John 226

Memory Selectric 48

Mencken, H. L. 127

Metzenbaum, Howard 21

military conscription 18

Miller, Jim 122

Miller, Johnathan 123, 150, 196

Mineta, Norman 124

Minh, Ho Chi 13, 17

Misery Index 22, 238

Mondale, Walter 78, 84, 95

Moon, Sun Myung 93

Morris, Edmund 23, 186,
    261–262

Moynihan, Daniel Patrick 226

MX basing systems 16

Mulroney, Brian 2

Murphey, Mike 29

mutual assured defense 182

mutual assured destruction
    (MAD) 97, 181

N

NAFTA (North American Free
    Trade Agreement) 280

Nakasone, Yasuhiro 129
    Ron-Yasu relationship
        129–130

Narcotics and Law Enforcement
    149

National Cathedral 1, 3–4

National Conservative Political
    Action Committee (NCPAC)
    29, 219

National Italian American Foun-
    dation 84

National Republican Congressio-
    nal Committee (NRCC) 14,
    229

National Restaurant Association
    83–84

National Review 16

national security advisor 132, 205,
    262, 273
    Oval Office meetings
        150–152, 203
    relationship 137
    report 282

National Security Council (NSC)
    83, 107, 122-127
    briefings 152

deputy executive secretary
124, 120
executive secretary 123
first family international
activity 141–145
functions 123
Contras and 147
presidential policy 275
senior staffer 180
Situation Room 44
system 151
team 46, 129, 271–275
NATO. *See* North Atlantic Treaty
Organization (NATO)
Nau, Henry 180
Naval Academy 22
Navy secretary 46, 226
NCPAC (National Conservative
Political Action Committee)
29, 219
Neuman, Mark 214, 216
Newsweek 237
Nighthawk Squadron 135
1988 presidential race 232–259
election eve 256–259
final weeks 252–255
power of incumbency
251–252
summer of Dukakis
245–251
1987 Washington Summit 193
Intermediate-Range Nuclear
Forces Treaty 183
1976 Ohio Republican primary
19
1972 Anti-Ballistic Missile (ABM)
Treaty 180
1972 presidential election 12
1968 presidential campaign 12

1966 Republican gubernatorial
primary 72, 230
Nixon Library 105
Nofziger, Lyn 47, 71, 275
Noonan, Peggy 107–108, 193
North American Free Trade Agree-
ment (NAFTA) 280
North Atlantic Treaty Organiza-
tion (NATO) 137, 187, 280
Pershing II missiles 137–138
North, Oliver 147–150, 196
NRCC (National Republican
Congressional Committee) 14,
229
NSC director 144, 175
NSC *See* National Security Coun-
cil (NSC)
nuclear initiatives 180
Zero Option 180
nuclear war 96, 127

O
Oakeshott, Michael 278
Oakley, Bob 149–150
Occidental Petroleum 188
Occupational Safety and Health
Administration (OSHA) 102
OEOB. *See* Old Executive Office
Building (OEOB)
Office of Administration 94, 123,
196
Office of Intergovernmental
Affairs 215
Office of Legislative Affairs (OLA)
85, 227
Office of Management and Bud-
get 73, 83, 122
Office of Political Affairs (OPA)
47, 50, 206, 214–215

Office of Political Affairs (OPA)
director 215
Office of Presidential Personnel
(OPP) 41–67
associate director 49
Office of Public Liaison (OPL)
47, 78–100
constituency outreach
81–82
organized outreach 82
Office of the Vice President 49,
253
Ohio Central Committee 247
OLA (Office of Legislative Affairs)
227
Old Executive Office Building
(OEOB) 43–44, 48, 57
Library 187
Oliver, Dan 122
O'Neill, Tip 266, 269, 279
OPA. *See* Office of Political Affairs
(OPA)
Operation Pedro Pan 46
communist Cuba 46
OPL (Office of Public Liaison)
47, 78–100
OPP (Office of Presidential Per-
sonnel) 41–42
Orwell, George 28
OSHA (Occupational Safety and
Health Administration) 102
Oswald, Lee Harvey 120

P

PAC (political action committee)
251
Panama Canal 23
Parker, Fess 45
parochial school 11
Pearson, Bob 200

Pelosi, Nancy 279–280
Pentagon 46, 187, 199, 206
Perk, Ralph 109
Phillips Academy 11
Pipe, Richard 153
law of bureaucracy 153
Plaza Accord 278
Pledge of Allegiance 250
plutocrat 44
pneumatic tube 48
Podhoretz, John 108, 115
Podhoretz, Norman 15
Poindexter, John 195–196
admiral 126, 134
congressional testimony 217
national security advisor
132, 150–153
National Security Council
(NSC) 138, 271
policy types
administration 82, 96, 127
defense 81
defense industrial 187
economic 43, 80
foreign 14, 43, 74, 191
health 100
international monetary 272
political
action committee (PAC)
251
analysis 27
communications 80
evaluation 5–6
identity 237, 249
philosophy 12, 14, 280
popularity theories 68–69
Political Office 233, 246, 257
Portuguese embassy 169
The Post-Standard 31